KRISTIN MORRISON

Canters and Chronicles

The Use of Narrative in the Plays of Samuel Beckett and Harold Pinter

THE UNIVERSITY OF CHICAGO PRESS
CHICAGO AND LONDON

KRISTIN MORRISON, associate professor of English at Boston College, is the author of *In Black and White* and the coauthor (with Michael Anderson, Jacques Guicharnaud, and Jack Zipes) of *Handbook of Contemporary Drama.*

The University of Chicago Press, Chicago 60637
The University of Chicago Press, Ltd., London

© 1983 by The University of Chicago
All rights reserved. Published 1983
Printed in the United States of America
5 4 3 2 1   83 84 85 86 87 88 89

Library of Congress Cataloging in Publication Data
Morrison, Kristin.
  Canters and chronicles.

  Bibliography: p.
  Includes index.
  1. English drama—20th century—History and
criticism.   2. Monologue.   3. Narration (Rhetoric)
4. Beckett, Samuel, 1906–   —Technique.   5. Pinter,
Harold, 1930–   —Technique.   6. Characters and
characteristics in literature.   I. Title.
PR739.M65M67   1983   822'.914'09   82-16086
ISBN 0-226-54130-4

Contents

Acknowledgments

My earliest debt is to Walter J. Ong for introducing me in 1959 to Beckett's work and to Hugh Kenner's dazzling analysis. Frederick J. Hoffman, Martin Esslin, John Russell Taylor, and Ruby Cohn subsequently all wrote books which further helped direct and illuminate my study of both Beckett and Pinter. As the volume of scholarship on these two playwrights grew, so too my debts. In particular I want to express gratitude to several scholars whose work I admire and whose kindness, interest, and criticism have in various ways cheered and aided me in the writing of this book: Lawrence Graver, Michael Anderson, James Knowlson, John Pilling, S. E. Gontarski, Ruby Cohn, Enoch Brater, Elin Diamond, Hersh Zeifman, and Linda Ben-Zvi. In addition, I am indebted to the Boston College Mellon Fund and Department of English for supporting this research, to the excellent staffs of the Beckett archives at Reading University and at Ohio State University for access to their collections, and to Samuel Beckett for allowing me to quote from manuscript materials. Finally, special thanks to Harold, whose terminal was only the beginning.

Many things may be told which cannot be shewed, if they know the difference betwixt reporting and representing.

—Sir Philip Sidney, *The Defense of Poesy*

Show! Hide! Show!

—James Joyce, *Ulysses*

"Get into my story
in order to get out"

A story is not compulsory, just a life," says the speaker of Samuel Beckett's "Texts for Nothing 4," lamenting his mistake in having wanted a story for himself "whereas life alone is enough."[1] But, ironically, neither does he have a life. No life, no story, no self, "in the true sense of the words" (p. 105). This tension between life and story, self and story, fills Beckett's work and has frequently been discussed as a key issue in his novels and shorter fiction. It is even more important in his drama, however, because there not only does this tension provide a major thematic concern but the narrative form itself has been employed as a significant new dramatic technique. When Winnie— on stage, buried up to her neck in earth—announces that it is time for her story,[2] she is not merely introducing a form taken from fiction and inserted supposedly unchanged into drama (like all those classics adapted for television, as if point of view and various other narrative structures were the same whether read or seen and heard). Her story in effect alters the drama, and the recital of story on stage radically alters the narrative. Beckett may not have suddenly

1. Samuel Beckett, *Stories and Texts for Nothing* (New York: Grove Press, 1967), p. 93.
2. Samuel Beckett, *Happy Days* (New York: Grove Press, 1961), p. 54.

1

and singly invented a new dramatic form, but sometime in this century narratives of a particular kind have begun to be used in drama, and his work, along with Pinter's, represents some of the best and most important examples of the phenomenon. What these narratives present is nothing less than a modern psychological equivalent of the soliloquy constituting an intrinsic part of the central dramatic action itself, the internal made external in a particularly revealing and dramatically convincing way.

In the past the accepted theatrical convention for revealing a character's hidden thoughts has been the soliloquy.[3] Used, of course, with varying degrees of subtlety and sophistication, it nonetheless functioned as a device which stopped the external "action" for a moment so that internal mind could be expressed. No matter how emotionally complex Hamlet is, the actor delivering his famous speculation, "to be or not to be," ordinarily draws apart from other characters into neutral playing space and thinks aloud to himself in lines which are clearly powerful as poetry and skillfully balanced as rhetoric. What the audience is given is controlled discourse; what it perceives is tormented spirit: the ready acceptance of an established convention makes such perception possible.

That the convention itself is difficult for playwrights of another century to use is demonstrated by Eugene O'Neill's experiments with psychological drama in *Strange Interlude*. As various characters voice their thoughts while other characters are on stage, it becomes necessary to distinguish in some theatrical way between those words the characters speak aloud and those they think silently in the privacy of their own minds. Philip Moeller, director of the first production of *Strange Interlude*, considered a number of theatrical

3. A number of recent studies of both Beckett and Pinter deal with traditional dramatic forms such as soliloquy, monologue, dialogue, and the various kinds of voices and languages used in the work of these two playwrights. See, for example, Andrew Kennedy, *Six Dramatists in Search of a Language* (London: Cambridge University Press, 1975); Ruby Cohn, "Outward Bound Soliloquies," *Journal of Modern Literature* 6 (February 1977): 17–38; Elin Diamond, "The Fictionalizers in Beckett's Plays," in *Samuel Beckett*, ed. Ruby Cohn (New York: McGraw-Hill, 1975); and Ruby Cohn, "All Mankind Is Us: Fictionalizers," *Just Play* (Princeton, N.J.: Princeton University Press, 1980).

possibilities to make this distinction clear: the use of an island of introspection where characters would deliver their mental asides, the use of a different quality of voice, a change of lighting, or (the convention finally chosen) having everyone on stage freeze while the lines are being delivered.[4] All four possibilites are artificial and thus, from one point of view, awkward, but not intrinsically more awkward than the convention of soliloquy itself, simply less well established. By arresting physical motion on stage, the technique chosen indicates that same interruption of what is usually considered to be the "action" of the play which soliloquy itself has always involved.

But as O'Neill insisted, "Everything is a matter of convention. If we accept one, why not another, so long as it does what it's intended to do?"[5] The convention that worked so well for one period of drama, the soliloquy, did not necessarily work well for another. Nor did O'Neill's own attempts with masks, asides, frozen motion, and other theatrical experiments seem appropriate for later playwrights, who by and large have not chosen to develop psychological aspects of drama through these conventions.

The newest convention for expressing psychological inwardness on stage is the technique of storytelling: "narrative" suddenly becomes "drama." There have, of course, always been narrative elements in drama, but never in the past used in quite the same way or to the same effect as is found in the work of Samuel Beckett and Harold Pinter. Now the telling of a story allows characters that quintessentially "modern," Freudian opportunity to reveal deep and difficult thoughts and feelings while at the same time concealing them as fiction or at least distancing them as narration. Although such psychological complexity could also be inferred from the soliloquy (through contrast between the character's hidden thoughts and overt behavior), that convention itself was fairly straightforward. But in the telling of a story, the conflict between facing issues and fleeing them is actually dramatized. In fact, in many plays by both Beckett and Pinter this conflict itself is the real action of the

4. Arthur Gelb and Barbara Gelb, *O'Neill* (New York: Harper & Row, 1962), p. 648.
5. Ibid., p. 628.

play. By choosing to tell a story, to *talk about* rather than to *perform*, to focus on a narrated past rather than on actual present, characters betray their deepest, most incompatible feelings. All that talk in Beckett's plays and in Pinter's plays is not for the sake of presenting thoughts and feelings directly, but rather for the sake of hiding them or at least disguising or distancing them.

When Pinter's Deeley in *Old Times* announces "What happened to me was this"[6] and then launches into a lengthy narrative about some strange event in the past, the audience wonders why this story is being told: there are other characters present (so this is not our old familiar convention, the soliloquy); there is to some extent a "realistic" social situation (so the introduction of this particular narrative seems odd); and on the surface at least there appears to be no connection between the content of the story and the "action" on stage (and so the entire segment seems inappropriate, both for Deeley to choose to tell and for Pinter to compose). Deeley appears to have stopped the "real action" of the play in order to tell a story; but the fact that he has chosen to tell a story rather than continue with the current conversation itself is the real action of that scene. He tells the story for the sake of the others who hear it and also for his own sake, because he needs both to establish something and to conceal something, both from the others and from himself. Functioning as a modern psychological equivalent of the soliloquy, such a narrative allows a character the relief of self-revelation while at the same time he continues to conceal from others, and to some extent even from himself, desires, motives, and emotions that are painful and in some way dangerous. This new device is psychologically more believable than the conventional soliloquy because it capitalizes on the fact that whether or not "people" speak thoughts aloud in private (an acceptable enough convention for theater), both real and fictional people actually do hide certain feelings not only from others but even from themselves. The audience knows this fact and recognizes the psychological significance of self-deception. Thus the story, whether told to other characters (as in this scene with Deeley) or merely recited solo,

6. Harold Pinter, *Old Times* (New York: Grove Press, 1971), p. 29.

can become a complex mechanism of revelation and concealment which uncovers, for the audience, depths of the speaker's interiority unfathomed by other theatrical conventions.

Beckett and Pinter are not, of course, the first to use narrative units in their plays. The history of English-language drama is full of a variety of narrative elements: scriptural stories, recited whole or suggested by allusion; *exempla,* taken from Scripture, mythology, history, literature, folktales, or simply invented to illustrate whatever point is being made; recounted dreams, usually presented as prophecy or as confirmation of some temporal event; Homeric similes, conceits, and other figures of speech which in effect present an anecdote of some kind; prologues and epilogues, in which a single character addresses the audience, not only commenting on the play and its lesson but in the process narrating part of the plot or some other story that relates to the play and its lesson; anecdotes recounted by a character within the play, either events from the past which have some bearing on the current action or fantasies which reveal something about the speaker himself; expository narration, in which one or more characters talk about previous events which account for the current dramatic situation; narrative frames, in which the play is begun as if it were a story being told by a single speaker addressing an audience (either the actual theater audience or a stage audience); ballads sung as part of the dramatic presentation but themselves succinctly retelling a story; jokes and witty stories by which the teller amuses or bests his fellows.

In whatever form—extended narratives recited as set pieces or compressed narratives with only a halo of story embellishing the dialogue—all these established narrative types function quite straightforwardly as familiar devices of poetry, rhetoric, and drama. For example, in his disquisition on the body politic (*Coriolanus* 1. i. 99–167) Menenius Agrippa tells a little story to the assembled masses in order to teach them a lesson: it is a strategy he as a good Renaissance Roman employs deliberately and one his plebeian audience recognizes and correctly interprets. Story here does not involve attempts at evasion or self-protection; Menenius Agrippa's narrative is, as a rhetorical convention of its time, directness itself. Even Brecht, to cite another user of narrative in drama, employs

5

story for quite different effect from the one Beckett and Pinter achieve: Brecht intends to destroy the illusion of "real life," to focus on social behavior rather than inner feelings and motives. When the Chaplain in *Mother Courage* (scene 6) develops a narrative, an *exemplum* to demonstrate how war is like peace, there is no unwitting self-revelation, no hidden emotions and motives revealed (as there are in Hamm's chronicle); the Chaplain would be the first to recognize that he is a gifted charlatan; indeed, that *is* the tradition he proudly represents.

When Brecht states that "the exposition of the story and its communication by suitable means of estrangement constitute the main business of the theatre" and that "everything hangs on the story; it is the heart of the theatrical performance,"[7] he refers to something quite different from the kind of narrative or the kind of story found in Beckett and Pinter. In Brecht, story is intended to flatten the drama, destroy the illusion, whereas in the plays of both Beckett and Pinter, the use of story increases psychological verisimilitude and invites sympathetic identification from the audience, who recognize and understand the complex deceptions which the character's use of story implies.

Often when critics use the term "story" or "narrative" in their discussions of drama, they actually mean plot: "It will have been noted by the attentive reader that what I have called a story, Mr Archer calls a plot," Shaw wrote in his 1893 preface to *Widowers' Houses*. And to some extent this is also what Brecht means when he refers to story. But in this discussion of the plays of Beckett and Pinter, the terms "story" and "narrative" do not indicate plot or "what you would have if you summarized the play." In this discussion those terms refer only to actual narrations (of whatever length) delivered during the course of the play by one of the characters in the play, units which comprise an important part of the dramatic action, units involving self-revelations and evasions of a most subtle kind on the part of the speaker himself: what he tells, when he tells it, and why he tells it are often the real drama.

7. Bertolt Brecht, "A Short Organum for the Theatre," in *Playwrights on Playwriting*, ed. Toby Cole (New York: Hill & Wang, 1961), pp. 102 and 98.

The essential distinction between the narrative and dramatic genres is that the one is told and the other performed. Obvious as this is, the complexity of modes by which the two genres are achieved can at times almost obliterate the distinction: the stream-of-consciousness technique has all the immediacy of drama, and radio plays are as much a telling as an acting. The basic difference between narrative and drama remains nonetheless. And when an actor performs a narrative text—as Joseph Chaiken has done with Beckett's *Texts for Nothing*—the piece is essentially altered. Telling involves the past in some way, even when the telling is done (like an instant replay) in the present tense; but performing, even in plays with flashbacks, involves time present; the action is always immediate. Narration requires the intermediation of a narrator (however subtly the voice structure may be contrived); drama is supposedly "happening" before our very eyes. In this sense, then, at its simplest and most naive expression, narrative is *about* something, and drama *acts* something. Both, of course, are conventions, but at the heart of the one convention is telling, at the heart of the other is doing.

When in drama (characters on stage doing things) there is included lengthy and significant telling, the phenomenon of telling becomes a form of doing; and, in the context of the action of the play itself, narrative begins to take the place of "life." In Pinter's *The Homecoming*, Lenny talks to Ruth about battering women; it is his way of violating her without physical contact. He would rather tell the story of an assault now, at this moment, than do it. There is method here—method Ruth recognizes, method the audience recognizes. And that recognition is made possible by the very fact that Ruth and audience all know there is a difference between saying and doing: the story is not identical with the event. But choosing to tell a story is its own kind of event. Lenny's stories of the pox-ridden slut and the demanding old woman and his vivid accounts of the beatings he gives them are not present in the play for the sake of exposition, and they are certainly not there because Pinter is unable to "handle action" and so, like many modern playwrights, resorts to talk. This particular talk, this storytelling, is itself the action. Like all narrative, it makes use of the essential distance involved in telling; it relies tantalizingly on the convention that in narrative the "author" and his story persona are not identical. It conveniently moves passions away from the body and into the mind, where the process of simultaneously admitting and denying something, facing and fleeing fascinating dangers can be achieved safely. When characters in Beckett's and Pinter's plays shift into narrative, it is often because they have gotten too close to painful emotional issues, which the conventions of narrative allow them to disguise. They substitute narrative for the present moment; events become confronted (or affirmed) as story while they are evaded (or negated) as life. And since issues connected with death and sex are among the most painful and threatening for many people, the evasions and revelations of Beckett's and Pinter's storytellers, usually centering on these issues, seem to an audience all the more plausible. Pain and fascination are not simply stated by a reflective character discoursing aloud to himself—a kind of hiatus in the midst of the dramatic action—but, rather, pain and fascination are actually dramatized by the character's telling a story, to deceive or shield himself, while at the same time considering problems which are significant in his own life. Thus the story (as "narration" a supposedly more objective device than soliloquy) actually becomes more intimate and inward, more genuinely dramatic. Evasion itself is often the main action. The subject evaded betrays something of great importance about the character, and the issues of love and death which permeate the evasions constitute some of the most important themes in both Beckett's and Pinter's plays. At one level, the stories as "mere fiction" are illusion, but at their deepest level they are truer than anything else in the play.

Canters and Chronicles

Waiting for Godot, Endgame, Happy Days

Although Beckett's early study of Proust is often quoted in connection with his own work—and there are single sentences and brief passages which seem very apt—the most obvious fact about Beckett's own characters in both fiction and drama is how very un-Proustian they are. That delicious sense of self-analysis that occupies Proust's narrator, the frissons of falsification and loss, the exquisite sufferings of the various couples (like so many parts of a fugue played again and again), the importance of time, which Beckett had discussed in his own literary criticism (and of which Marcel-narrator is, even more than any critic, most intensely aware)—all this cultivated feeling and concomitant awareness of feeling is lost on Beckett's characters. Belacqua, perhaps, is a kind of parody of Marcel-narrator, but for the rest, all those *M*'s of Beckett's novels, there is a progressive negation of sensibility, a descent into apathy that seems the very antithesis of Marcel's recaptured past with its momentarily recaptured past self. The dazzling richness of the gifts of involuntary memory are never available to Beckett's characters; they never experience what Beckett describes Marcel experiencing in his second visit to Balbec: "he has not merely extracted from this gesture the lost reality of his grandmother: he has recovered the lost reality

of himself, the reality of his lost self."[1] Instead, Beckett's characters
tend to *be* lost selves, painfully conscious of their loss without any
of that self-conscious cherishing which paradoxically allows Marcel
to possess himself *as lost*. More than once in his analysis of Proust,
Beckett asserts that the only true paradise is the paradise that has
been lost (p. 55). But for Beckett's own characters there is no
paradise of any kind.[2]

Different as Beckett's own characters are from Proust's, his
essay nonetheless illuminates an important element in his own
characterization: Beckett's discussion of habit in Proust's work
makes even clearer why characters in his own work have recourse
to narration. Storytelling is a way to avoid the "suffering of being"
and thus makes it possible for life to go on.

Life is made up of moments of boredom occasionally pierced
by "the suffering of being," a time when "the free play of every
faculty" (p. 9) makes attention real and suffering inevitable. To
illustrate this suffering, Beckett discusses the famous passage in
A la recherche du temps perdu when the narrator in his room at the
Grand Hotel on his first visit to Balbec-Plage encounters an "inferno of unfamiliar objects" (p. 12); habit has not yet reduced
them to his own "formula" of perception and containment, and so
he suffers. The particular phrase Beckett uses to describe Marcel—
protective habit for the moment suspended—is very interesting in
relation to Beckett's own plays: Winnie, Hamm, even the "imaginative" Joe, Croak, and Krapp, and the witty Vladimir and Estragon, none of these characters has "the free play of every faculty."
They are in a permanent state of boredom and partake of boredom's
chief advantage—a feeling of safety, specious (as these complex
characters at some level of awareness all too painfully realize) but

1. Samuel Beckett, *Proust* (New York: Grove Press, n.d.), p. 27.
2. Vera G. Lee observes that "What seems most significant is that this
universally pessimistic view [Beckett's view of Proust] obscures totally the fact
that *A la Recherche du temps perdu* is, in the last analysis, an optimistic novel";
"Beckett on Proust," *Romanic Review* 69 (1978): 202. See also "Beckett, Proust,
and Schopenhauer," in Steven J. Rosen, *Samuel Beckett and the Pessimistic Tradition*
(New Brusnwick, N.J.: Rutgers University Press, 1976), pp. 137–52.

superficially reassuring nonetheless. The function of habit is to
"empty the mystery of its threat" (p. 11); their faculties do not
play with the "essence" of whatever objects they encounter. Instead,
they dull their perceptions with repetitive behavior and give themselves the semblance of variety and freedom by creating fictions,
imaginary worlds where there are no unfamiliar objects and where
every object seems controlled and thus made safe (Winnie's uneasy
refusal to be disconcerted by her flaming parasol is only the most
dramatic of dozens of examples which could be cited). It is a very
nice touch, of course, that what Beckett says of Proust's characters—being in an inferno when habit is momentarily suspended—
is quite literally true of the "real situation" of all of Beckett's own
characters, from Estragon's "I'm in hell," through Winnie's scorch-
ing ground, to the various psychological hells of the later plays.[3]
Were these "lost ones" to allow themselves to look clearly at their
situation, they would be more overwhelmed than Marcel at Balbec,
the suffering of being would flood them. But they flee such realization by whatever means they can, boredom being a chief means
of escape. Beckett writes in his essay:

> "Of all human plants," writes Proust, "Habit requires the least
> fostering, and is the first to appear on the seeming desolation of
> the most barren rock." Brief, and dangerously painful. The fun-
> damental duty of Habit, about which it describes the futile and
> stupefying arabesques of its supererogations, consists in a perpet-
> ual adjustment and readjustment of our organic sensibility to the
> conditions of its worlds. Suffering represents the omission of that
> duty, whether through negligence or inefficiency, and boredom its
> adequate performance. The pendulum oscillates between these
> two terms: Suffering—that opens a window on the real and is
> the main condition of the artistic experience, and Boredom—with

3. This motif is most explicit in a later fictional piece, *The Lost Ones*, which
has clear allusions to Dante's *Inferno* and an unavoidable reminder of one of
Beckett's earliest stories, "Dante and the Lobster," in which a central theme of
Beckett's work is first stated: "Well, thought Belacqua, it's a quick death, God
help us all," followed by the brief but powerful narrative commentary, "It is not";
More Pricks than Kicks (New York: Grove Press, 1972), p. 22.

its host of top-hatted and hygienic ministers, Boredom that must be considered as the most tolerable because the most durable of human evils.

[P. 16]

This passage reveals as much about Beckett's work as it does about Proust's. The "real" causes suffering, and yet paradoxically it also makes possible a sense of life as "delicious" *because* threatened by death. The implication here, and elsewhere in the essay, is that habit lulls one into a sense that the world remains the same (objects are always "familiar") and thus, because there is no change, there is no deterioration, loss, or death. The price of this comforting illusion is boredom, an evil more tolerable than the unsettling realism of facing death. Beckett has thus given a very accurate description of the situation of the characters he would later create in his plays: they are unredeemed Proustians, unredeemed by any moments of contact with "the real" or any grace of "involuntary memory." They are perpetually engulfed in boredom and apparent attempts to relieve it (attempts which are, however, actually modes of maintaining that boredom). They "tell stories," engage in various canters, revive voluntary memories (just another form of falsity from a Proustian point of view), all in an effort to distract themselves, lull themselves with what is specious-familiar. This is not to say that Beckett's characters have no awareness, no conflicts, and no terrors. Indeed, they do, but the struggle is always, as Krapp puts it, to "keep 'em under!" The "seeming desolation of the most barren rock" is the abiding terrain of Beckett's characters, made bearable and ordinary by their apparently complacent acceptance of it; all the volatile emotions, the disquieting variables of real life get translated into "story," something the character-narrator can control, something that, in any case, by its very repetition becomes "fixed" and thus pseudo-immortal. Winnie distances her own terrors by the comforting recital of little Millie's misadventure; Krapp's real women and his experiences with them are held forever on tape, sexual "magnetism" become simply a detail of technology; Henry, Croak, and Joe all relive experiences that are fraught with feeling, but they control their experience of that feeling, beginning and

12

ending it as deliberate narrative, not the great wash of involuntary memory or the shattering experience of "the real." That they so carefully control and evade and distance in itself betrays how strong those feelings really are and how painful they are to face. With one anguished sentence of denial, Beckett's Krapp distills all the loss on which Proust's Marcel spent three thousand pages of exquisite reflection: "No, I wouldn't want them back"—years, loves, talents, even the longing is apparently lost. But not really lost at all, and that is what the stories are about.

Waiting for Godot and *Endgame* illustrate very well two extremes of narrative presence: on the one hand, a mere suggestion of story in various sequences and allusions; on the other, fully developed stories presented in the play explicitly *as story;* Vladimir and Estragon have their little canters, and Hamm his chronicle. Here, very early in Beckett's playwriting career, are the basic elements of narrative he will progressively refine in later works.

In *Waiting for Godot* the "story" elements are only suggested, present in the form of allusions, both biblical and mythological, references to past history very briefly described, dreams barely mentioned, a joke uncompleted, a song, and a final powerful metaphor. Related to these actual story-type narratives, with their characters and "plot," is another form of narrative that involves the telling of a series of ideas rather than a series of events. The chief example of this kind of narrative is Lucky's parody of philosophical disquisition; Pozzo's rhetorical affectations constitute a minor rendition of Lucky's theme. Unlike subsequent plays, *Waiting for Godot* has no extended narrative sequences, only shadows and suggestions of story, but those in abundance.

In this first produced play Beckett did not capitalize on the possibilities of storytelling as a way to reveal character, as he was to do later in *Endgame* and subsequent plays. Instead, most of the narrative elements in *Waiting for Godot* serve to accentuate themes and prolong and vary tones sounded throughout the play. The few longer narratives, especially those that involve biblical allusions, do help reveal something of Vladimir's "world view" and attempts at self-deception, but they do not approach the soliloquizing nature and subtlety of Hamm's chronicle, Henry's Bolton-Holloway story,

Krapp's vignettes, and the haunting voices of the later plays. Here
Beckett's tendency to write "story units" is illustrated in various
muted forms and in bits and pieces interesting as predecessors of
those moving narratives which will distinguish his subsequent drama.

The play itself is structured as a series of segments which, if
they are not themselves "stories," have the same effect that a series
of jokes or anecdotes would. Estragon refers to them at one point
as little canters, verbal excursions on a theme which help Vladimir
and Estragon to pass the time in between their realizations (and
repeated announcements) that they are waiting for Godot.[4] Unlike
the usual plotted drama (or even loosely episodic plays, in which
there is nonetheless some sense of development or movement forward), the structure of *Waiting for Godot* is much more like a music-
hall review or, to use a more literary analogy, a frame narrative
such as *The Decameron* or *The Canterbury Tales*. In *Waiting for Godot*
the "frame" is the abiding static situation of waiting, and the various
episodes Vladimir and Estragon engage in are the means by which
they enhance the "beauty of the way." Their various "canters" have
as much variety in subject matter, style, and pace as does any
collection of tales marshaled to hearten pilgrims. "For trewely,
confort ne myrthe is noon / To ride by the weye doumb as a stoon"[5]
is a judgment Vladimir and Estragon would share; and if they seem
less genuinely merry than Chaucer's sondry folk, it may be simply
that for them martyrdom is both more immediate and certainly less
meaningful. Nonetheless, they set themselves "to talen and to
pleye."

Most of these playful sequences are comic in their effect, such
as the following three:

VLADIMIR: ⎱ *(turning simultaneously)* Do you—
ESTRAGON: ⎰
VLADIMIR: Oh pardon!
ESTRAGON: Carry on.

4. Samuel Beckett, *Waiting for Godot* (New York: Grove Press, 1954), p. 42.
The pages of this edition are numbered consecutively only on the verso; pages
with numbers will be cited here by their designated number, and the next, facing
page will be given that same number and the designation " + ."
5. Geoffrey Chaucer, "General Prologue," *The Canterbury Tales*, ll. 773 f.

VLADIMIR: No no, after you.
ESTRAGON: No no, you first.
VLADIMIR: I interrupted you.
ESTRAGON: On the contrary.
>	*They glare at each other angrily.*
VLADIMIR: Ceremonious ape!
ESTRAGON: Punctilious pig!
VLADIMIR: Finish your phrase, I tell you!
ESTRAGON: Finish your own!
>	*Silence. They draw closer, halt.*
VLADIMIR: Moron!
ESTRAGON: That's the idea, let's abuse each other.
>	*They turn, move apart, turn again and face each other.*
VLADIMIR: Moron!
ESTRAGON: Vermin!
VLADIMIR: Abortion!
ESTRAGON: Morpion!
VLADIMIR: Sewer-rat!
ESTRAGON: Curate!
VLADIMIR: Cretin!
ESTRAGON: (*with finality*) Crritic!
VLADIMIR: Oh!
>	*He wilts, vanquished, and turns away.*
ESTRAGON: Now let's make it up.
VLADIMIR: Gogo!
ESTRAGON: Didi!
VLADIMIR: Your hand!
ESTRAGON: Take it!
VLADIMIR: Come to my arms!
ESTRAGON: Your arms?
VLADIMIR: My breast!
ESTRAGON: Off we go!
>	*They embrace. They separate. Silence.*
VLADIMIR: How time flies when one has fun!
>	*Silence.*
ESTRAGON: What do we do now?

>	[Pp. 48 +, 49]

Each one of these sequences has its own rhythm and tone: first, the balance and restraint of formal courtesy, next, the staccato ugliness of vilification, and finally, the breathless enthusiasm of affectionate reconciliation. Yet all three are amusing as parodies, and the whole tripartite sequence has its own climax in the silly punch line, "How time flies when one has fun!" Then the basic "narrative frame" is restored with "What do we do now?" and a pause before yet another sequence occurs.

But not all these sequences are comic, as the following example indicates:

ESTRAGON: In the meantime let us try and converse calmly, since we are incapable of keeping silent.
VLADIMIR: You're right, we're inexhaustible.
ESTRAGON: It's so we won't think.
VLADIMIR: We have that excuse.
ESTRAGON: It's so we won't hear.
VLADIMIR: We have our reasons.
ESTRAGON: All the dead voices.
VLADIMIR: They make a noise like wings.
ESTRAGON: Like leaves.
VLADIMIR: Like sand.
ESTRAGON: Like leaves.
    Silence.
VLADIMIR: They all speak at once.
ESTRAGON: Each one to itself.
    Silence.
VLADIMIR: Rather they whisper.
ESTRAGON: They rustle.
VLADIMIR: They murmur.
ESTRAGON: They rustle.
    Silence.
VLADIMIR: What do they say?
ESTRAGON: They talk about their lives.
VLADIMIR: To have lived is not enough for them.
ESTRAGON: They have to talk about it.
VLADIMIR: To be dead is not enough for them.
ESTRAGON: It is not sufficient.
    Silence.
VLADIMIR: They make a noise like feathers.
ESTRAGON: Like leaves.

VLADIMIR: Like ashes.
ESTRAGON: Like leaves.
   Long silence.
VLADIMIR: Say something!

[Pp. 40 f.]

Here, although the lines are short and alternate between speakers, the effect is lyrical, not comic; the music-hall manner gives way to meditative poetry. The cadences are mellifluous and gently repetitive, the sounds are onomatapoetic, the language imagistic, and the mood melancholy. And what the sequence states is important. Like so many other of Beckett's protagonists, Vladimir and Estragon hear voices telling stories, and their *own* talk is in part an attempt to avoid hearing *that* talk. In death there is no peace, but a constant repetition of the story of one's life: such a harrowing prospect is more than Vladimir and Estragon can face, and so they fill the haunted silence with their own verbal sequences, some of which are the comic canters previously described and some of which are actually or incipiently stories.

The first and one of the most explicit of these stories is Vladimir's discussion of the two thieves. Very early in the play, after remarks about anonymous beatings and painful boots, Vladimir suddenly announces, "One of the thieves was saved" (p. 8 +), thus introducing a long dramatic segment that sets a tone and theme for much else that will occur in the play. Not to be put off by various digressions (existential repentance, prostate pain, biblical maps, ragged poetry, and swelling feet) Vladimir tenaciously holds on to his topic: "Do you remember the story?" "Shall I tell it to you?" (p. 9). Undaunted by Estragon's "No" and subsequent interruptions, Vladimir persists in recounting his chosen anecdote—"Two thieves, crucified at the same time as our Saviour. ... One is supposed to have been saved and the other ... damned"—and then proceeds to raise a standard question from the Higher Criticism, "how is it that of the four Evangelists only one speaks of a thief being saved." "One out of four. Of the other three two don't mention any thieves at all and the third says that both of them abused him" (pp. 9–9 +). But Estragon is not to be lured into this nineteenth-century discussion of the harmony of the Gospels: "Well? They don't agree and that's all there is to it." The sequence concludes with two pairs of remarks, comic and pointed. "Why believe him rather than the others?" is answered by "Who believes him?"—a question that both shocks and amuses the audience, shocks because we are "supposed" to believe the Bible, we belong to a culture that officially accepts it, and yet personally, individually, we may not really believe "the old stories." So there is a gasp of surprise and a laugh of recognition. The next pair of lines continues in similar fashion to make the audience both ally and enemy: "Everybody [believes him]. It's the only version they know" is met by the judgment "People are bloody ignorant apes" (p. 9 +). And once again the audience is shocked and amused— and caught. Yes, yes, at one time we studied the Bible (at least Beckett's French, English, and Irish audiences did, if not his American) but in fact most of us only vaguely remember the details, have a sort of lingering composite version in which, yes, there is something about two thieves. Estragon's remark indicts the very people who, sitting there to be entertained or to get "culture," have vaguely remembered the story Vladimir tells, who no doubt are willing on occasion to consider *other* people to be "bloody ignorant apes," then find themselves suddenly included. This shock of recognition, as well as the many startling reversals of expectation ("Our Saviour . . ." "Our what?") constitutes part of the comedy of this particular sequence.

But the sequence is more than merely comic. Beckett could have chosen any story for Vladimir to recount, scriptural or not. Why this particular story? Its apparent gratuitousness, of course, emphasizes Vladimir's desperation to fill the time somehow. But the story does have a subject, one Vladimir and Estragon spend several minutes considering, one the audience hears and necessarily integrates into its general impression of what is "happening." The very same sequence could have been played with the story of the Nativity, which also is liable to shocking humor based on textual difficulties. However, that basically happy and hopeful event would strike the wrong note; crucifixion provides the appropriate theme and tone for this play, which is, after all, about slow death and absent salvation. The story of the two thieves may have "spontaneously" popped into Vladimir's head; what is important is the fact that it *is* a story he knows, remembers, and chooses to tell when he finds himself in a desperately boring situation. It is among the first of several things he and Gogo find to give themselves the impression they exist (p. 44 +). That they are in any way associated with people who have significance and history, gives these two derelicts some slight claim to significance and history themselves; but if the history is only fiction, significance becomes problematic. Was the thief ever really saved? From hell? From death? Or is that only a story, with various versions? Will Godot ever come? And if he does, will they really be saved (p. 47 +) or is that hope, too, only a fiction? The fact that Vladimir tells Estragon this story of the two thieves, emphasizing its textual uncertainties, betrays his own conflicting hope and despair. The fact that Beckett places this story early in the play indicates his authorial concern to establish the theme of blighted hope, the tone of grieving despair early in the play.

There are many other biblical allusions in the play which bear out this early one. The crucifixion motif is kept on the edge of the audience's perception by a few brief references. Vladimir reprimands Lucky for his alleged mistreatment of Pozzo: "How dare you! It's abominable! Such a good master! Crucify him like that! After so many years!" (p. 23). And later Estragon compares himself to Christ as justification for going barefoot:

VLADIMIR: Christ! What has Christ got to do with it? You're not going to compare yourself to Christ!
ESTRAGON: All my life I've compared myself to him.
VLADIMIR: But where he lived it was warm, it was dry!
ESTRAGON: Yes. And they crucified quick.

[P. 34 +]

These references to crucifixion may indeed be "Irishisms," but they are not so entirely colloquial that their original meaning is forgotten. If the terrible slow torture of crucifixion is considered quick and preferable to Estragon and Vladimir's lingering life, then the pain and despair of their situation is accentuated by these references.

Other less obvious allusions also contribute to the sense of despair that permeates the play. Just before launching into his story about the two thieves, Vladimir had suddenly, through a process of understandable free association, come up with the quotation: "Hope deferred maketh the something sick, who said that?" (p. 8). Whether or not the audience recognizes Proverbs 13:12, knows that "something" is "heart," and considers God the ultimate author of the Bible is not really important; there is enough force to the incomplete quotation to achieve its tragicomic effect (what has been deferred is Vladimir's urinating). This ironic use of Scripture continues several minutes later when Vladimir's false alarm concerning Godot's arrival is met with Estragon's "Pah! The wind in the reeds" (p. 13 +). Again, the line has enough meaning on its own to make sense to any member of the audience; but those familiar with the Bible will immediately remember that the same image is used to refer to the Messianic herald who goes unheeded.[6] Thus the line has an overlay of ironic meaning. Literally the phrase means "there is nothing," but through its biblical reference the line suggests that once there was something or someone who went unrecognized and that those who awaited but did not detect him were not saved. The irony of this line in this particular play does not come from any suggestion that there really *is* salvation for Vladimir and Estragon if only they could see it (those who give the play an optimistic Christian interpretation badly misread it), but quite the contrary, that there truly is "nothing." All the many references to hope and salvation which occur in the play—whether as metaphors and idioms readily available, stories to be told, quotations to be identified—reveal the extent to which Vladimir and Estragon have been misled by their culture. They carry around

6. "Jesus began to say unto the multitudes concerning John, What went ye out into the wilderness to see? A reed shaken with the wind? But what went ye out for to see? A man clothed in soft raiment? behold, they that wear soft clothing are in kings' houses. But what went ye out for to see? A prophet? yea, I say unto you, and more than a prophet. . . . [Yet] John came neither eating nor drinking, and they say, He hath a devil. The Son of man came eating and drinking, and they say, Behold a man gluttonous, and a winebibber, a friend of publicans and sinners" (Matthew 11: 7–19).

with them shards of belief and fragments of philosophy and theology (as does Lucky in his speech) which only tantalize them with desire for the impossible. Estragon is closer to their real situation when he remarks, "There's no lack of void" (p. 42 +).

There are many other biblical or theological and religious references in the play that serve similar ironic functions: Pozzo as a parody of God the Father, though "not particularly human" (p. 19 +), happy to meet the meanest creature (p. 20), "Of the same species as Pozzo! Made in God's image!" (p. 15 +), "even when the likeness is an imperfect one" (p. 16 +); Vladimir and Estragon as parodies of mankind, Estragon giving his name as "Adam" (p. 25) and later mocking Pozzo by calling him "Abel" and then "Cain," concluding humorously that "He's all humanity" (p. 54); the image of Godot as a parody of popular images of God, with white beard (p. 59), Blake's and Shaw's old Nobodaddy; and many other miscellaneous references to God, saints, and things religious.

All of these various ironic references serve to keep alive in the play what the story of the two thieves had suggested, that there is no salvation for Vladimir and Estragon. Allusion to two specific parables makes this point even clearer. At the end of act 1, when the boy, the messenger,[7] arrives to say that Mr. Godot "won't come this evening but surely to-morrow" (p. 33 +), and Vladimir proceeds to question him about his "credentials," the boy reveals that he minds the goats and his brother minds the sheep. These two words together are enough to suggest one of the best known of Jesus's parables, one frequently used in art and sermon, the parable of the sheep and the goats:

> When the Son of man shall come in his glory, and all the holy angels with him, then shall he sit upon the throne of his glory: and before him shall be gathered all nations: and he shall separate them one from another, as a shepherd divideth his sheep from the goats: and he shall set the sheep on his right hand, but the goats on the left. Then shall the King say unto them on his right hand, Come, ye blessed of my Father, inherit the kingdom

7. The word "angel," of course, means "messenger," and European art is full of "boy" angels, cherubs.

prepared for you from the foundation of the world. . . . Then
shall he say also unto them on the left hand, Depart from me, ye
cursed, into everlasting fire, prepared for the devil and his
angels.

[Matthew 25:31–46]

This is, of course, a narrative about salvation and damnation; the
sheep are the saved, the goats are the damned. It is significant that
the messenger who attends Vladimir and Estragon is the goatherd
(Vladimir and Estragon seem not to recognize the significance of
this fact, but Beckett's informed audience does). And previous
ironies about the nature of this parodied God are intensified by
his perverse beating of the boy who tends the sheep, not the one
who tends the goats (the damned are damned and the saved get
beaten). Act 2 ends with a similar messenger (apparently not the
same one, but not necessarily his shepherd brother either). It is
this boy, who in response to questions, provides the information
that Godot has a white beard, frightening Vladimir and Estragon
into pleas for mercy and expectations of punishment (pp. 59 f.).

A second parable which contributes to the sense that Vladimir
and Estragon will not be saved is the parable of the wise and foolish
virgins. The textual allusions to this narrative are quite brief, and
it is arguable to what extent Beckett might have expected the
reference to be recognized. But it is a reference he has used
elsewhere in his work, most notably in *Endgame,* written immediately
after *Waiting for Godot,* and it is a parable so frequently used in
sermons and in art that a reasonably well-informed audience would
know it. The single line that carries the reference might not arrest
attention but could nonetheless have its effect subliminally.

One of the critical lines in the parable of the wise and foolish
virgins is the statement, "Behold, the bridegroom cometh, go ye
out to meet him."[8] These lines from the parable are echoed in
Vladimir's triumphant announcement, "It's Godot! We're saved!
Let's go and meet him!" (p. 47 +). Like attendant virgins of ancient
ceremony, these two derelicts have awaited one who they are sure
has a special claim on them and in waiting have proved themselves

8. The full text of the parable is given in the discussion of *Endgame* on pp.
34 f.

worthy. "What are we doing here, *that* is the question. And we are blessed in this, that we happen to know the answer. Yes, in this immense confusion one thing alone is clear. We are waiting for Godot to come—" (p. 51 +). In the parable the bridegroom *does* finally arrive and takes those who are ready into the wedding feast (an image for the "kingdom of heaven" or salvation). But in this play Vladimir is wrong, they are not saved (or blessed), and Estragon is right, they're "in hell" (p. 47 +). Once again the parable has served as ironic contrast to the dramatic scene: the received wisdom of Vladimir's world is untrue; he may regulate his behavior and set his expectations according to the old stories, but in fact these stories do not "work": *he* may keep *his* appointment, but the bridegroom does not. In the parable, of course, the bridegroom tarries, arriving finally at midnight; and it is precisely this detail of the story that traps Vladimir, the never knowing if he has waited long enough: perhaps Godot will come tomorrow, "without fail" (p. 58 +).

Vladimir is not, of course, consciously referring to this parable; but its ethic resides in him, as his echo of its words suggests. And the audience, recognizing the reference, sees one more grimly comic moment of blighted hope. "Your only hope left is to disappear" (p. 47 +). But they continue to wait, hoping for a salvation, a deliverance, even though all their stories of salvation—the two thieves, the sheep and goats, the ten virgins—mock any real hope they might have.

Lucky's monologue presents yet another kind of narrative, a mock account of the history of Western thought concerning the relationship between God and man. This narrative, this mock discourse, like the parables, presents an image of blighted hope. Despite the apparent chaos of the presentation, there are enough intelligible phrases with enough connections that a semblance of meaning does emerge from the welter of repetitions, puns, and pseudo-philosophical jargon. A paraphrase of that meaning could go something like this: despite the supposed existence of a personal God—both popular (with white beard) and philosophical (God *qua* God)—who supposedly loves mankind (while at the same time having neither sensitivity to man's suffering nor power to help him and in some cases even tormenting some men), and despite the supposed intellectual and physical progress of man himself, mankind wastes and pines. No distractions of physical activity or mental contrivance can hide the fact that man is only a "skull," fading, dying, only a skull that has been abandoned unfinished.[9] An audience, of course, does not "catch" this whole "statement" and does not need to. Students of philosophy will hear the "quaquaquaqua" and be amused at Beckett's mockery of Latinate pedantry ("now, consider a table, *qua* table"); those swift with puns will enjoy the scatology; the athletic intellectuals will chortle over "conating" and "camogie" as allied activities; and anyone with an ear for poetry and a heart for misery will hear the sonorous repetitions of "wastes and pines" and the delicate lamentations of "alas"; and by the end, all will have given up attempts at logic, so that repetitions alone will arrest attention: "the skull the skull the skull the skull," and the last word, literally the last word on the subject, "unfinished." The discourse is unfinished; man, that mere skull, is unfinished.

9. See pp. 28+ to 29+. Walter D. Asmus describes Beckett's own analysis of Lucky's monologue thus: "Beckett starts to talk about Lucky's monologue. It is not as difficult as it may seem, he says. We are going to divide it into three parts and the second part is going to be divided again into two sections. The first part is about the indifference of heaven, about divine apathy. This part ends with, 'but not so fast . . .' The second part starts off with 'considering what is more,' and is about man, who wastes and pines and furthermore fades away. These two points represent the two under-sections of the second part. The theme of the third part is 'the earth abode of stones' and starts with 'considering what is more, much more grave.' Beckett is very concerned to be exact in his explanations [in German] and repeats certain ideas, underlining them with short gestures.

"The actor would like to know, how should he deal with the end of the monologue. Beckett explains that the different elements, belonging to the first three sections, are returning here, at the end. He compares these with a cadence in music: The threads and themes are being gathered together. The monologue's theme is: to shrink on an impossible earth under an indifferent heaven"; Program Notes, Brooklyn Academy of Music (May 25–June 18, 1978), leaf 4 r. This description is borne out by Beckett's own notes for the Berlin production in 1975 (Samuel Beckett Collection, Reading University Library, MS 1396/4/3, p. 94, and MS 1396/4/4, p. 57; hereafter manuscripts from this collection will be cited as RUL).

All the various fragments of Lucky's monologue will not add up to an actual disquisition for the audience any more than it does for the three auditors on stage. But it disturbs them; yes, because it is, as Beckett terms it in the stage directions, a *tirade,* something vituperative, censorious in its language, something that has unpleasant content and meaning (and not just the "form" of apparent chaos). If the three listeners on stage become progressively more agitated, more violent in their reactions, it is in response to something they hear in what Lucky is saying. And if the audience has, along with its amusement at the parody and hi-jinks, a feeling of discomfort, that too comes from something Lucky is saying.

In a play where the word "saved" is used frequently and desperately, in a play that virtually begins with a "sacred" but untrustworthy story about salvation, it is unsettling to hear even a fragmentary denial of the possibility of that salvation. And the word "skull" does not help. Not only does "skull" obviously suggest death and disintegration, but also lodged somewhere in the memories of most people in Beckett's audience is the name "Golgotha," that place of the skull where the two thieves were crucified. If, as Lucky's monologue suggests, man is only a skull—carrying his hill of salvation around inside him as a mere image, like Moll in *Malone Dies* with her earrings and carved tooth[10]—then special places like Golgotha and special salvations from dying Gods or delaying Godots are the mere delusion Vladimir uneasily fears they are. Lucky's "narrative" thus becomes one more story to put beside Vladimir's story of the two thieves, both ironic commentaries on the present situation of blighted hope.

10. "He thrust Moll's face away from his on the pretext of examining her ear-rings. But as she made to return to the charge he checked her again with the first words that came into his head, namely, Why two Christs? implying that in his opinion one was more than sufficient. To which she made the absurd reply, Why two ears? But obtained his forgiveness a moment later, saying, with a smile (she smiled at the least thing), Besides they are the thieves, Christ is in my mouth. Then parting her jaws and pulling down her blobber-lip she discovered, breaking with its solitary fang the monotony of the gums, a long yellow canine bared to the roots and carved, with the drill probably, to represent the celebrated sacrifice"; Samuel Beckett, *Three Novels* (New York: Grove Press, 1965), pp. 263–64.

Pozzo's own rhetorical manner provides a fitting complement to Lucky's garbled speech. The answer to a simple question becomes an occasion for oratory. Pozzo vaporizes his throat for better delivery and demands complete attention from his audience, through both eye and ear (pp. 20+, 24+, 25). What he finally says becomes a little story containing scenic description, "main character," and an event, all told with expression:

> Ah yes! The night. (*He raises his head.*) But be a little more attentive, for pity's sake, otherwise we'll never get anywhere. (*He looks at the sky.*) Look! (*All look at the sky except Lucky who is dozing off again. Pozzo jerks the rope.*) Will you look at the sky, pig! (*Lucky looks at the sky.*) Good, that's enough. (*They stop looking at the sky.*) What is there so extraordinary about it? Qua sky. It is pale and luminous like any sky at this hour of the day. (*Pause.*) In these latitudes. (*Pause.*) When the weather is fine. (*Lyrical.*) An hour ago (*he looks at his watch, prosaic*) roughly (*lyrical*) after having poured forth even since (*he hesitates, prosaic*) say ten o'clock in the morning (*lyrical*) tirelessly torrents of red and white light it begins to lose its effulgence, to grow pale (*gesture of the two hands lapsing by stages*) pale, ever a little paler, a little paler until (*dramatic pause, ample gesture of the two hands flung wide apart*) pppfff! finished! it comes to rest. But—(*hand raised in admonition*)—but behind this veil of gentleness and peace night is charging (*vibrantly*) and will burst upon us (*snaps his fingers*) pop! like that! (*his inspiration leaves him*) just when we least expect it. (*Silence. Gloomily.*) That's how it is on this bitch of an earth.
>
> [Pp. 25 f.]

Unlike Lucky's speech, Pozzo's performance has more coherence, more calculated variety of effect, and a more clearly specified moral. But it is thus merely the deliberate rhetorician's version of Lucky's pessimism, as Pozzo's final speech in act 2 makes clear:

> (*suddenly furious*). Have you not done tormenting me with your accursed time! It's abominable! When! When! One day, is that not enough for you, one day he went dumb, one day I went blind, one day we'll go deaf, one day we were born, one day we shall die, the same day, the same second, is that not enough for

you? (*Calmer.*) They give birth astride of a grave, the light
gleams an instant, then it's night once more.

[P. 57 +]

Even here there is the vestige of story: scene (grave; gleam of
light); characters ("they," so powerfully present as to need no
antecedent); and an event (birth). The statement is philosophical;
that universal "they" refers to all progenitors (and ultimately to
all mankind, for who exists without having been part of them?),
and the universal statement made is that all life is short, womb and
tomb are adjacent. But the mode of statement is fictional, not
philosophical; the story, the vivid metaphor, carries the meaning.

Waiting for Godot is full of such little stories and suggestions of
story: all those dreams that Vladimir cannot bear to have recounted
("DON'T TELL ME!" pp. 11 and 57 +); the joke about the En-
glishman in the brothel, another story begun but not finished (p.
11 +); the song that opens act 2, an endless narrative about dogs
(pp. 37 f.); mythological references of several kinds, each carrying
its halo of story. These vestigial stories are dispersed throughout
the apparently static dramatic situation of waiting, and along with
them the somewhat longer forms of narrative already discussed:
biblical stories and parables, rhetorical and philosophical disquisitions, culminating in Pozzo's final arresting metaphor of death
in which the whole of human existence is concentrated in a miniature
story with universal applicability. In writing these various forms of
story and storylike elements into his first produced play, Beckett
is beginning to move toward that technique which he develops
powerfully in *Endgame* and even more subtly and effectively in his
later drama.

After the little canters of *Waiting for Godot,* Beckett composed
a substantial "chronicle" for *Endgame,* providing one of the best
examples of extended narrative as an essential part of drama: the
presence of story is unmistakable here, both to the audience and
to characters within the play. Hamm refers by name to his "chronicle" and is self-conscious in his narration of it, aware of himself
assuming the role of historian, aware of himself adopting a special
voice and manner setting off these words from his other speech.

His chronicle itself has to do both with origins and with ends; it "accounts for" an entire world by presenting critical events and interpreting their meaning. Hamm is the Moses of a garden desolate, the Polidore Virgile of a wrecked kingdom. He records bereft existence, a modern inversion of "providential history." The whole point of *Endgame* lies in the interrelationship between this chronicle, this value-laden record of past events, and the words and actions which make up the dramatic present of the play. The play ends when the narrative ends.

The chronicle is presented at length in two different versions at two different times. The occasions for recital of the story, the interruptions and editorial changes all suggest the extent to which this narrative is emotionally and philosophically important to Hamm, a way to give "meaning" to his life, a way to justify his behavior. First reference to the story occurs about halfway through the play, after Hamm and Clov have attempted various other diversions to make their existence bearable. Hamm's announcement "It's time for my story"[11] is much like Winnie's in *Happy Days;* there is a sense that the best distraction has been saved till last. The story—Hamm corrects the word to "chronicle"—is one which Clov states "you've been telling yourself all your days" (p. 58). It has an ongoing continuity suggested by Hamm's comments "where was I?" (p. 50) and "No, I've done that bit" (p. 51). It gets Hamm through difficult moments and leads him to that final moment when "time is over, reckoning closed and story ended" (p. 83).

Basically, this chronicle has to do with a man and his son, the son starving, the man petitioning Hamm for aid. As is usual throughout Beckett's work, the account contains a number of clear scriptural references, three of which epitomize Christian belief: the time is Christmas Eve (when life and light are born into the world), the boon sought is bread (the divine gift that sustains life), the child has been deep in sleep for three days (prototype of death and resurrection). The bare event itself has many counterparts in Biblical stories where a parent intercedes on behalf of a dying child

11. Samuel Beckett, *Endgame* (New York: Grove Press, 1958), p. 48.

(or in some cases, a master tries to save a beloved servant). In most of these stories the passionate commitment of the parent is shown by his or her traveling a distance and being undeterred by difficulties (whether awe of the prophet from whom aid is sought, rebuke of his or her efforts, or the premature arrival of death itself). The story of Jairus's daughter[12] and the story of the centurion and his servant[13] are well known versions.[14] In John, the event involves a solicitous father, not put off by rebuke, and a dying son:

> And there was a certain nobleman, whose son was sick at Capernaum. When he heard that Jesus was come out of Judea into Galilee, he went unto him, and besought him that he would come down, and heal his son: for he was at the point of death. Then said Jesus unto him, Except ye see signs and wonders, ye will not believe. The nobleman saith unto him, Sir, come down ere my child die. Jesus saith unto him, Go thy way; thy son liveth. And the man believed the word that Jesus had spoken unto him, and he went his way. And as he was now going down, his servants met him, and told him, saying, Thy son liveth. Then inquired he of them the hour when he began to amend. And they said unto him, Yesterday at the seventh hour the fever left him. So the father knew that it was at the same hour, in which Jesus said unto him, Thy son liveth: and himself believed, and his whole house.
>
> [John 4:46–53]

In the story of Elijah and the widow of Zarephath, there is the added element of imminent starvation, both food and life being restored to the woman and her son by the man of God in response to the widow's prayers.[15] But as is also the case in Beckett's other work, these remote biblical allusions suggest ironic contrast: Hamm

12. Matthew 9:18–26; Mark 5:21–43; Luke 8:40–56.
13. Matthew 8:5–13; Luke 7:1–10.
14. See also Mark 9:14–29, Matthew 17:14–21, and Luke 9:37–43 for the story of the father seeking cure of his epileptic son; and Matthew 15:21–28 and Mark 7:24–30 for the Syrophoenician woman's persistence on behalf of her afflicted daughter.
15. 1 Kings 17:8–24.

questions the suppliant father's belief that "there's manna in heaven still for imbeciles like you" (p. 53). There is "no cure" for being on *this* earth, no providential bread in *this* wilderness; the great faith of this father does not move Hamm's "divinity" to provide miraculous sustenance. On the contrary, Hamm tempts the man to betray his role as father, to abandon his own beneficence. Such a twist to the prototypical stories suggests what is central in Hamm's own bitter disappointment about his own existence.

One of the clues to the importance of this malevolent twist comes from the fact that Hamm interrupts his narrative before getting to his "punch line":

> Well to make it short I finally offered to take him into my service. He had touched a chord. And then I imagined already that I wasn't much longer for this world.
> *He laughs. Pause.*
> Well?
> *Pause.*
> Well? Here if you were careful you might die a nice natural death, in peace and comfort.
> *Pause.*
> Well?
> *Pause.*
> In the end he asked me would I consent to take in the child as well—if he were still alive.
> *Pause.*
> It was the moment I was waiting for.
> *Pause.*
> Would I consent to take in the child . . .
> *Pause.*
> I can see him still, down on his knees, his hands flat on the ground, glaring at me with his mad eyes, in defiance of my wishes.
> *Pause. Normal tone.*
> I'll soon have finished with this story.
> *Pause.*
> Unless I bring in other characters.
> *Pause.*

But where would I find them?
    Pause.
Where would I look for them?
    Pause. He whistles. Enter Clov.
Let us pray to God.

[Pp. 53–54]

He rationalizes that he will soon have finished his story, implying that he does not want to get to the end too quickly and thus needs to stop for a while. But what he turns to when he stops reveals indirectly what there was in the narrative itself that he needed to avoid. Apparently out of the blue he says, "Let us pray" (that "oremus" of sacred liturgy which introduces commentary on the "lesson" or scriptural narrative just recited) and the prayer he gets Nagg and Clov to participate in results in an important assertion ("Our Father which art—") and an even more important judgment: "The bastard! He doesn't exist!" (p. 55).

Here is the source of Hamm's desolation: there is no father to care for him, no heavenly father, no earthly father to hear his cries and to provide solace. "The bastard! He doesn't exist!" serves as commentary both on traditional prayer and also on the story Hamm was just telling. The cause of all this desolation is Hamm's relationship with Nagg; the effect of it all is seen in Hamm's relationship with Clov and other "creatures." In order to understand the painful significance of the content of Hamm's chronicle, it is necessary to look carefully at both his experience as son and his experience as father.

First, Hamm's own experience as son. His hatred for Nagg ("Accursed progenitor!" p. 9) is revealed early in the play and is connected with hatred for his own existence: "Why did you engender me?" (p. 49) is not a question so much as an expression of resentment. Hamm's lament about existence, the desire to end, has its root in his first experience of existence, his infancy and childhood. If he curses the ideal father, "that bastard" who doesn't exist, it is due to neglect from his actual father; the passage that establishes this fact comes immediately after the prayer sequence, as Nagg complains about being wakened unnecessarily:

31

Whom did you call when you were a tiny boy, and were frightened, in the dark? Your mother? No. Me. We let you cry. Then
we moved you out of earshot, so that we might sleep in peace.
>*Pause.*

I was asleep, as happy as a king, and you woke me up to have
me listen to you. It wasn't indispensable, you didn't really need
to have me listen to you.
>*Pause.*

I hope the day will come when you'll really need to have me
listen to you, and need to hear my voice, any voice.
>*Pause.*

Yes, I hope I'll live till then, to hear you calling me like when
you were a tiny boy, and were frightened, in the dark, and I was
your only hope.

[P. 56]

This passage connects several important elements in *Endgame*:
Hamm's childhood fear, the dark, his father's neglect, the need to
call out, the need to have a listener. The story Hamm tells now—
the prayer sequence and this subsequent passage are only an interruption of that chronicle, which will eventually resume—is simply
an adult version of his childhood cry. Then, and now, he *does* need
someone to listen to him, and then, as now, his "only hope," his
father, fails him by refusal. Later in the play, as an introduction
to his final, terminal soliloquy, Hamm repeats a number of these
elements in a passage similar to Nagg's. After thinking of fearful
events, of being deserted by a father, "all kinds of fantasies," Hamm
says: "Then babble, babble, words, like the solitary child who turns
himself into children, two, three, so as to be together, and whisper
together, in the dark" (p. 70).

The adult, as well as the child, finds remedy for desertion in
storytelling: the babbles, the whispers, the pretense that others are
there make the dark not so lonely, so frightening. This passage of
Hamm's, like the earlier one of Nagg's, comes immediately after
Hamm has speculated about the ending of the story he has been
telling.[16] If he ends his story, he will indeed be alone in the dark,

16. "I'll soon have finished with this story. (Pause.) Unless I bring in other
characters" (p. 54) and "Perhaps I could go on with my story, end it and begin
another" (p. 69).

a solitary child abandoned, no father to listen and comfort. And, as is the case with all of Beckett's use of narrative, it is not the mere fact of storytelling that is important, but the very content of the story itself is crucial, allowing the character simultaneously to reveal and conceal himself. Hamm's chronicle does not serve as mere distraction; it betrays his deepest fear and need, as his final brief reference to it reveals in the important last minutes of the play.

But before discussing that ending, it is necessary to examine Hamm's own experience as "father" and note how that correlates with his experience as son. Fatherhood is, in Hamm's case, a metaphor for power, a power he exercises in three ways. First, like a biological father, Hamm has given a specific son his chance in life; he says to Clov, "I was a father to you," "my house a home for you" (p. 38). Second, he has supplanted his own father; now he is the one to dispense pap, to promise and withhold sugarplums; now he controls Nagg, not vice versa, and in that process he duplicates Nagg's own earlier treatment of him; for example, he objects to Nagg's keeping him awake now by storytelling (p. 18) just as earlier Nagg had objected to having his own sleep interrupted by Hamm's infant cry. But Hamm's third and greatest assertion of power is established by his references to himself as divine, the ultimate and most powerful of fatherhoods.

Hamm is an ineffectual god of a "corpsed" world, parodying the traditional role of divinity in a number of ways. He is master-generator whose will is carried out by a servant-son. He is right at the center of his world but also, through that son, visits the perimeters (p. 25), beyond which is hell, that "other hell" (p. 26) since as a god manqué his own paradise is itself infernal. Both he and Clov use the regal or Trinitarian plural on one occasion.[17] Enthroned at the center of his world, he trains his blindness on the earth and "sees"—through his son, Clov—"a multitude . . . in transports . . . of joy" (p. 29).[18] Since Clov's telescope is turned

17. "CLOV: So you all want me to leave you. . . . HAMM: You can't leave us" (p. 37).

18. This biblical-sounding phrase is not a direct quotation, but it has the resonance of many passages in Revelation (see, for example, 19:1–8). This

toward the auditorium when he makes this grim little biblical joke, the audience, too, is included in that gray lifeless world outside of Hamm's room. That world is dead because Hamm has failed as savior: "All those I might have helped. (Pause.) Helped! (Pause.) Saved" (p. 68). Throughout the play Hamm manifests a desire to have creatures pray to him; he likes to have his dog "gazing" at him, "asking," "begging," "imploring" him (p. 41). But whether it be a bone for the dog, bread and crumpets for the starving multitudes (p. 68), or meaning for the audience (p. 33), Hamm does not provide any manna[19] in this wilderness, any light in this darkness. He implies, in fact, that the desolation of the earth is due to his own absence from it: "I was never there. . . . Absent, always. It all happened without me" (p. 74).

Thus in Hamm traditional divine attributes—benevolence, omnipotence, ubiquity, omniscience—are all inverted. Toward the end of the play Beckett introduces a biblical allusion that illustrates how deadly Hamm's pseudo-divinity is. Despite Hamm's protestation that he does not himself know what has happened (p. 74) or whether it matters (p. 75), Clov challenges Hamm's feigned innocence: "When old Mother Pegg asked you for oil for her lamp and you told her to get out to hell, you knew what was happening then, no? (Pause.) You know what she died of, Mother Pegg? Of darkness" (p. 75). This passage with its oil lamp and outer darkness contains clear reference to the New Testament parable about the wise and foolish virgins:

> Then shall the kingdom of heaven be likened unto ten virgins,
> which took their lamps, and went forth to meet the bridegroom.
> And five of them were wise, and five were foolish. They that
> were foolish took their lamps, and took no oil with them: but the
> wise took oil in their vessels with their lamps. While the bride-

association is particularly ironic since Revelation is permeated with the refrain "behold, I come quickly."

19. In an early draft of the play, Hamm's important connection with food (crumpets, pap, sugarplums, Turkish Delight, porridge, corn, etc.) is suggested by an emotional moment in which the character (there called X) shows great emotion about his failure to garden: "(Pleurant) J'aurais dû être horticulteur! . . [sic] J'ai rate ma vie! . . [sic]"; *Avant fin de partie*, RUL MS 1227/7/16/7, p. 16.

groom tarried, they all slumbered and slept. And at midnight there was a cry made, Behold, the bridegroom cometh; go ye out to meet him. Then all those virgins arose, and trimmed their lamps. And the foolish said unto the wise, Give us of your oil; for our lamps are gone out. But the wise answered, saying, Not so; lest there be not enough for us and you: but go ye rather to them that sell, and buy for yourselves. And while they went to buy, the bridegroom came; and they that were ready went in with him to the marriage: and the door was shut. Afterward came also the other virgins, saying, Lord, Lord, open to us. But he answered and said, Verily I say unto you, I know you not. Watch therefore; for ye know neither the day nor the hour wherein the Son of man cometh.[20]

Parables are literary forms (stories) used to teach a lesson. Beckett picks up the images and basic message of this particular well-known parable and inverts it for his own purposes. Hamm is thus the god who damns by withholding or being unable to provide the means which make life possible, whether it be bread in the wilderness or light in the darkness. After facing this revelation about himself (which clearly rankles, because the phrase "Of darkness!" interrupts Hamm's speculations about his own death a few minutes later), Hamm moves on to what he calls his "last soliloquy" (p. 78), that moment which will end Hamm, end the play, and reveal how very significant his chronicle really is.

As son, Hamm was mistreated and abandoned, and as father, he has mistreated and failed his own creation. His chronicle is an attempt to offset the pain of these two basic related experiences.

The chronicle deals with the paternal benevolence Hamm never experienced, a father's selfless efforts to try to save a starving son. As he recounts this chronicle, Hamm uses three voices: his special narrating voice to tell the story, the father's voice as quoted by the narrating voice, and his own voice to comment on the other two.

20. Matthew 25:1–13. See also the parable of the marriage feast, which ends with lines associating darkness and damnation: "Then said the king to the servants, Bind him hand and foot, and take him away, and cast him into outer darkness; there shall be weeping and gnashing of teeth. For many are called, but few are chosen"; Matthew 22:1–14.

The narrating voice describes the scene and most of the action: "The man came crawling towards me, on his belly. Pale, wonderfully pale and thin, he seemed on the point of—" (p. 50). And then his own voice ("normal tone," Beckett calls it) comments: "No, I've done that bit" (p. 51). After describing at length the harshness of this Christmas day, the narrating voice gets to the main issue, narrating, commenting, and quoting:

> It was then he took the plunge. It's my little one, he said. Tsstss, a little one, that's bad. My little boy, he said, as if the sex mattered. Where did he come from? He named the hole. A good half-day, on horse. What are you insinuating? That the place is still inhabited? No no, not a soul, except himself and the child—assuming he existed. Good. I enquired about the situation at Kov, beyond the gulf. Not a sinner. Good. And you expect me to believe you have left your little one back there, all alone, and alive into the bargain? Come now!
>
> [P. 52]

The narration continues in this manner to recount the man's plea for bread for his child, the narrator's scorn and anger, his denial that "there's manna in heaven still" or that there is any resurrection (the earth will not awake in spring nor will one deep in sleep for three days arise), and concludes with a temptation: "I finally offered to take him into my service." At this point Hamm interrupts his narrative, worrying that his story will soon end, forcing Nagg and Clov to join in prayer, tormenting Nagg about the sugarplum, and finally talking with Clov about the dog and Clov's leaving. Then he resumes the story. This entire interruption reveals why he stops the story where he does and why he resumes it when he does. The temptation directed toward the fictional father is a crucial one: here is a man, himself starving (or so Hamm's description suggests), who seems to care more for his son than for himself. Rather than face the pain which the spectacle of such benevolence inflicts on Hamm—he so much wishes he had had that kind of love as a child—he turns away from narration in order to berate those fathers who failed him (Our Father and Nagg) and to dominate those who stand as his "sons" (the dog and Clov).[21] Then, having vented his hostility in two directions, against both fathers and sons, he is able to resume narration (p. 58) only to break off again at the same point: "Before accepting [the proffered job] he asks if he may have his little boy with him" (p. 60). Hamm seems not to be able to move the narrative beyond this point. What if the man does indeed care for the child's welfare more than for his own? What if he refuses the narrator's offer of help if it does not include his son? How can Hamm face such altruism?

In both his narrative and his "normal" speculations, Hamm argues against benevolence and altruism by suggesting that earthly existence is an incurable disease. In his narrating voice he says to the suppliant father, "Use your head, can't you, use your head, you're on earth, there's no cure for that!" (p. 53) and repeats the line word for word later, in his "normal tone" as he speculates about all those he might have saved. But this repeated violent outburst is not followed, as it is in the chronicle, by a return to innocuous description of the weather; instead it continues, parodying the chief injunction of the New Testament: "Get out of here and love one another! Lick your neighbor as yourself!" (p. 68). Hamm himself has refused the starving multitude bread (and crumpets); it is a small matter for his fictive narrator to deny one small boy life.

Throughout *Endgame*, Hamm has been talking about ending, bringing all life to a halt, his own as well. In the final moments of the play there is the suggestion such a winding down to absolute zero does occur. And one of the elements that makes cessation possible is final desertion among fathers and sons: "I'll have called my father and I'll have called my ... (he hesitates) ... my son" (p. 69). If they are gone, he will again be a solitary child alone in the dark, telling himself stories. And when the story ends, Hamm will end. In the last few moments of the play, his "last soliloquy," when Nagg and Clov are silent and Hamm thinks they are both irrevocably gone, Hamm finishes his story and "gives up" (p. 82). The last words of his story reveal the real nature of his hatred and

21. The similar servile role for these two is further suggested by Beckett's production notes for *Endspiel* (1967): "Clov's pose when trying to make dog stand. Parallel backs"; RUL MS 1396/4/5, leaf 15 r.

desolation. He picks up the narrative now at its critical point, where he had abandoned it twice before—"If he could have his child with him. . . ." (p. 83)—and he continues to comment:

> It was the moment I was waiting for.
> *Pause.*
> You don't want to abandon him? You want him to bloom while you are withering? Be there to solace your last million last moments?
> *Pause.*
> He doesn't realize, all he knows is hunger, and cold, and death to crown it all. But you! You ought to know what the earth is like, nowadays. Oh I put him before his responsibilities!
> *Pause. Normal tone.*
> Well, there we are, there I am, that's enough.
>
> [P. 83]

"That's enough" of the story because Hamm has finally stated what is particularly offensive to him in this altruistic father-son relationship. The narrator's apparent argument—life on earth is so bad that a father's real responsibility is to *avoid* sustaining his son's existence—is really only a mask for the narrator's true feelings of resentment. The words "bloom" and "wither" betray the narrator's real motive, Hamm's real feelings. The corollary of a son's life is the father's death. By the natural order of human development, as the one grows into prime, the other passes beyond it, and the only term of that beyond is death. Hamm resents the fact that he will degenerate while another flourishes; thus his determination that there be no more potential procreators in this world, no fleas nor small boys from which humanity might start all over again (p. 33). His is the resentment of age toward youth, compounded by his own personal sense of never having had the solace he needed, not in childhood and not now in his old age. So he berates the father in his story, presuming to lay bare that father's true motive, to prove it not altruistic but selfish: "Be there to solace your last million last moments?" But this accusation that the father only wants to help the son so that the son will help him has no foundation in the narrative as Hamm recounts it; this is pure projection at the most critical moment of the story. Hamm is the one unsolaced.

This story has allowed Hamm to reveal his deep sense of not having been cared for (his own father moved him out of earshot and certainly did nothing so beneficent as try to save his life at the expense of his own) and his deep resentment that such care could ever exist for anyone else: the father in his story must surely be a fake altruist, as the narrator's arguments about responsibility are supposed to prove.[22] At the same time, the story has allowed him to disguise this revelation as fiction: he is not saying anything about him and Nagg; he is only making up events and details to pass the time. And yet this story is also a reckoning, a way to account for his life and himself. He is able to give up, to end, to die only when "time is over, reckoning closed and story ended" (p. 83). These words introduce that final moment of his narrative, which has just been discussed. He can terminate that narrative only after he has reached the stage in it when he can say, however colloquially, "there I am"; only then is the story "enough." He has recounted his deepest feelings of neglect, resentment, and hatred (felt as a child and re-enacted in reversed roles as an adult), but in doing this he has also disguised and protected himself. He has never had to say "I" except as a supposedly fictional narrator.

22. In *Avant fin de partie* (p. 19), there is a story about a mother and a son, in which the son expresses great care for the mother: he alone knows her well enough to realize that her disappearance is a serious matter; he alone knows where she is to be found ("Cherchez, cherchez, elle est dans le coin"); and he alone nearly perishes from shock when her battered body is finally discovered, like a sponge, every bone broken, every fracture open. Somehow, she survives and after fifteen years in casts and on a bland diet, actually recovers, nursed by her watchful son. A sense of terrible disaster and abiding loss permeates the story (years later the narrator keeps repeating not the lines about recovery but the lines "cherchez-la dans le coin, je la connais," as if that moment of fear were perpetually present to him). These emotional elements are much like those in Hamm's chronicle, but the reversed roles and the alternate parent are significant differences. As Beckett finally chose to formulate the play, mothers are negligible and fathers are of central importance; and the son's pain comes not from loss of the parent (by death) but from loss of the parent's *care* (which results in the *child's* death).

The final seconds of the play dramatize what the story has also revealed. Thinking he has already lost both father and son, Hamm continues to divest himself of the things that give him solace—he throws away the dog, he throws away the whistle, he repeats the announcement "Discard" (p. 84). Only one possession remains, his handkerchief, and his word for it betrays with concentrated irony everything that the chronicle has revealed. "Old stancher!" he says, "You ... remain." At the beginning and at the end of the play, Hamm's first and last words contain this rather unusual term, "old stancher." Its immediate meaning is available to the audience without a dictionary, but in its etymology it carries a grim pun that establishes once more how bereft Hamm feels.

The *Oxford English Dictionary* lists several meanings of the basic term "stanch:" to stop the flow of water, the flow of blood; to stop a leak, to make something watertight; to quench, repress, extinguish (thirst, appetite, hatred, anger); to weary. And under the noun form "stancher" ("One who or that which stanches"), two examples are particularly apt: "This is the first and chiefest Bloud stencher" and "Friendship, stancher of our wounds and sorrows."[23] The two most familiar modern uses of this word correspond to these two earlier literary examples. The audience does not need a dictionary in hand because it certainly knows the clichés "a staunch friend" and "to stanch a wound." "Friend," "wound," love and death: Beckett makes capital of these two apparently distant associations contained in Hamm's exclamation, "Old stancher! (Pause.) You ... remain."

Literally this stancher is the "large blood-stained handkerchief" which covers Hamm's face when the play opens and which he replaces when the play ends. It stops the flow of blood, and thus is a true and loyal friend. It literally stands by him when all else fails and must be discarded. The irony of this reference and its associations comes from the fact that "blood" itself has failed Hamm, blood relationships. Fathers and sons, sources of life and sustenance during both infancy and old age, have not been loyal and true. Fathers and sons seem, in fact, to cause "wounds and

23. *The Compact Edition of the Oxford English Dictionary* (New York: Oxford University Press, 1971), 2:3012.

sorrows," not to bind them up. There is no young boy (as in the chronicle) to solace Hamm's "last million last moments." He is left with just a bloody rag of extinction, himself and his story ended.

In addition to this extensive use of a single narrative, *Endgame* also contains shorter narrative forms of the kind already seen in *Waiting for Godot:* the joke and the anecdote. When Hamm begins his brief recital "I once knew a madman," he is ostensibly recounting an event he actually experienced, as distinct from his chronicle, which is presented in its form and context as first-person narrative fiction. This anecdote is brief, moving, self-contained, recounted once and not referred to again:

> I once knew a madman who thought the end of the world had come. He was a painter—and engraver. I had a great fondness for him. I used to go and see him, in the asylum. I'd take him by the hand and drag him to the window. Look! There! All that rising corn! And there! Look! The sails of the herring fleet! All that loveliness!
> *Pause.*
> He'd snatch away his hand and go back into his corner. Appalled. All he had seen was ashes.
> *Pause.*
> He alone had been spared.
> *Pause.*
> Forgotten.
> *Pause.*
> It appears the case is . . . was not so . . . so unusual.
> [P. 44]

This flash of memory into Hamm's mind makes perfect sense in context: he and Clov have been talking about the desolation all around them, the unburied dead who once were bonny "like a flower of the field" (p. 42); they both are present in a room which, like that asylum, imprisons them, opening out, through windows, on the world outside. It is not unusual that the wreck of this present world should remind Hamm of that painter in the past who only perceived ashes and devastation. What is important about the memory in this context is that it shows the madman to have been a prophet. Even Hamm, in those days, saw the rising corn, the herring fleet, "all that loveliness" of fecund, nourishing nature. The painter seemed then to be insane, but he is proved, by the passage and development of time, to have been visionary—not mentally crippled, but swift. Hamm's hesitating concession, "the case is ... was not so ... so unusual" betrays both how pained he is by the loss of that golden world (that corn which would have fed some child, if there were beneficence) and also his awareness (kept down, like Lear's early realizations) that the madman indeed spoke true, that apparent madness was in fact real sanity.

Much critical commentary on *Endgame* has associated the play with postnuclear destruction. It is interesting in this regard to compare Hamm's anecdote of the mad painter with Alain Resnais's film *Hiroshima Mon Amour,* where scenes of lovemaking are counterpointed with memory flashes of maimed and burned bodies. Or, for that matter, to go back in time to the medieval and renaissance tradition of *memento mori* with its countless woodcut emblems showing the beautiful woman (to take only one example) gazing into her mirror which reflects the skeleton she will become. This apocalyptic vision, to see the ashes of "all that loveliness" even while it still flourishes is, apparently, as Hamm reluctantly realizes, "not so unusual." His reply to Clov's observation that "There are so many terrible things" has an interesting double meaning to it: "No, no, there are not so many now" seems a denial if the focus is on "now" and also a confirmation of the devastation if the focus is on "many."

Nagg and Nell's amusement over similar devastations serves as "subplot parallel" to Hamm's anecdote and chronicle. Nagg and Nell laugh heartily remembering "When we crashed on our tandem and lost our shanks" (p. 16), and Nagg's favorite joke about the tailor puts into comic relief the miserable state of that world, that botched creation, in which such horrors regularly occur (pp. 22–23). This "engagement joke" so tickled Nell that she capsized the canoe on Lake Como where Nagg first told it to her. "By rights we should have been drowned" (p. 21) does not, of course, testify to an odd kindness on the part of the cosmos but rather to that continuing misfortune which has plagued Hamm's life. With no Nagg, no Nell, no marriage, no engendering, Hamm would not have found himself where he is now, surrounded by ashes and the memories and stories by which he both looks at his misery and tries to evade it.

Happy Days presents a particularly complex use of narrative because Beckett employs a number of different kinds of canters and chronicles: allusions that serve as highly condensed stories, memories of past events that are ultimately anecdotal, and, most important, "when all else fails,"[24] Winnie's actual story itself, another of Beckett's important extended narratives.

Winnie's frequent quotations,[25] poorly remembered fragments of poetry, usually allude to events and not mere sentiments in their original; a listener with better memory than hers could summon up a scene with characters, action, and perhaps even climax; in short, a little "story." For example, Winnie's first foray into the sustaining tradition of English literature nets her a fragment of *Hamlet:*

> —what are those wonderful lines—(*wipes one eye*)—woe woe is me—(*wipes the other*)—to see what I see—(*looks for spectacles*)— ah yes—(*takes up spectacles*)—wouldn't miss it—(*starts polishing spectacles, breathing on lenses*)—or would I?
>
> [Pp. 10–11]

This moment is in itself highly comic: the surprising conjunction of "wonderful" and "woe," the intellectual double take of "or would I," the silly literalizing of "see"—all these are techniques of rhetoric and farce of which Beckett is the acknowledged master. But the comedy (and its underlying desperate unhappiness) is intensified for any listener who recognizes Winnie's allusion and has a brief flash of Ophelia, just insulted and rejected by Hamlet, lamenting over his madness, herself "of ladies most dejected and wretched."[26] Robust and determined Winnie is the very opposite of fragile Ophelia, and yet the story of Ophelia and Hamlet lurks in Winnie's

24. Samuel Beckett, *Happy Days* (New York: Grove Press, 1961), p. 54.

25. The fullest list of identified quotations and allusions is to be found in S. E. Gontarski's *Beckett's Happy Days: A Manuscript Study* (Columbus, Ohio: Ohio State University Libraries, 1977), p. 59–74, 76–77.

26. *Hamlet* III. i. 158–69.

mind in ironic counterpoint to her own situation. A few moments later, Winnie again invokes a scene from Shakespeare as she rouges her lips: "Ensign crimson" and "Pale flag" (p. 15) may perhaps sound like Revlon's latest colors, but they are in fact Romeo's words as he bends over the body of sleeping Juliet, thinking her dead and celebrating her surviving beauty.[27] A whole story—tragic love, fated youth—is suggested by this allusion, used so grotesquely by Winnie in her aged and loveless sterility.

Not all the poetic allusions are so eventful, but many are ultimately narrative nonetheless: "Hail, holy light" (p. 49) calls up the elaborate action of *Paradise Lost,* as does Winnie's mangled "Oh fleeting joys ... oh something lasting woe" (p. 14).[28] Here the whole divine economy and plenum of creation, Adam and Eve's great sin and happy fault, cosmic loss and gain stand in ironic contrast to Winnie's nullity. Even her brief reference to the *Rubáiyát* suggests a highly condensed little story. After asking Willie if he found her lovable and, as usual, receiving no answer, she goes on to comfort herself with a dash of optimism climaxing in poetry:

And you have done more than your bit already, for the time being, just lie back now and relax, I shall not trouble you again unless I am compelled to, just to know you are there within hearing and conceivably on the semi-alert is ... er ... paradise enow.

[Pp. 31–32]

Suddenly there flashes on the skrim of memory (even for an audience just semi-alert) the prototypical idyllic desert scene: amorous man and maiden, cool jug of wine, wholesome loaf of bread, an event of great passion commemorated in elegant miniature, complete antithesis to Winnie and Willie in their burning sand.[29]

Memories provide even more explicit narrative units than do allusions in *Happy Days.* Most of Winnie's memories have to do with romantic or erotic relationships. After Willie has read aloud from the newspaper, "His Grace and Most Reverend Father in God

27. *Romeo and Juliet* V. iii. 91–96.
28. *Paradise Lost* 3:1 and 10:741–42.
29. Edward FitzGerald, *The Rubáiyát of Omar Khayyám,* st. 12.

Dr Carolus Hunter dead in tub," Winnie goes off in an ecstasy of "fervent reminiscence":

> Charlie Hunter! (*Pause.*) I close my eyes—(*she takes off spectacles and does so, hat in one hand, spectacles in other . . .*)—and am sitting on his knees again, in the back garden at Borough Green, under the horse-beech. (*Pause. She opens eyes, puts on spectacles, fiddles with hat.*) Oh the happy memories!
>
> [Pp. 15–16]

And when again Willie reads, "Opening for smart youth," Winnie continues her recollections (with probably unintentional double entendre worthy of Willie's announcement):

> My first ball! (*Long pause.*) My second ball! (*Long pause. Closes eyes.*) My first kiss! (*Pause. . . . Winnie opens eyes.*) A Mr Johnson, or Johnston, or perhaps I should say John*stone*. Very bushy moustache, very tawny. (*Reverently.*) Almost ginger! (*Pause.*) Within a toolshed, though whose I cannot conceive. We had no toolshed and he most certainly had no toolshed. (*Closes eyes.*) I see the piles of pots. (*Pause.*) The tangles of bast. (*Pause.*) The shadows deepening among the rafters.
>
> [P. 16]

These little anecdotes of early love are flanked by the tragic and romantic poetic allusions just discussed and are followed by a more fully developed memory of a more recent event:

> (*She turns to bag, rummages in it, brings out finally a nailfile, turns back front and begins to file nails. Files for a time in silence, then the following punctuated by filing.*) There floats up—into my thoughts—a Mr Shower—a Mr and perhaps a Mrs Shower—no—they are holding hands—his fiancée then more likely—or just some—loved one. (*Looks closer at nails.*) Very brittle today. (*Resumes filing.*) Shower—Shower—does the name mean anything—to you, Willie—evoke any reality, I mean—for you, Willie—don't answer if you don't—feel up to it—you have done more—than your bit—already—Shower—Shower. (*Inspects filed nails.*) Bit more like it. (*Raises head, gazes front.*) Keep yourself nice, Winnie, that's what I always say, come what may, keep yourself nice. (*Pause. Resumes filing.*) Yes—Shower—Shower—

45

(*stops filing, raises head, gazes front, pause*)—or Cooker, perhaps I should say Cooker. (*Turning a little towards Willie.*) Cooker, Willie, does Cooker strike a cord ? (*Pause. Turns a little further. Louder.*) Cooker, Willie, does Cooker ring a bell, the name Cooker? (*Pause. She cranes back to look at him. Pause.*) Oh really! (*Pause.*) Have you no handkerchief, darling? (*Pause.*) Have you no delicacy? (*Pause.*) Oh, Willie, you're not eating it! Spit it out, dear, spit it out! (*Pause. Back front.*) Ah well, I suppose it's only natural. (*Break in voice.*) Human. (*Pause. Do.*) What *is* one to do? (*Head down. Do.*) All day long. (*Pause. Do.*) Day after day. (*Pause. Head up. Smile. Calm.*) The old style! (*Smile off. Resumes nails.*) No, done him. (*Passes on to next.*) Should have put on my glasses. (*Pause.*) Too late now. (*Finishes left hand, inspects it.*) Bit more human. (*Starts right hand. Following punctuated as before.*) Well anyway—this man—Shower—or Cooker—no matter—and the woman—hand in hand—in the other hands bags—kind of big brown grips—standing there gaping at me—and at last this man Shower—or Cooker—ends in er anyway—stake my life on that—What's she doing? he says—What's the idea? he says—stuck up to her diddies in the bleeding ground—coarse fellow—What does it mean? he says—What's it meant to mean?—and so on—lot more stuff like that—usual drivel—Do you hear me? he says—I do, she says, God help me—What do you mean, he says, God help you? (*Stops filing, raises head, gazes front.*) And you, she says, what's the idea of you, she says, what are you meant to mean? It is because you're still on your two flat feet, with your old ditty full of tinned muck and changes of underwear, dragging me up and down this fornicating wilderness, coarse creature, fit mate—(*with sudden violence*)—let go of my hand and drop for God's sake, she says, drop! (*Pause. Resumes filing.*) Why doesn't he dig her out? he says—referring to you, my dear—What good is she to him like that?—What good is he to her like that?—and so on—usual tosh—Good! she says, have a heart for God's sake—Dig her out, he says, dig her out, no sense in her like that—Dig her out with what? she says—I'd dig her out with my bare hands, he says—must have been man and—wife. (*Files in silence.*) Next thing they're away—hand in hand—and the bags—dim—then gone—last human kind—to stray this way. (*Finishes right hand, inspects it, lays down file, gazes*

front.) Strange thing, time like this, drift up into the mind.
(*Pause.*)

[Pp. 41–44]

This long anecdote,[30] made even longer by Winnie's interruptions and interpolations, serves to pass the time, as indeed do all of Winnie's various activities, but more than that, it constitutes a specific commentary on Winnie's situation. The fact that she recounts this event at all, the particular details which she remembers, the attitude she has toward them, all reveal something of great importance about Winnie, something which her fictional narrative will later corroborate, that is, her sexual disability.

The principal image of sexual disability is Winnie's physical immobilization. For the whole of act 1 she is "imbedded up to above her waist" in earth (p. 7), which she calls that "old extinguisher" (p. 37). That it is sexuality which has been extinguished is indicated by this anecdote about Mr. and Mrs. Shower (as well as by her comments on the dirty postcard and by her repeated references to hog setae). As she chatters to herself she recounts the remarks made by the last people to see her, Mr. and Mrs. Shower: "What's the idea? he says—stuck up to her diddies in the bleeding ground—coarse fellow—What does it mean? he says—What's it meant to mean?" This question finds the beginning of an answer in his further suggestion: "Why doesn't he dig her out? he says—referring to you [Willie] my dear—What good is she to him like that?—What good is he to her like that?—and so on—usual tosh." When this "coarse fellow" asserts that he would dig her out even with his bare hands, Winnie assumes the couple are man and wife. This incident indicates that what is lost by Winnie's burial is not merely physical mobility (for that, a friend or relative might dig one out), but access to sexual organs: Winnie is no good, as a wife, to Willie, nor is Willie any good as a husband while she is buried up to her waist; a real man, a coarse fellow,

30. S. E. Gontarski refers to the Shower-Cooker story as "a play within a play, complete with dialogue" (*Beckett's Happy Days: A Manuscript Study,* p. 71); yet what is important about this passage is precisely that it is *not* a play, however vivid, but a narrative, with *quoted* voices, not dialogue.

Two

would dig her out even with his bare hands. By dwelling at such length on this memory-anecdote, Winnie emphasizes how keenly she suffers from her sexual impairment, despite her determined optimism.

That Willie leaves her where she is because of his own sexual disability is suggested by the incident of the postcard and the hog setae. Throughout the first part of act 1 Winnie has, with great comic difficulty, been struggling to read the words inscribed on her toothbrush. Her eventual triumph—"fully guaranteed genuine pure hog's setae"—occurs while Willie relishes a postcard which Winnie judges to be "genuine pure filth" (p. 19).[31] She rejects the pornographic picture and returns to her intellectual pursuits, wondering for the rest of the act about the meaning of the word "hog" (and not, as one might expect, about the presumably more obscure word "setae"). A climax for these apparently unrelated details occurs at the end of act 1 when Willie finally speaks to her, announcing the definition of "hog" to be "castrated male swine" (p. 47); thus the one question he chooses to answer makes explicit yet another image of sexual impairment. Whether from some actual physical incapacity of his own or simply from Winnie's rejection of "filth," Willie, too, is associated with sexual deprivation.

The ambivalence which these various forms of narrative betray— Winnie's ready pleasure in the blighted loves of Juliet and Ophelia, her Persian idealization of scorched sand, her own sexual deprivation and indignation—this ambivalence finds its safest outlet in the story Winnie chooses to tell herself. Now she is not relying on a literary tradition, the hallowed words of others, nor on memory, bounded supposedly by fact; now she is in the free realm of fantasy, able to conjure whatever characters, events, and details she likes. And what she chooses to tell herself, the story that is so precious she saves it for last, for the time "when all else fails," is the suggestive story of little Mildred. This story, like the Bolton-Holloway story in *Embers,* serves to focus the various sexual references in the play

31. Beckett's production notebook for the Old Vic revival (1975) indicates that he intends Winnie to appear ambivalent about sex; he states that she "*feels* for glasses and mag. glass without taking eyes from card," thus suggesting her fascination despite her stated disgust. (See RUL MS 1396/4/11, leaf 11 r.)

on death, not on life. The story concerns a little girl, Milly, who gets up early and begins to undress her doll (Milly herself, it would seem, sleeps naked since one of Winnie's corrections in her narrative involves backtracking to add that Milly "slipped on her nightgown," p. 55). As Winnie gets to the description of undressing the doll, with its associations of surreptitiousness and wickedness ("crept under the table," "scolding her"), she mentions a mouse and for some reason begins to feel uneasy, leaving the narrative and calling on Willie for attention. He, as usual, ignores her, so she begins a long digression, including reference to sadness after song (less explicable to her than sadness after intimate sexual intercourse, which she takes for granted) and another reference to Mr. Shower and her own buried legs. After it becomes apparent that Willie is not going to reply to her repeated call for help, she suddenly plunges back into her narrative at the point where she had abandoned it, describing the mouse running up Mildred's thigh, imitating her piercing screams, and listing all the family members who came running to see "what on earth could possibly be the matter." But they arrive "Too late. (Pause.) Too late" (p. 59). The story itself is innocent enough, and quite general in its description of a childhood terror. What makes it seem fraught with special meaning is its association with the various sexual references in the digression and the concern with nakedness and surreptitiousness in the narrative itself. Whatever "up her little thigh" means to Winnie (whose legs are fully protected by burial in sand), it is clear that something terrible has happened, something irrevocable.[32] Winnie's only solace after this ritualistic reliving of an intense and climactic moment is to comment that it "can't be long now, until the bell for sleep. (Pause.) Then you may close your eyes, then you *must* close your eyes—and keep them closed. (Pause.) Why say that again?" (p. 59). Why, indeed, except that a return to buried sleep is the only refuge from the dangers to which little

32. In an early draft of *Happy Days* in the "Eté 1956" manuscript notebook, Beckett used the phrase "ran up her right leg" (RUL MS 1227/7/7/1, p. 42); the later change from "leg" to "thigh" increases the erotic suggestiveness of the line.

Milly's thigh so fatally awoke. Sexual disability is safer than sexual activity.

This extended narrative has allowed Winnie to face and to re-experience a desire and a fear about which she feels ambivalent: romantic, erotic love is attractive (in stories about Ophelia and Juliet), but it ought to fail, it ought to be frustrated (just as Ophelia and Juliet found death, not sexual consummation). When the passion succeeds, goes beyond just a first kiss in a "toolshed," when the titillating mouse scampers all the way up her thigh, she feels like a little girl who has done something dangerous, something terrifying, all on her own, beyond help from mama and papa, something irrevocable.

In her story she ritualistically relives this desire and this fear. But in real life, outside her story, Winnie has avoided sexual activity by immobililty and by choosing a man she knows will fail. This fact, and its association of sexuality with death, is most explicit in the final, culminating scene. Right after Winnie ends her narrative and begins a coda of miscellaneous memories, Willie finally emerges from behind the mound and begins to advance toward her on all fours. After so much visual tedium, this physical action shocks the audience: something, at last, is about to "happen." According to Beckett's stage directions, Willie is "dressed to kill" (p. 61): dressed up in "top hat, morning coat, striped trousers, etc." but also ready for physical violence. After taunting him ("Reminds me of the day you came whining for my hand") and encouraging him ("Come on, dear"), Winnie asks an important question: "Is it a kiss you're after, Willie . . . or is it something else?" (p. 63). The "something else" is, of course, that "revolver conspicuous to her right on mound" (p. 49).[33] Is it murder or love he is after? The question is never answered because Willie does not complete his climb; the play ends with a tableau of the two of them looking at each other. What is important dramatically is not the actual answer but the charge of emotion this potential violence (either murderous

33. The phallic suggestiveness of the revolver is indicated by Beckett's production notebook for the Berlin performance (1971): "old fashioned pistol, disproportion between short butt & long muzzle, conspicuous on mound" (RUL MS 1396/4/10, p. 81).

or erotic) gives to the climax of the play. Once again Willie has come courting, once again he approaches her mound, her *mons veneris*. In surprised excitement she gleefully urges him to "put a bit of jizz"[34] into his efforts, but now, as in the past, he fails: "There was a time when I could have given you a hand. (Pause.) And then a time before that again when I did give you a hand. (Pause.) You were always in dire need of a hand, Willie" (p. 63). Her psychological/sexual put-down sends him slithering "back to foot of mound," and once again sexuality is rendered impotent and grotesque, the man grovelling, the woman buried. Winnie's fear of the mouse running up her thigh and Willie's lack of "jizz" constitute mutual sexual disability which results in that barren mound in which Winnie lives, rigid and extinguished, a state even more fatal than the death, the revolver Willie cannot reach.

In these three important plays, written relatively early in Beckett's playwriting career, the main elements of storytelling stand out very clearly indeed, from the halo of story that attends various allusions and metaphors to the full-blown and deliberately accentuated extended narratives which various characters use ostensibly for diversion but actually to allow themselves simultaneously to face and to flee excruciatingly painful emotional issues. Vladimir has his parables of hope and salvation to mask an annihilating despair; Hamm composes a chronicle of impossible altruism to ease the pain of paternal hatred; Winnie occupies herself with a fiction about childish fear to help exorcise her own burning terror. And at the heart of these stories are two ultimate issues—both the appeal and the threat of death or of sex—issues which will permeate Beckett's later plays through ever more refined forms of story and storytelling.

34. "Jizz" and "jazz" are probably derived from "jism." As well as meaning "vigor, speed, animation, excitement" (as in the sentence "Put a little jism into it"), "jism" also has the taboo meaning semen. Harold Wentworth and Stuart Berg Flexner, *Dictionary of American Slang* (New York: Thomas Y. Crowell, 1960), p. 292.

On Saying "I"

Krapp's Last Tape, Not I, Footfalls

Since carefully controlled evasion is part of a character's motivation in choosing to tell a story, the convention which separates author from narrator provides one of the chief advantages of this mode of speaking. The character relies on the fact that teller and told are not the same. There is safety in the ostensible vicariousness of narrative; nothing is betrayed or experienced directly. The speaker, the character, as "author" never really has to say "I."

This division of the self into speaker and spoken is very clear in Beckett's fiction, but the plays, too, have their equivalent kinds of splits and doubles. Even in the early unpublished "Eleuthéria," where there are no significant stories told, the tendency toward doubling is suggested by the O'Neill-like stage set with its simultaneously viewed areas for "l'action principale et l'action marginale."[1] In later plays the characters themselves, as couples, have been viewed by various critics as aspects of the same "being." Beckett's own comments in his production notebook for the 1975 Berlin *Godot* reinforce the notion of the characters as comple-

1. Photocopy of typescript of "Eleuthéria," a three-act play in French by Samuel Beckett, copied from a typescript in the possession of A. J. Leventhal, c. 1947 (RUL MS 1227/7/4/1, p. 2).

mentary pairs: "E–V: perpetual moving apart and coming together again"[2] he directs, and also E's "play with removed boot mirrors V's with hat" (leaf 3 r.). The words "mirror," "echo," and "parallel" appear frequently in this notebook, suggesting visual and auditory equivalents of an identity and a split which later will be expressed through stories such as Winnie's account of the little girl and the mouse. Originally Winnie had been named Mildred (and Willie, Edward), but this blatant equation of speaker and spoken was later softened to a more subtle suggestion through similarity of sound.[3] And even then, at critical moments, Winnie calls the little girl by a formal "Mildred," thus keeping her at a "safe" distance; elsewhere she uses the more intimate "Milly" (a close echo of "Winnie," just as their first initials, as has been frequently noted of Beckett's many *M* and *W* characters, are mirror images of each other). By speaking of a little girl, not of a mature woman, by speaking of someone with a different name, Winnie manages to avoid confronting herself directly, to evade the identity which binds teller and told.

This evasion becomes all the more obvious when the material narrated is not presented as fiction (as in Hamm's chronicle or Winnie's story) but clearly involves personal anecdote of some kind. Two plays of Beckett's deal directly with this matter of not saying "I" while dealing with autobiographical material. The earlier and more complicated one, *Krapp's Last Tape,* is composed almost entirely of narrative units in which the character on stage treats his past self as "other," a strategy made possible by Beckett's innovative use of the tape recorder.[4] Beckett's whole dramatic career has evidenced an interest in the phenomenon of voice, isolated at times from any visible gesture, as in the radio plays, or with a minimum of gesture, as in *Play* and *Not I.* At the end of the

2. RUL MS 1396/4/3, leaf 2 v.
3. See the early draft of *Happy Days* in the "Eté 1956" notebook (RUL MS 1227/7/7/1, p. 42) and Gontarski, *Happy Days,* p. 9.
4. According to Martin Esslin, Beckett had become fascinated with the newly developed tape recorder and experimented in this play with its dramatic possibilities; "Samuel Beckett and the Art of Broadcasting," *Encounter* 45 (September 1975): 42.

typescript of *Embers,* for example, he has listed the various kinds of voices used and throughout the manuscript he has written "dialogue tone" and "monologue tone" at various spots in the margin;[5] in his production notebook for *Happy Days* (Royal Court Theatre, June 1979), he has also made an extensive list headed "Winnie's Voices," including "usual," "to herself," "to Willie," "Description Dolly," "Narrative (Mildred, Showers)," and "Quotes."[6] Here in an early one-act, *Krapp's Last Tape,* he presents a single character at various stages in his life, hoarding the madeleines of memory, reveling in a whole autobiography fixed on tape, immortalized by his own voice. The concept is a brilliant one, and the play, for all its brevity, is tantalizingly complex.

The "voice structure" of the play presents multiple impressions of the titular character. Krapp, on his sixty-ninth birthday, is physically on stage, speaking in his own voice (at a time which Beckett teasingly calls "a late evening in the future";[7] that "future," however, constitutes the dramatic present of the play and will be considered here as time present). He performs his birthday ritual of making a tape in which he reflects on his past year; this recording is partially made during the performance. He also listens to parts of tapes he made on earlier birthdays, one from his thirty-ninth birthday with its own references to another from his late twenties (for purposes of simplicity, hereafter referred to as his twenty-ninth birthday tape). Thus there are three different "voices" presented to the audience: Krapp-on-stage-at-sixty-nine; Krapp-on-tape-at-thirty-nine; Krapp-on-tape-at-twenty-nine-as-quoted-by-Krapp-on-tape-at-thirty-nine. There is a certain "interaction" among these voices, as Krapp, both on stage and on tape, responds to, comments on, and repudiates himself at earlier periods.

In addition to these interlaced voices, the play is made up of interlacing themes: constipation and defecation; love (present or

5. RUL ACC 1658. This manuscript also includes the designation "story monologue" and "non-story monologue," p. 11.

6. RUL MS 1730, leaf 8 v.

7. Samuel Beckett, *Krapp's Last Tape* (New York: Grove Press, 1960), p. 9. For detailed discussion of the play as a whole see James Knowlson, ed. *Samuel Beckett: Krapp's Last Tape (Theatre Workbook 1)* (London: Brutus Books, 1980).

absent, either erotic or maternal), art (writing), inspiration and accomplishment, and "insight" (realization about the "meaning" of one's life). Not only do these themes weave throughout the various voices that comprise the play, they also have a relationship to each other. The fact that they are all concerns of Krapp's and seem to have preoccupied him his whole adult life reveals something about his character, just as the fictional narratives have in other plays.

The most obvious theme is that of constipation and defecation. The character's name and the title of the play provide a double meaning which is carried out in many other phrases and images. Like any "anal-compulsive type," Krapp hoards and will not let go what he treasures. Thus he has been physically constipated all his life and comments in his various tapes on his problems with "un-attainable laxation" (p. 17) and "the sour cud and the iron stool" (p. 25). But he has other forms, too, of constipation: he cannot give his words away and he cannot give his love away. Although he has been a professional writer, his real magnum opus seems to have been composed for himself alone: that collection of tapes, his own logorrheic musings about his own life listened to by himself. He fondles his life by replaying it; he fondles his own words. (And some of this fondling is suggestively associated with his physical constipation: he revels in the word "spool," which sounds like "stool"—both spool of recording tape and stool of crap constitute treasured, hoarded relics of himself.)

Nor can Krapp give his love away. Several of the anecdotes, the memories, which he has recorded involve "love" relationships: his mother's death, his early affair with Bianca and later with the woman in the boat, and finally, Fanny, that "bony old ghost of a whore" (p. 25) who visits him in his old age. In all these there is indication, one way or another, of his emotional or sexual "holding back."

His actual writing has had its effect on these love relationships, as a closer look at them will reveal, and has also served as a kind of "unloading" of himself which has failed. Only the logorrhea and constipation of those hoarded tapes remain in his old age. Whatever "insight" he may have gained in the process of living has been rejected by the sixty-nine-year-old Krapp in favor of self-deception and cynicism. All four of these principal themes—constipation, love, writing, and "insight"—are expressed in the various anecdotal units Krapp includes in his taped narratives; and they are best examined as they exist there, intertwined with the complexity of poetry.

After the comic opening of the play (Krapp's clownlike look, his farcical maneuvers with the banana, his silly/suggestive relish of the word "spool," and the tantalizing delays of all the counting and finding of tapes), the first anecdote is introduced.[8] He is consulting a ledger (his summary of the various tapes) and reads aloud the items to be found on spool five:

> Mother at rest at last ... Hm ... The black ball ... (*He raises his head, stares blankly front. Puzzled.*) Black ball? ... (*He peers again at ledger, reads.*) The dark nurse ... (*He raises his head, broods, peers again at ledger, reads.*) Slight improvement in bowel condition ... Hm ... Memorable ... what? (*He peers closer.*) Equinox, memorable equinox. (*He raises his head, stares blankly front. Puzzled.*) Memorable equinox? ... (*Pause. He shrugs his shoulders, peers again at ledger, reads.*) Farewell to—(*he turns the page*)—love.
>
> [P. 13]

Here are two important sets of recorded events: those involving "love" (his mother, the dark nurse, and his farewell to love, read out with music-hall comic delay) and those involving items he cannot now remember or recognize (the black ball and the memorable equinox, apparently not so memorable). When Krapp-at-sixty-nine plays this tape by Krapp-at-thirty-nine, he begins at the beginning and must pass through a series of other comments before reaching the important anecdote of his mother's death. The tape contains references to his constipation and "fatal" consumption of bananas; his concern with the meaning and value of his life (those

8. In various later productions Beckett has tended to cut back on the stage business; for example, the elaborate and repeated maneuvers with keys, drawers, reels, and banana were minimized for the revival at the Royal Court Theatre in 1973 (see annotations in production copies of the text, RUL MS 1227/7/10/1 and RUL MS 1479/1).

grains which he wants to separate from the chaff, those grains which in *Endgame* constitute a paradoxical image of parts which may or may not mount up to a whole); his certainty that he never sings (in a few moments Krapp-at-sixty-nine will burst into a quavering few lines of "Now the Day is Over"); comments about an earlier tape he has just been listening to, with *its* reference to an early love relationship, resolutions not to drink so much, problems with constipation, his magnum opus, his sneers at himself when even younger, closing with a "yelp to Providence," punctuated with derisive laughs by both the narrating Krapp-at-thirty-nine and the listening Krapp-at-sixty-nine (who then pops off stage for a moment to have a quick drink, as he will do several times during the play). Only then does the tape (narrated by Krapp-at-thirty-nine) get to the critical anecdote of his mother's death:

> TAPE: ... there is of course the house on the canal where mother lay a-dying, in the late autumn, after her long viduity (*Krapp gives a start*), and the—(*Krapp switches off, winds back tape a little, bends his ear closer to machine, switches on*)—a-dying, after her long viduity, and the—
> *Krapp switches off, raises his head, stares blankly before him. His lips move in the syllables of "viduity." No sound. He gets up, goes backstage into darkness, comes back with an enormous dictionary, lays it on table, sits down and looks up the word.*
> KRAPP: (*reading from dictionary*). State—or condition of being—or remaining—a widow—or widower. (*Looks up. Puzzled.*) Being—or remaining? ... (*Pause. He peers again at dictionary. Reading.*) "Deep weeds of viduity" ... Also of an animal, especially a bird ... the vidua or weaver-bird ... Black plumage of male ... (*He looks up. With relish.*) The vidua-bird!
> *Pause. He closes dictionary, switches on, resumes listening posture.*
> TAPE: —bench by the weir from where I could see her window. There I sat, in the biting wind, wishing she were gone. (*Pause.*) Hardly a soul, just a few regulars, nursemaids, infants, old men, dogs. I got to know them quite well—oh by appearance of course I mean! One dark young beauty I recollect particularly, all white and starch, incomparable bosom, with a big black hooded perambulator, most funereal thing. Whenever I looked in her direction she had her eyes on me.

And yet when I was bold enough to speak to her—not having
been introduced—she threatened to call a policeman. As if I
had designs on her virtue! (*Laugh. Pause.*) The face she had!
The eyes! Like ... (*hesitates*) ... chrysolite! (*Pause.*) Ah well
... (*Pause.*) I was there when— (*Krapp switches off, broods,
switches on again*)—the blind went down, one of those dirty
brown roller affairs, throwing a ball for a little white dog, as
chance would have it. I happened to look up and there it was.
All over and done with, at last. I sat on for a few moments
with the ball in my hand and the dog yelping and pawing at
me. (*Pause.*) Moments. Her moments, my moments. (*Pause.*)
The dog's moments. (*Pause.*) In the end I held it out to him
and he took it in his mouth, gently, gently. A small, old, black,
hard, solid rubber ball. (*Pause.*) I shall feel it, in my hand,
until my dying day.

[Pp. 18–20]

What is important in this lengthy anecdote is Krapp's attitude
toward what he narrates. A mother's death, however loving-hating
a relationship it might have been, is a situation fraught with emotion
(and usually, of course, the relationship is considered to be a loving
one and appropriate response to its loss to be grief). Krapp's
manner, however, is curiously detached. The listening Krapp does
not intend to be comic when he puzzles over the word "viduity,"
but the effect of the replay and the sudden stops is comic nonetheless
(Bergson's theory of comic repetitions, man acting like a machine,
here literalized in the taped voice); and Krapp's foray into the
dictionary, emerging with his mouth full of pleasure in the phrase
"the vidua-bird!" increases the humor of the moment. Thirty years
later Krapp may indeed have forgotten words he knew and used
at age thirty-nine, he may indeed feel a bit detached from his
mother's death; but surprisingly, the voice on tape is also detached,
even though the death occurred recently. Krapp-at-thirty-nine recounts that moment of death: he was not with her but rather sat
outside watching her window, "in the biting wind, wishing she were
gone." His account is filled with extraneous detail ("nursemaids,
infants, old men, dogs") and in particular, one "dark beauty" whose
bosom and eyes capture his attention more than does his mother's
fate. And yet he does *not* act on this interest—he has no designs

on her virtue—because neither maternal attachment nor erotic possibility can really get him to go out from himself.[9] He will sit, merely, at a distance and observe. At the moment when the shade in his mother's room is lowered, signaling her death, he is playing with a dog; thus the great event and a trivial detail—the ball he is throwing—are associated in his mind, so he thinks, forever. But Krapp is not Marcel, and the remembrance of things past does not flash through his aging solipsism. Beckett has already supplied the ironic indictment of Krapp's thirty-nine-year-old conviction "I shall feel it, in my hand, until my dying day"; and that indictment appeared in the first moments of the play when Krapp puzzled over his tape summary, having no recollection of the black ball or its significance. Not only has he not remembered it; he does not even recognize it. The conscious experience of powerful emotion, then and now, is not Krapp's strong point.

There is a second anecdote on the tape, immediately after the anecdote of his mother's death; and this one, too, his "memorable equinox," has been forgotten by the aged Krapp:

> Spiritually a year of profound gloom and indigence until that memorable night in March, at the end of the jetty, in the howling wind, never to be forgotten, when suddenly I saw the whole thing. The vision, at last. This I fancy is what I have chiefly to record this evening, against the day when my work will be done and perhaps no place left in my memory, warm or cold, for the miracle that . . . (*hesitates*) . . . for the fire that set it alight. What I suddenly saw then was this, that the belief I had been going on all my life, namely—(*Krapp switches off impatiently, winds tape forward, switches on again*)—great granite rocks the foam flying up in the light of the lighthouse and the wind-gauge spinning like a propellor, clear to me at last that the dark I have always struggled to keep under is in reality my most—(*Krapp curses, switches off, winds tape forward, switches on again*)—unshatterable associa-

9. In his notebook for the production of *Das letzte Band* in Berlin in 1969, Beckett has devoted several pages to what he thinks of as the Manichaean elements in *Krapp's Last Tape,* including the "ascetic ethics, particularly abstinence from sensual enjoyment. Sexual desire, marriage, forbidden" (RUL MS 1396/4/16, p. 45). For a fuller discussion of this issue see James Knowlson, *Light and Darkness in the Theatre of Samuel Beckett* (London: Turret Books, 1972).

tion until my dissolution of storm and night with the light of the understanding and the fire—(*Krapp curses louder, switches off, winds tape forward . . .*)

[Pp. 20–21]

This is a provocative passage, clearly full of "significance" for Krapp yet not at all explicit about what that significance is. But there are some clues. First of all, the event was important and a "good experience"; the words that describe it—"memorable," "vision," "miracle," "fire"—are positive in their connotations. The scene in which the revelation occurs is romantic, nature providing sympathetic tumult for the insight which emerges from Krapp's personal gloom. The experience itself had something to do with "world view" or "life philosophy" or "self-knowledge," something which could be called spiritual or religious.[10] The basic image of the insight is light and fire, something which illumines Krapp's understanding and enflames his imagination. And what exactly *was* that insight? Krapp-at-sixty-nine cannot bear to continue to listen, and so he stops the tape, moves it forward, plays another fragment, moves it forward. These interruptions, reinforced by the stage directions, betray the agitation Krapp feels: he does not want to listen to this part of his earlier life. When he saw the phrase "memorable equinox" in his ledger, he could not remember what that was; now, hearing the passage, he prefers to leave that experience buried in forgetfulness. The passage is disturbing, annoying; and, consequently, the audience recognizes it to be of great importance. But what precisely was the nature of the insight so exhilarating to Krapp-at-thirty-nine and so annoying now to Krapp-at-sixty-nine? Here Beckett relies on a rhetorical device he frequently uses to great effect: giving part of a phrase and letting the

10. Beckett himself has used the word "religion" in reference to this play. Martin Held, who rehearsed Krapp under Beckett's direction, recounts Beckett's own view of Krapp: "He told me the character was eaten up by dreams. But without sentimentality. There's no resignation in him. It's the end. He sees very clearly that he's through with his work, with love and with religion." Quoted by Ronald Hayman, *Samuel Beckett* (New York: Frederick Ungar, 1973), pp. 79–80.

audience fill out the rest. This technique requires a certain triteness
in the phrasing, a certain set to the syntax, so that the rest of the
phrase is fairly obvious. The first fragment—"the belief I had been
going on all my life," is cut off by Krapp before the insight can
be specified: "the dark I have always struggled to keep under is
in reality my most—" This last phrase, however, does have some
revealing groups of words: "dark" and "struggled" have negative
connotations, but the rest of the phrase indicates that what appeared
negative is instead something positive (the adversative "but" is
reinforced by the phrase "in reality"; and "most" suggests that the
positive thing is quite positive indeed). What this comes down to
in effect is the suggestion of some kind of mid-life crisis, a complete
change of belief or orientation. At thirty-nine Krapp seems to have
discovered his "dark" side and found it exhilarating. His life thus
far seems misspent; now he will go in new directions, fired and
illuminated. How valid or how successful this conversion has been
is suggested by the older man's displeasure and agitation as he
listens to his earlier ecstatic account of "vision" and "miracle."

There is a third anecdote on this same tape, following just after
the anecdotes of the mother's death and the son's vision. This final,
critical event concerns an erotic experience and seems to be the
only part of his earlier life Krapp wants to hear:

—upper lake, with the punt, bathed off the bank, then pushed
out into the stream and drifted. She lay stretched out on the
floorboards with her hands under her head and her eyes closed.
Sun blazing down, bit of a breeze, water nice and lively. I noticed
a scratch on her thigh and asked her how she came by it. Pick-
ing gooseberries, she said. I said again I thought it was hopeless
and no good going on, and she agreed, without opening her eyes.
(*Pause.*) I asked her to look at me and after a few moments—
(*pause*)—after a few moments she did, but the eyes just slits, because of the glare. I bent over her to get them in the shadow
and they opened. (*Pause. Low.*) Let me in. (*Pause.*) We drifted in
among the flags and stuck. The way they went down, sighing,
before the stem! (*Pause.*) I lay down across her with my face in
her breasts and my hand on her. We lay there without moving.

But under us all moved, and moved us, gently, up and down, and
from side to side.

[Pp. 22–23]

The language and cadence of this passage is idyllic. There is
nothing grotesque or bawdy here; the imagery is precise; the double
meanings have the richness of poetry, heightening the beauty of
the erotic moment: "The way they went down, sighing, before the
stem!" This is one of the few times Krapp has gone out from
himself; "Let me in" is his plea for both personal communion and
sexual union. But the moment is one of termination, not renewal
(as his ledger had capsulated the event: "Farewell to . . . love").
The older Krapp listens to the whole passage (he knows where it
ends; snipping off the last few words in this first playing is of no
consequence because he had heard the important part). Then he
broods. His mood now is not agitation but reverie.[11] What he has
left to him are his old vices: the banana, the drink, and making
another tape. Love has indeed gone, and his final tape indicates
how grievous a loss that has been.

Krapp begins to record the tape for his sixty-ninth birthday,
debunking the tape he has just listened to. But his "Thank God
that's all done with anyway" does not sound convincing followed
by "The eyes she had!" and his consequent brooding (p. 24). "Let
that go!" is undercut by "Maybe he was right." And the rest of
the tape reveals just what went wrong in Krapp's life to make him
the sour creature he now is.[12] His constipation has been abiding.

11. Beckett's production notebooks often contain lists of themes, gestures,
images, sounds, suggesting a kind of rhythm that each of the many elements
of the play has. In the German production of *Krapp's Last Tape* (1969), there
are frequent references to Krapp's being caught up in a dream (e.g., "dream
seizes hold of him . . . he can't move," RUL MS 1396/4/16, p. 97) and also to
his being arrested by "Hain" (e.g., "turn slowly left and long look behind into
dark absolutely still," p. 86): the dream is of past love, still present as memory;
the "Hain" is of future death, perpetually lurking as unavoidable fate. These
two nonverbal actions lend dramatic support to the themes of love and death
present in Krapp's monologues.

12. For discussion of how various productions have highlighted the fact of
Krapp's "lifetime of unfulfilled aspirations," see James Knowlson, " 'Krapp's Last
Tape': The Evolution of a Play, 1958–75," *Journal of Beckett Studies*, 1 (Winter

His only happiness has been reveling in his own words, but those, alas, in the form of his magnum opus, have been a failure: "Seventeen copies sold, of which eleven at trade price to free circulating libraries beyond the seas" (p. 25). He may consider this "getting known" but the audience recognizes this line as comic self-deception. Now old, he is still "drowned in dreams," whose romantic nature is betrayed by his reading: "Scalded the eyes out of me reading *Effie* again, a page a day, with tears again. Effie . . . (Pause.) Could have been happy with her, up there on the Baltic, and the pines, and the dunes. (Pause.) Could I? (Pause.) And she?" (p. 25). This is what Krapp wants: an imaginary relationship, a story about love, not the real woman. (It was he, after all, who terminated that idyllic relationship with the woman in the boat: "I said again I thought it was hopeless and no good going on.") What he actually has left to him in his old age is imaginary grand passion (through *Effie Briest*) and actual grotesque sex (in the manner of Watt and Mrs. Gorman): "Fanny came in a couple of times. Bony old ghost of a whore. Couldn't do much, but I suppose better than a kick in the crutch. The last time wasn't so bad. How do you manage it, she said, at your age?" (pp. 25–26). His answer to this question is both a flippant cliché and an unwittingly precise revelation: "I told her I'd been saving up for her all my life." Just that: saving up, hoarding himself, his feces, his words, his sex, his love. Here in the evening of his life, emphasized by his song for Vespers, he suddenly realizes his poverty. At twenty-nine he had resolved on a "less . . . engrossing sexual life" (p. 16); at thirty-nine he had bidden farewell to love altogether in order, presumably, to follow the fire of his imagination, to write that opus magnum;[13] and now he is plagued by "last fancies," tries unsuccessfully to "keep 'em under" (p. 25), tries to recapture love by reading *Effie Briest* and "managing it" with a bony old whore. Yet the sense of a lost, a wasted life pursues him. Like Henry, in *Embers*, he tries to conjure up scenes from the past: "Be again in the dingle on a Christmas

1976): 55 f.

13. For an interesting connection between Racine and Beckett and specifically the theme of conflict between love and ambition in *Krapp's Last Tape*, see Vivian Mercier's *Beckett/Beckett* (New York: Oxford University Press, 1977), pp. 79–80.

Eve, gathering holly, the red-berried. (Pause.) Be again on Croghan on a Sunday morning, in the haze, with the bitch, stop and listen to the bells. (Pause.) And so on. (Pause.) Be again, be again" (p. 26). But these Wordsworthian moments of childhood are gone forever, dismissed as "all that old misery." He tries to reconcile himself to time past and lost by devaluing those early experiences: "Once wasn't enough for you." Yet his next line, and the last words Krapp-on-stage says, reveals how poignant is his loss: "Lie down across her."

The final moments of the play are made up of Krapp listening again to that idyllic erotic anecdote, having wrenched off his current tape and thrown it away. This self-deceiving, self-debunking man of sixty-nine is not what he wants to hear or to be; he goes back to the only event in which he was for a moment not solitary: one with another person and one with nature. The specifically erotic nature of this episode and Krapp's displacement of that eroticism away from an actual woman and onto his tapes themselves is suggested by Beckett's own production notes for the revival of the play at the Royal Court Theatre (January 1973). As Krapp listens for the last time to the boat episode, Beckett indicates, "Head gradually down to rest finally on table, righ[t] hand in to touch base of TR, left on switch to switch off while head down"; this direction written just opposite the lines "I lay down across her ... my hand on her" links girl and tape recorder in a single embrace.[14]

This time Krapp plays the tape through to the end, not just that exquisite, richly poetic experience but also his thirty-nine-year-old's commentary: "Perhaps my best years are gone. When there was a chance of happiness. But I wouldn't want them back. Not with the fire in me now. No, I wouldn't want them back" (p. 28). It is all too clear, both to the motionless man on stage and to the audience, that Krapp *does* want them back; that he forfeited the

14. See Beckett's marginalia in Faber paper-covered edition (1970), RUL MS 1227/7/10/1, p. 17. The Grove edition (1960), also used for the Royal Court revival, was initially even more explicit as Beckett directed Krapp to put his "left arm round the tape recorder" (he later struck out those words in favor of touch by hand only; see RUL MS 1479/1, p. 22).

only real fire he ever had (that real woman moving gently with him) for the sake of an illusory fire of the imagination which did not produce an opus magnum but rather left him with merely the narrated residue of himself, repudiated yet intensely desired. Krapp has given up those eyes like chrysolite, his own equivalent of Othello's tragic loss, for the only eye and light left him at the end of the play. Beckett's Royal Court directions specify, "Slow Fade of stage light and cubby hole light till only light that of 'eye' of tape recorder."[15] That machine's inanimate glow finally replaces both the "eyes" of love and the "I" of selfhood, leaving Krapp, as Beckett wrote in his Faber edition, "dead still" indeed.[16]

An even more explicit repudiation of personal history occurs in *Not I*, where the character's attempts at evasion and disguise are particularly poignant and where telling a "story," providing an "account" of something becomes a dramatization of the character's struggle simultaneously to face and to avoid a deeply personal issue. *Not I* is structured entirely to appear as narrative, having two of the basic components of telling, speaker and listener. There is almost no physical motion in this play; the stage appears dark except for a faintly-lit "Mouth" and a faintly-lit shrouded character called "Auditor." Except for movements of the mouth while speaking and the auditor's three "gesture[s] of helpless compassion,"[17] the play is "dead still throughout." Voice, word holds the attention of the audience. What "happens" in the play, happens there, in that narration (made up of groups of anecdotes and attempts at evasion). Critical to the dramatic effect of the play are the question of the relationship between the speaker, Mouth, and the event she recounts and the fact that teller and told are closer than the speaker will acknowledge.

The "story" Mouth tells concerns a woman, from the time she is born, abandoned, reared in an orphanage, until the time she is nearly seventy wandering aimlessly in a field; the interval, her life, is marked by lovelessness, lack of pleasure, sense of sin and pun-

15. Annotation in Grove edition, RUL MS 1479/1, p. 28.
16. RUL MS 1227/7/10/1, p. 19.
17. Samuel Beckett, *Not I*, in *Ends and Odds* (New York: Grove Press, 1976), p. 14.

ishment, and, above all, by a feeling of isolation characterized particularly by her inability to speak to others. Three rather specific anecdotes[18] establish this verbal incapacity. The first describes her silence in the supermarket:

> practically speechless ... all her days ... how she survived! ... even shopping ... out shopping ... busy shopping centre ... supermart ... just hand in the list ... with the bag ... old black shopping bag ... then stand there waiting ... any length of time ... middle of the throng ... motionless ... staring into space ... mouth half open as usual ... till it was back in her hand ... the bag back in her hand ... then pay and go ... not as much as goodbye ... how she survived!
>
> [P. 18]

The second shows her in court, silent when she ought to defend herself:

> speechless all her days ... practically speechless ... how she survived! ... that time in court ... what had she to say for herself ... guilty or not guilty ... stand up woman ... speak up woman ... stood there staring into space ... mouth half open as usual ... waiting to be led away ... glad of the hand on her arm ...
>
> [P. 21]

And the third describes a frantic but failed attempt at speech:

> practically speechless ... even to herself ... never out loud ... but not completely ... sometimes sudden urge ... once or twice a year ... always winter some strange reason ... the long evenings ... hours of darkness ... sudden urge to ... tell ... then rush out stop the first she saw ... nearest lavatory ... start pouring it out ... steady stream ... mad stuff ... half the vowels wrong ... no one could follow ... till she saw the stare she was getting ... then die of shame ... crawl back in ...
>
> [P. 22]

18. In his synopsis of *Not I* Beckett lists five "life scenes": (1) "field," (2) "shopping centre," (3) "Croker's Acres," (4) "courtroom," and (5) "rushing out to tell." The field, repeated several times throughout the play, is there also at its end and provides the present context into which the other narrated segments fit (RUL MS 1227/7/12/10).

These three anecdotes indicate the woman to be painfully unable to communicate verbally and intensely in need of doing so. A fourth anecdote reveals that the cause of this isolation is lifelong repression of feeling:

> or that time she cried ... the one time she could remember ... since she was a baby ... must have cried as a baby ... perhaps not ... not essential to life ... just the birth cry to get her going ... breathing ... then no more till this ... old hag already ... sitting staring at her hand ... where was it? ... Croker's Acres ... one evening on the way home ... home! ... a little mound in Croker's Acres ... dusk ... sitting staring at her hand ... there in her lap ... palm upward ... suddenly saw it wet ... the palm ... tears presumably ... hers presumably ... no one else for miles ... no sound ... just the tears ... sat and watched them dry ... all over in a second ...
>
> [P. 20]

What is the context for these anecdotes? The woman who is their subject, now old and wandering in a field on an April morning, finds herself suddenly "face down in the grass" (p. 21), insentient in the dark, a buzzing in her ears, a ray of light moving in her head, sudden flashes of memory (p. 15), her mouth uttering strange sounds (p. 18), and "the brain ... raving away on its own ... trying to make sense of it" (p. 20). Beckett never specifies what has happened, but the details clearly suggest a stroke; the entire monologue thus becomes her thoughts as she lies there, at the mercy of her failing body. The situation psychologically is a kind of "last judgment" for her: review of her past life, with need to "make sense of it." Several times she repeats the phrase "something she had to— ... what?" (p. 21) without finishing the sentence, impeded by her own inability to face her terrible omission; finally, the critical word slips out, "something she had to ... had to ... tell ... could that be it? ... something she had to ... tell ... " (p. 21). She does not, however, tell "it" but resumes her lament from the beginning, moving into the third anecdote, already quoted, in which she is "on trial" (as indeed she is now in her "last judgment"). She has the need, and the obligation, to "tell how it

had been . . . how she had lived . . . lived on and on . . . " (p. 21),
but she is bereft of that insight just as she has been bereft of love
and speech all her days.[19] She must "tell her story" and yet she
cannot.

That "cannot" has an interesting quality—refusal rather than
actual inability, a refusal governed by a certain self-deception.
Beckett makes this clear by having his narrator betray herself by
doing what she says she cannot do and not even, apparently, noticing
that she has given herself away. Describing "her" in the field, she
says "couldn't make the sound . . . not any sound . . . no sound of
any kind . . . no screaming for help for example . . . should she feel
so inclined . . . scream . . ." and then the stage directions indicate
that she actually screams, twice (p. 17). Clearly she is able to
attempt communication "should she feel so inclined." What impedes
her? The answer to this question reveals the significance of the
relationship between the narrator, Mouth, and the woman in the
narration. Mouth is that woman, forced by her moving lips, cheeks,
jaws, tongue to babble out her life's story, unable because of her
stroke to stop the flow of speech that has been dammed up all her
days. Her trial and her punishment consist in her having to listen
to her own words as she persists in the "sin" for which she is being
punished: her inability to say "I." Three times in the course of the
monologue, the narrating voice says "what? . . . who? . . . no!
. . . she!" (pp. 15, 18, 23). The title of the play supplies the
important complementary phrase, *Not I*, and Beckett's stage directions corroborate the connection by referring to Mouth's "vehement refusal to relinquish third person" (p. 14).

Mouth tells the story of herself, but she must make the fact a
fiction, must talk of some other *she*, not *I*. Thus she can evade
admission of her personal grief while at the same time expressing
it as if it were another's. The poignancy of *Not I* comes mostly
from this evasion: the woman's miserable life is appalling, but her

19. Beckett's manuscript revisions are particularly revealing in this regard.
The positive word "showered" in the phrase "no such love as normally showered
on the . . ." is altered at various points to negative terms such as "visited,"
"vented," "inflicted," finally arriving in print as "vented" (see RUL MS 1227/
7/12/5, p. 1 and RUL MS 1227/7/12/6, p. 1).

resignation to lovelessness is worse than the lovelessness itself ("no love . . . spared that . . ."); her inability to face herself ("who? . . . no! . . . she!") is worse than her inability to speak to others. She holds herself at bay throughout her life and throughout her story.

Evasions of this sort occur frequently in Beckett's work, but especially in the later pieces such as *Play, Words and Music,* and *Eh Joe* where personal anecdotes, like the other narrative forms, both reveal and conceal, shielding the character while at the same time showing where he is most vulnerable.

An ultimate point in self-evasion is reached in *Footfalls.* Unlike *Not I,* where the denial of self is vehement and thus obvious, this evasion is so subtle as to pass easily unnoticed; this speaker has refined her deceptions so that listeners, perhaps herself included, will only hear the regular beat of her pacing and wheeling, seeing only the physical turns, not noticing the moment when her narrative itself turns.

The play begins with May, "dishevelled grey hair, worn grey wrap hiding feet," pacing up and down in a dimly lit place.[20] Two voices are heard, May's and her mother's. Their opening exchange establishes a number of pieces of information: the mother is very old, perhaps ninety, and bedridden; May, in her forties, takes care of her mother and pursues her own sleepless pacing, thinking about something which has apparently plagued her for a long time. There is the suggestion that May's life has been a curse, not a blessing, because her mother asks forgiveness, again, for having had her (p. 44). A second sequence is composed of a monologue in which the mother reminisces about May's peculiar life: "outwardly un-moved," reclusive, obsessed since childhood with the bizarre mea-sured pacing which the audience has witnessed; the motion is important to May, the sound of the footfalls is important; she rarely sleeps (and that, standing); her occasional speech is only an attempt, alone, "to tell how it was" (p. 46). That "it" which she constantly revolves in her poor mind and which she struggles to tell, grows

20. Samuel Beckett, *Footfalls,* in *Ends and Odds* (New York: Grove Press, 1976), p. 42.

more portentous without ever having any clear antecedent. The third and final sequence is composed of May's monologue, and it is here that the skillful self-evasion occurs.

May introduces her monologue with the word "sequel"; she paces two lengths and repeats that term. Then she begins to talk, presumably about herself but in the third person. These two factors alone tend to distance her narrative, making it seem more like story and less like autobiography. She recounts slipping out at night, getting somehow into the church and pacing up and down the transept. Suddenly her mode of narration changes style and becomes even more explicitly literary: "Old Mrs. Winter, whom the reader will remember, old Mrs. Winter, one late autumn Sunday evening . . ." (p. 47). The audience suddenly finds itself put in the place of "reader," plunged into the midpoint of a story about Mrs. Winter and her daughter Amy. The narrative event here is different from anything May and her mother have spoken about, but there are a number of important elements to suggest that Mrs. Winter and her daughter are fictional analogues for May and her mother. Both mothers are old; both daughters are living with their mothers but are scarcely girls any more; the repetitions of phrasing which are present in May's mother's account of their dialogue also characterize the speech patterns Amy and her mother use ("What do you mean, May, not enough, what can you possibly mean, May, not enough?" p. 45, and "What do you mean, Amy, to put it mildly, what can you possibly mean, Amy, to put it mildly?" p. 48, and, of course, "Amy" is an anagram of "May").[21] With these suggestions of a relationship between May and her mother and the fictional Amy and Mrs. Winter, the content of the narrated fictional discussion takes on additional meaning. When Mrs. Winter asks Amy "How could you have responded if you were not there?" (p. 48), what is at issue is not simply her actual presence or absence from the church service, but the much larger issue of May's "presence" in life and her inability to respond to that life. May is the author of this story about Amy and Mrs. Winter; significantly the

21. In early drafts May was first named Mary and Amy was named Emily; the change for both was made in the same typescript and reinforces the similarity between the two women (see RUL MS 1552/4).

reference which triggers her narration occurs in both her reminiscence about "her" and her story about "Amy." The phrase "during Vespers" marks the end of the reminiscence and is a kind of verbal pivot, like the ball of the foot on which May physically wheels, that turns her away from reminiscence about herself (distanced as "she") and toward a fictional story of a daughter whose presence "at Evensong" is mysteriously unclear. May wheels into fictional narrative at precisely the moment when her reminiscence is getting too close to an admission that her life is excruciatingly painful. "His poor arm" and "that poor arm" refer, of course, to the transept of the church, which is laid out in the form of a cross, so that the poor arm she ponders is a crucified one. Her nights are thus taken up with pain, not with the comfort and sense of protection that Vespers is supposed to convey. And as she begins to talk about that pain, her traversing that poor arm, she risks losing hold of her stoic manner ("outwardly unmoved") and so pivots quickly into fictional narrative which allows her in disguise to reveal the true source of her misery, her inability to respond to "the love of God, and the fellowship of the Holy Ghost" (p. 48), in fact her inability to respond to any fellowship at all, not lacrosse with other girls her age (p. 45), not erotic love (as early manuscript versions suggest),[22] not in fact to any human life outside the old home "where she began" (p. 45).[23]

22. Earlier versions make the sexual element in May's strangeness more explicit. In the first typescript when the mother refers to having May, May complains "Could you not have waited?" and the mother explains, "I lost control of myself a moment," but that suggestion of passion is immediately revised to "I forgot myself a moment" (RUL MS 1552/1, p. 1A). Thus having learned, to her sorrow, the dangerous results of passion, May avoids sexuality for herself by her obsessive pacing. The question "When did this begin?" has the specifically sexual answer, "Well before puberty" and she is referred to now as certainly being still a maid (p. 2).

23. "Along with this sense of existence by proxy goes 'an unconquerable intuition that being is so unlike what one is standing up,' and intuition of 'a presence, embryonic, undeveloped, of a self that might have been but never got born, an être manqué'"; Beckett in conversation with Lawrence Harvey in 1961 and 1962, Lawrence E. Harvey, Samuel Beckett: Poet and Critic (Princeton: Princeton University Press, 1970), p. 247. For a full discussion of May as one of Beckett's many êtres manqués, as someone never properly born, see James

Three

Other characters in Beckett's plays have shifted into fictional narrative when they began to get too close to painful emotional issues—Winnie and Hamm most notably—but May has brought her escape to a point of perfection. The fictional narrative suddenly loses its "closing bracket" and becomes the present reality, taking over the play and repeating the dialogue of the opening sequence between May and her mother: "Amy. (Pause.) Yes, Mother. (Pause.) Will you never have done?" (p. 48). And so the passage continues, repeating the exact words from the end of the opening sequence, but there the dialogue was spoken by two voices, while here the dialogue is spoken by only one voice, one person, the author of the story who quotes both parts. May has successfully annihilated the "I" she began with in the opening sequence, and she has done it almost imperceptibly by moving slowly from "she" understood to be herself, to a fictional "she" named "Amy" who now takes over May's lines and place. The last fade up of light shows a stage with, finally, "no trace of May" (p. 49). Through narrative she has escaped the pain of saying, of being, "I."

Knowlson and John Pilling, *Frescoes of the Skull* (New York: Grove Press, 1980), pp. 220–28.

FOUR

Telling a True Tale

All That Fall, Play

Repudiation of self is not the only lie powering these stories. In a few plays Beckett has, somewhat more conventionally, raised the question of the accuracy of the story material itself and placed that question unavoidably in the spectator's way. In these cases, too, the phenomenon of deception betrays something about the speaker and the speaker's relationship to others in the play.[1]

In *All That Fall* there are two kinds of deception at issue: the deliberate misleading of one character by another character and the blurring uncertainties of a character's attempts at self-deception. Linking the two and providing a shocking climax to the play is the final question which the climactic story contains, a question which can never be answered with certainty. That the play has a climax is itself unusual in Beckett's drama. That the climax is delivered in a "punch line" at the very end of the play is unusual for any kind of drama. And the fact that that punch line contains a miniature

1. The question of the reliable narrator has frequently been discussed in relation to Beckett's fiction. See, for example, Raymond Federman's "Beckettian Paradox: Who Is Telling the Truth?" in *Samuel Beckett Now,* ed. Melvin J. Friedman (Chicago: University of Chicago Press, 1970), pp. 103–17.

story quite strikingly emphasizes the issues of truth and falsity which the audience is left to ponder but can never quite resolve.

Like *Not I*, *All That Fall* depends upon a recounted event, an anecdote, which illumines something important about one of the characters. But that "story," unlike the biography which comprises Mouth's monologue, is told very briefly and straightforwardly in the last moments of the play and constitutes a sudden shocking revelation. In addition to this unusual use of narrative, the play also includes more typical narratives in the form of allusions and memories.

As a radio drama, *All That Fall*, like *Embers*, is composed of a series of voices and sounds. Radio dramas are, by their very form, akin to narrative: they are "told" not seen. And although, strictly speaking, still drama—made up of individual voices rather than a single narrating voice (which may or may not quote other voices)—they nonetheless, like narrative, require a listener, not a spectator. They employ words and sounds, not spectacle. They play to the imagination alone and are essentially more private than staged drama. Listening to a radio drama is more like reading a book than sitting in a theater: at any moment interruptions, distractions, boredom, disgust, outrage, any number of personal motivations can make the listener turn off the set without hesitation or qualms, as easy as closing a book.[2] Theater, on the other hand, captures its audience more variously: the plot may be foolish but the heroine beautiful, the words may be stilted but the stage effects

2. In countering remarks that Beckett's plays for radio have not been particularly successful, Clas Zilliacus points out, "The estimated 0.4 per cent of the adult population that made up the first-night audience of *All That Fall* translate into some one hundred and fifty thousand people. Such a crowd would have filled the Royal Court Theatre every night of the week for one year"; *Beckett and Broadcasting: A Study of the Works of Samuel Beckett for and in Radio and Television* (Abo: Abo Akademi, 1976), p. 25. Martin Esslin observes that the experiments with sound effects for this particular play "directly led to the establishment of the BBC's Radiophonic Workshop. Beckett and *All That Fall* thus directly contributed to one of the most important technical advances in the art of radio (and the technique, and indeed technology, of radio in Britain.)"; "Samuel Beckett and the Art of Broadcasting," *Encounter* 45 (September 1975): 40.

interesting; or there may simply be too many long legs between the restless spectator and the aisle to make early escape feasible.

Radio drama is already a kind of "telling." What is especially interesting about Beckett's radio drama is that here, too, he includes actual narrative units of various lengths within that telling. And here, too, those narrative units function, as they do in the stage plays, to "explain" the action, to reveal character, to comment on situation.

The plot line of *All That Fall* is quite clear: Mrs. Rooney, an old fat woman who has recently been hospitalized, is laboring along a road and up a hill to the railway station to meet the 12:30 train in order to escort her blind husband home. Along the way she meets many people, has various kinds of exchanges with them, and is troubled when she discovers that the train is late. What has happened to delay it? The answer to that question constitutes the shocking climax of the play.

A number of themes thread their way through Mrs. Rooney's encounters and conversations: inquiry about the health of the relatives of the people she meets; lament over the loss of her own little Minnie; expressions of distress concerning her own inability to communicate with language, to be noticed by others, to be given love; and considerable erotic innuendo with greatly comic effect. Many of these encounters involve the telling of brief anecdotes, little stories with no apparent relationship to the whole, except perhaps as jokes, grim and grotesque. For example, when Mrs. Rooney laments her lack of love, her remarks contain a vignette of her ideal relationship: "Love, that is all I asked, a little love, daily, twice daily, fifty years of twice daily love like a Paris horse-butcher's regular, what normal woman wants affection? A peck on the jaw at morning, near the ear, and another at evening, peck, peck, till you grow whiskers on you."[3]

Even the mystical Miss Fitt cannot talk about herself—as she does at length—without including a number of anecdotes: "Ah yes, I am distray, very distray, even on week-days. Ask Mother, if

3. In Samuel Beckett, *Krapp's Last Tape and Other Dramatic Pieces* (New York: Grove Press, 1960), p. 37.

you do not believe me. Hetty, she says, when I start eating my doily instead of the thin bread and butter, Hetty, how can you be so distray?" (p. 55)

These various anecdotes in the first part of the play are merely brief illustrations or corroborations of some point one of the characters is making, a biographical event from the past that rather obviously helps explain something in the present. But as the play progresses, Mrs. Rooney expands to longer narratives, memories of past events that she finds still significant but which the audience may find puzzling. When she at last meets Mr. Rooney and he begins to tell her his version of the train's delay, she interrupts with an apparently unrelated memory:

MRS. ROONEY: I remember once attending a lecture by one of these new mind doctors, I forget what you call them. He spoke—

MR. ROONEY: A lunatic specialist?

MRS. ROONEY: No no, just the troubled mind, I was hoping he might shed a little light on my lifelong preoccupation with horses' buttocks.

MR. ROONEY: A neurologist.

MRS. ROONEY: No no, just mental distress, the name will come back to me in the night. I remember his telling us the story of a little girl, very strange and unhappy in her ways, and how he treated her unsuccessfully over a period of years and was finally obliged to give up the case. He could find nothing wrong with her, he said. The only thing wrong with her as far as he could see was that she was dying. And she did in fact die, shortly after he washed his hands of her.

MR. ROONEY: Well? What is there so wonderful about that?

MRS. ROONEY: No, it was just something he said, and the way he said it, that have haunted me ever since.

MR. ROONEY: You lie awake at night, tossing to and fro and brooding on it.

MRS. ROONEY: On it and other ... wretchedness. (*Pause.*) When he had done with the little girl he stood there motionless for some time, quite two minutes I should say, looking down at his table. Then he suddenly raised his head and exclaimed, as if he had had a revelation, The trouble with her was she had never been really born! (*Pause.*) He spoke throughout without notes. (*Pause.*) I left before the end.

[Pp. 82–84]

Rarely is Beckett as direct and obvious as he is here: "the only thing wrong with her as far as he could see was that she was dying" is a clear statement about "the human condition," as timeless as any *memento mori* of medieval devotion; "The trouble with her was she had never been really born" encapsulates the plight of every Beckettian character, whose partial life is a living death. But why should Mrs. Rooney make these remarks? Why should she tell at length such a story, especially when she has trouble with language (p. 80) and fears to alienate others every time she speaks a few simple words from her heart (p. 54)? The importance of the memory is that it is *hers* and thus reveals something about her. And that she remembers it at this moment, while Mr. Rooney is urging her to speak, reveals something about their relationship.

The memory-narrative itself contains a number of details which connect with other remarks Mrs. Rooney has made in the course of her odyssey. Most important, this is a story about a "story of a little girl." Mrs. Rooney has repeatedly lamented someone called "little Minnie," probably a daughter who died young. She feels bereft in this mother-daughter relationship, and her emotion spills over into her conversations with the various people she meets (most of her questions involving relatives concern the welfare of either mothers or daughters). And just as this little girl in the neurological case history was deficient in some way, unsavable, so too the various daughters Mrs. Rooney knows have serious defects, which are presented as a form of sterility: were little Minnie alive today she would be menopausal (p. 42) and Mr. Tyler's daughter has had her "whole bag of tricks" removed (p. 38). Even that "lifelong preoccupation with horses' buttocks" seems to connect bizarrely with Mrs. Rooney's concern with daughters and with sterility: when Christy offers the Rooneys a load of dung, Mrs. Rooney's comic reply (coming after Christy's horse has farted) is "Dung? What would we want with dung, at our time of life?" (p. 35). She is beyond "fertilizer" now, tired of "light old hands on [her] shoulders and other senseless places" (p. 39). And yet such loss grieves her, as her frantic cry to Mr. Tyler—"Come back and unlace me behind the hedge!" (p. 43)—and her giggling hoist by Mr. Slocum (p. 46) indicate. Her association of fertility, either positive or negative, with horses' buttocks is further indicated by the many references to the hinny and her persistent interest in whether or not they can procreate.[4] (The play has sounds of animal maternity, e.g., a woolly little lamb with its mother, which serve to emphasize the sterility of the hinny.)

Mrs. Rooney's story of the story of the little girl may not explain either to herself or to her husband her preoccupation with horses' buttocks, but it does focus for the audience an important group of associations: sterility and death, hopeless maternity and grievous loss. These themes preoccupy Mrs. Rooney and thus reflect her own bereavement. The fact that she recounts the memory at length to Mr. Rooney at precisely the moment when she does also reveals something about their relationship or her view of him. Since his late arrival she has been pestering him with her anxiety; he has responded "coolly" (p. 66), has refused to kiss her (no Paris horse-butcher he), has repulsed her efforts to cling to him, refuses to tell her why the train was delayed. Finally, after an interval when they are jeered by two children and he verbalizes the ordinarily repressed feeling, "Did you ever wish to kill a child?" (p. 74), he begins to narrate his experience on the train, his "story"; the stage directions include the phrase "narrative tone" (pp. 76–77) and Mr. Rooney refers to his "composition" (p. 81). Oddly enough, this narrative does not in any way explain the delay, but it does include a long account of Mr. Rooney's speculations about retirement and

4. One particularly revealing passage is the discussion of rotting leaves (p. 85) and subsequent references to the laburnum losing its tassels (reproductive organs) and the rain as "golden drizzle" (Jove's shower somewhat abated), then the sudden apparently illogical but psychologically clear leap to the question of hinnie's productivity. In the typescript for Grove Press, the reference to the laburnum is absent from the text but is written in the margin, an important addition to make intelligible the phrase "golden drizzle" and to help emphasize the references to fertility (see RUL MS 1526/1 photocopy of original document held by Washington University Libraries, St. Louis, Missouri, p. 23).

the subsequent "horrors of home life" retirement brings, including reference to "the brats, the happy little hearty little howling neighbours' brats" (p. 79). Mrs. Rooney, at this point in the narrative, suddenly feels "very cold and faint"—a state which may or may not be due to her scanty dress and lack of food; Mr. Rooney, in any case, is annoyed that she has apparently stopped listening to him (p. 80). He continues his narration, asserting lack of interest in what was "amiss" with the train, and concludes with an irrelevancy about Grimm's law and a request to his wife: "Say something, Maddy. Say you believe me" (p. 82). Why is belief an issue? Is there anything in what he has said, in her response to it, in anything she knows about him to prompt disbelief? Rather than reassure him or respond directly to his narrative, she begins her own (the story of the little girl just discussed).

And so story balances story. The man speaks of wanting to kill a child, "nip some young doom in the bud" (p. 74), and is unconcerned about what may be amiss. The woman speaks of a girl whose life is so flawed by death that the doctor washes his hands of her. And between the two stories is sandwiched the suggestion of frightening insight (Maddy suddenly cold and faint) and fear of discovery ("Say you believe me"). These stories, these personal anecdotes, are not mere diversion, not the sign of a couple talking at cross purposes; they present characters who, as Pinter says of his own people,[5] communicate all too well.

What is it Maddy fears to learn, Mr. Rooney fears to have discovered? The punch line of the play, the critical anecdote revealing what happened on the train, answers that question. And appropriately enough, that anecdote is recounted not by either principal, but by a minor character who can tell it simply and without disguise because he is not involved. Jerry catches up with

---

5. In a BBC TV "Monitor" interview Pinter denied that his plays are about an absence of communication: "I don't think there's an inability to communicate on the part of these characters. It's rather more that they communicate only too well in one sense. Their tentacles go out very strongly to each other, and I think communication is a very fearful matter, to really get to know someone, to participate with someone"; quoted by Kay Dick, "Mr. Pinter and the Fearful Matter," *Texas Quarterly* 4 (Autumn 1961): 264–65.

the old couple to bring Mr. Rooney something he left behind in the train, a "kind of ball," and Mrs. Rooney takes advantage of his presence to ask about the delay. Mr. Rooney tries to prevent Maddy from seeing the ball, from questioning Jerry, but she is not to be stopped. When Jerry replies quite simply, "It was a little child, Ma'am," Mr. Rooney groans. Then the last spoken lines of the play finally reveal what happened: "It was a little child fell out of the carriage. On to the line, Ma'am. (*Pause.*) Under the wheels, Ma'am" (pp. 90–91).

These final lines provide an unusually shocking climax to the play, because coming after Mr. Rooney's expressed hatred of children, his pretense not to know what caused the delay, his attempt to keep Jerry from speaking, his present groan and Mrs. Rooney's earlier fear, there is the implication that he may have acted on his desire to "nip some young doom in the bud": What was he doing with the ball? Had he used it to lure the child? Had he taken it away from the child? Did he push the child?

This suggestion of child murder is made all the more significant by Beckett's use of biblical allusions, his references to yet another form of narrative, parables and anecdotes from the New Testament. The play takes its title from one such reference, which Maddy quotes answering Mr. Rooney's question about the text for tomorrow's sermon: " 'The Lord upholdeth all that fall and raiseth up all those that be bowed down' " (p. 88). Their response to these optimistic lines is "wild laughter." Maddy had learned from her biblical questioning to be cynical; earlier when she had been talking about hinnies, she suddenly remembered something she had learned from "the Regius Professor": "It wasn't an ass's colt at all. . . . it was a hinny, he rode into Jerusalem or wherever it was on a hinny. (Pause.) . . . It's like the sparrows, than many of which we are of more value, they weren't sparrows at all" (p. 86). In this particular passage, Mrs. Rooney combines two biblical references—the event of Jesus' entry into Jerusalem[6] and his parable about the birds of

6. Like Shakespeare, Beckett is master of the "missing antecedent." When Lear finally states, "I did her wrong" (*King Lear* I. v. 25), there is no question to whom that pronoun refers, even though Cordelia has not been seen nor named

the air[7]—and finding factual inaccuracies in both implies that they are thus unreliable. There may have been no messianic triumph; man may not be of special worth, object of special care (as Mr. Rooney's ironic comment—"Does that put our price up"—indicates).

Mr. and Mrs. Rooney know from their own experience that the Lord does *not* uphold all that fall: Mr. Rooney is blind and "bowed down" (pp. 84–85), Mrs. Rooney is "destroyed with sorrow and pining and gentility and church-going and fat and rheumatism and childlessness" (p. 37), lamentable Little Minnie is dead, everybody's relative is sick or suffering, and a little child has just been crushed by the train, falling under the wheels, not upheld by any special providence. The biblical stories, both historical event and didactic parable, and the text of the sermon suggest a beneficence, a triumph of good, absent from the Rooneys' world. The sacred stories are not true and do not comfort. Personal narratives, like those of Mr. and Mrs. Rooney, allow for expression of human distress, pent-up resentment, spasms of hostility and destructiveness, while at the same time shielding the speaker from too immediate a revelation. The Lord does not sustain Mr. and Mrs. Rooney. Instead, according to the final sound effects of the play, they move on, with dragging steps, holding each other up, into the tempest of wind and rain, shielded from too fierce an assault of emotional tempest by the various deceptions their own stories have allowed, turning their backs altogether on the "true" story, the "real" event which Jerry blurts out at the end (p. 91).

The need to tell one's story—and the need to falsify it—is even more explicit in *Play* than it is in *Not I*. Here, too, voice is

---

for some time; this use of pronoun, rather than noun, in fact, betrays how very powerful Cordelia's presence has been to Lear's mind. So, too, here does the pronoun betray an obsession precisely because the noun is absent: no need to name the one whose life and words have so troubled Maddy Rooney.

7. "Are not two sparrows sold for a farthing? and one of them shall not fall on the ground without your Father. But the very hairs of your head are all numbered. Fear ye not therefore, ye are of more value than many sparrows" (Matthew 10:29–31; see also Luke 12:6–7).

paramount and gesture minimal, but in this drama there are three characters on stage, a man and two women, each with head protruding from the neck of a gray urn, faces fixed front and "impassive throughout."[8] A fourth "character" is present in the form of a spotlight. Beckett's stage directions refer to this light as "a unique inquisitor" (p. 62) and its projection on the other characters' faces as a "solicitation" (p. 45). They, in turn, refer to the light as "you" (pp. 52–60). The three immobilized characters speak only when the mobile light strikes their faces. Beckett is precise in his description of how the light should move (three separate fixed spots would be unsatisfactory), and aside from this incorporeal motion, the audience sees no other movement but the speaking mouths, producing in toneless voices three versions of the same story.

Quite literally, this is a play with a variety of "points of view," a term normally applied to narration, not to drama.[9] The man, his wife, and his mistress each presents a unique perspective on their triangular relationship, and the spotlight presents yet another view by suggesting through its impatient shifting that all three spoken stories are not entirely true. Because the light activates the speakers, it is, in a sense, the very world in which they live and move and have their being. It provides the "frame" into which their spoken stories fit. By making the play virtually all story and by emphasizing contrasts among versions of that story, Beckett has created yet another variation in his use of narrative in drama and yet another example of the tension between candor and deception which story allows.[10]

8. Samuel Beckett, *Play,* in *Cascando and Other Short Dramatic Pieces* (New York: Grove Press, 1977), p. 45.

9. For discussion of different uses of the term "point of view" in fiction—point of view as "speaker" and point of view as "seer"—see my article "James's and Lubbock's Differing Points of View," *Nineteenth-Century Fiction* 16 (1961): 245–55.

10. It is interesting that George Devine in his manuscript notes for the first production of *Play* in England (Old Vic, 1964) emphasizes these narrative elements in the drama; one of his directions reads, "Stress the novelletish quality. The more lurid 'that' is the better this ["Comedy/Tragedy"] will be understood" (RUL MS 1581/15, p. 3). Essential to this "novelletish quality" is the relationship between external narrative and internal feeling ("Narrative more hectic. Inward

The story told is this: A man (M) has had regular sexual relations with two women, one (W1) probably his wife (someone with a claim on him), and another (W2) probably his mistress (the "other woman"). Both women are well-to-do; W2 has a butler ("I rang for Erskine and had her shown out," p. 47) and W1 is even wealthier than W2 ("I sometimes wondered if he was not living with her for her money," p. 49). M is a man of great sexual prowess (when his wife finds out she has been sharing him, her "first feeling was one of wonderment. What a male!" p. 48). He, for his part, treats both women the same; of both he says, "So I took her in my arms and swore I could not live without her. I meant it, what is more. Yes, I am sure I did" (pp. 48 and 51). The wife confronts the other woman and then her husband, precipitating a situation in which he must choose between them (he tries to pretend to have given up W2 while still continuing the relationship, but neither woman will allow that). Since he cannot live without both of them and since the triangle cannot continue, death for all three seems the only solution. A number of lines in the play suggest that each commits suicide (or possibly murder): W1 carries a razor in her vanity bag and looks "more and more desperate" (pp. 49–50); W2 feels "like death" (p. 50); and M finds that "it was all too much" (pp. 51–52). The first segment of the play—the narration of these stories—ends with these lines of despair, suggesting that both women have lost him, and that he has lost them.

After a brief blackout, the second segment of the play begins, establishing the current dramatic situation. A "change" has occurred for all three: they are no longer living in the state in which the story happened, and there is every suggestion that they are dead and in a limbo where they are required to recount the events that brought them to the gray pitiless world in which the audience finds them. Throughout the earlier segment, each character had spoken only when the light shone on it and had stopped, even in midsentence, when the light moved away. None of the characters seemed to hear the others but pursued instead his or her own

more painful," p. 3) as the characters are driven to tell their three conflicting versions of the same story, "playing" with the truth.

interrupted monologue. But in the second segment it is clear that the speakers are aware of having an auditor, the spotlight itself, which seems to compel them to speak and to react to it personally: "When you go out—and I go out. Some day you will tire of me and go out . . . for good" (p. 53). And in that reaction, they begin to betray why they speak (and why the spot shifts impatiently away from them). M worries, "Is it that I do not tell the truth, is that it, that some day somehow I may tell the truth at last and then no more light at last, for the truth?" (p. 54). And W1 tries to account for why she still lingers on: "it must be something I have to say. How the mind works still!" (p. 54). Yet her evasions continue: "But I have said all I can. All you let me. All I—" (p. 55). As the spotlight shifts suddenly away there is the sense that it is annoyed with W1, that she is still wasting time, blaming another, refusing to take responsibility. If the spotlight did not want to let her say all she can, it would not focus on her in the first place; it can keep her quiet by leaving her in the dark. Thus it is not the spotlight that tries to squelch the story by moving, but the woman herself with her lies.

What are these lies? All three characters have been guilty of them. In addition to the basic lie of the relationship (M telling each woman he is not having sex with the other), there are the more subtle lies of self-deception. W1, in her version of the triangular love story, states that her rival is "just a common tart" (p. 50), and yet W2's lines reveal by their calm and dignified manner a woman of culture, and the presence of a butler suggests a certain elegance in her life. But "common tart" is the lie W1 needs in order to deceive herself and boost her own value: "What he could have found in her when he had me—" (p. 50). And W2 makes use of a similar ploy increasing her own esteem by derogating W1's looks: "Her photographs were kind to her. Seeing her now for the first time full length and in the flesh I understood why he preferred me" (pp. 46–47). Yet there is no indication of preference: despite her termagant tongue, M has been as "assiduous as ever" toward W1 and claims to have loved her with all his heart (p. 47). He claims, in fact, to love them equally, to be unable to live without either of them. Yet even that claim of wholehearted love is something of a lie, as one of his remarks betrays: "At home all heart to heart, new leaf and bygones bygones. I ran into your ex-doxy, she said one night, on the pillow, you're well out of that. Rather uncalled for, I thought. I am indeed, sweetheart, I said, I am indeed. God what vermin women. Thanks to you, angel, I said" (p. 51). Lies marked their relationship, and now they are allowed no peace by the spotlight until they tell the story straight. But they persist in self-deception. M, in fact, goes on to further fantasies of an impossible idyllic relationship: "To think we were never together"; "Never woke together, on a May morning, the first to wake to wake the other two. Then in a little dinghy—"; "A little dinghy—"; "A little dinghy, on the river, I resting on my oars, they lolling on air-cushions in the stern . . . sheets. Drifting. Such fantasies"; "We were not civilized" (pp. 59–60). Each of these remarks is interrupted by unrelated statements from W1 and W2, the speech of each character being triggered by the glare of the spotlight, which keeps moving away in its inquisitorial probe when the characters fail to "bring it up" (p. 58), that "it" of the truth they are hiding. When grouped together, these remarks by M constitute a little story, with authorial comment, by which he continues to deceive himself that his conflicting loves might have co-existed harmoniously if only they had been "civilized," and so he continues to dwell on the comforting fantasy rather than answer the difficult question that gets squeezed out of him, "Am I hiding something?" (p. 57).

The persistence of these three characters in self-deceiving versions of their story is emphasized by the fact that after the two basic segments have been completed (narrating the story and commenting on their current situation), the entire play is repeated (p. 61). It is important, too, that the replay ends not with the final word of the second segment but with the opening lines of what would be a third go-round of the whole play, were the audience and actors willing to endure again what these characters will apparently spend an eternity reciting. The very last line of the play is the first line of M's version of his story—"we were not long together"—thus emphasizing for the audience that this is a play in which a spotlight plays over characters who play with the truth, altering it to story that in some way justifies their behavior and comforts M at least with a completely fabricated idealized fantasy. Once again Beckett has written a piece for the stage in which narration, and what it reveals about its narrators, is at the very heart of the drama.

The Absent Face

Embers, Words and Music, Eh Joe, A Piece of Monologue

Th…here are frequent references, especially in Beckett's later plays, to a face. Often the face is a ghostly one, haunting the speaker's memory, the face of a beloved woman, once present, now apparently forever absent. Sometimes this spectral image is associated with the phenomenon of voice, and the attempts of the face to speak are of crucial emotional importance to the play's main character. Sometimes this main character is prompted to speak because of the face, and about the face, recounting the suggestive story of a past love lost.

These female faces are present fairly early in Beckett's playwriting career. Krapp, of course, though he also remembers the incomparable bosom and the scratched thigh, is most taken with eyes and dwells painfully on that feature of the girl in the boat, that perfect chrysolite he, like Othello, has thrown away. Theatrically, too, faces have been important in Beckett's work; Winnie dwindles to just a head, and in later plays the *mise en scène* also dwindles so that a face, or part of a face, is all the audience really sees (the three faces protruding from urns in *Play,* the dominant face in *That Time,* finally down to the isolated mouth in *Not I*). In *Film* the face is deliberately turned away from the camera, and the persistent final peering in at the face constitutes the climax of that study. In "... but the clouds ..." visitation by the face is earnestly sought and when it comes, gigantically large on the TV screen, the mouth and its labored attempt to speak fascinate the central character.

Important as these visionary faces are, the absent face takes on even greater importance in Beckett's later work. The first significant absent face occurs in *Embers,* that radio play in which two voices interact, Henry a character "really present" and Ada the faceless but articulate shade of his wife. The main story element in this play belongs to the kind previously discussed as a "chronicle," an extended narrative of the kind Winnie and Hamm tell. But the dramatic frame for the play—an interchange among faceless voices—foreshadows a theatrical mode which will become increasingly important in later plays.

Because *Embers* is a radio drama, both voices are actually faceless for the audience. That fact only heightens the sense of mysterious absence associated with the face of Ada, whom Henry can hear but not see. Before looking at the later plays in which absence of the face constitutes a major element, it will be useful to examine *Embers* and the significance of its extended narrative in order to isolate issues which are more obscurely expressed in the later plays.

The main voice in *Embers* is that of Henry, a lonely tormented man who speaks to himself and conjures up the voices of others in order to cover the sound of the sea, which he constantly hears and hates. The dramatic situation is thus a kind of monologue, and although there is another voice heard at length, that of Ada, his wife, it is clear her voice "exists" in his mind. She is not physically present there on the beach with him (stage directions indicate his movements make noise on the shingles, hers do not).[1] These imaginary conversations include his father (who now will not answer him, will not "appear") and some brief anecdotes concerning his daughter, Addie, with her music master and with her riding master. Interspersed with these voices are the sounds of galloping hooves and clashing stones summoned by Henry to "drown out" the

1. Samuel Beckett, *Embers,* in *Krapp's Last Tape and Other Dramatic Pieces* (New York: Grove Press, 1960), p. 104.

sucking sound of the sea (heard constantly throughout the play, sometimes softer, sometimes louder). In addition to creating these imaginary sounds and voices, Henry also tells himself a story about an old man named Bolton and a doctor named Holloway. These, then, are the pieces of the structure of the drama: fragments of narrative, snatches of sound, memories worked into imaginary conversations, various characters who relate to Henry in terms of his feelings about them. Among these relationships the most important is that of Henry (as son) to his father and mother, and Henry (as father) to his daughter; of lesser importance is the relationship of Henry (as husband) to his wife. Less clear (but tantalizingly important) is the relationship between Bolton and Holloway and their joint relation to Henry. As I have demonstrated elsewhere, what ties all these elements together is a thematic concern with sterilization and abortion, a suggestion that sexuality leads to death, not to life.[2] The structural technique that clinches this theme is Beckett's use of narrative within the dramatic form. Henry's story about Bolton and Holloway reveals what there is in Henry's relationship with his wife, his father, his daughter which accounts for his current situation. Once again, the dramatic character's extended narration serves as unwitting self-revelation and commentary.

On the surface, the Bolton-Holloway story seems gratuitous, entirely unrelated to Henry's "real life." It seems, at most, simply to provide escape, as if any subject would do. But timing, as in *Endgame,* indicates how apt psychologically the story itself is, and some of its details have close resemblance to elements in Henry's own life, specifically his father's suicide, his own wish never to have been born, and his disgust with sex, that unpleasant activity which unfortunately produces life in the first place.

The story itself is concerned with death. Bolton is, according to Henry's description, "an old man in great trouble" (p. 98) who has called his doctor on a cold wintry night and begged a special service, something the doctor has repeatedly refused despite Bolton's desperate pleas. The most that Holloway is willing to do for

2. Kristin Morrison, "Defeated Sexuality in the Plays and Novels of Samuel Beckett," *Comparative Drama* 14 (Spring 1980): 18–34.

Bolton is give him an injection. Nothing more explicit is stated, but the details of the scene—the deteriorated old man, his tearful pleas, the candle "guttering all over the place" (p. 120), the cold embers—all suggest that Bolton is begging to be put out of his misery, to be given something more permanent than a standard pain-killing injection. This association with voluntary death is reinforced by the fact that Henry has resumed his story at this point immediately after reflecting on his father's suicide and his speculation that Ada may have witnessed it (pp. 118–19); the story seems, in fact, to be an escape from that memory, a more acceptable distraction, or perhaps a disguised way of thinking about his father's death (both Bolton and his father have "eyes drowned," p. 121).

In his impatience to get away, to avoid any involvement in Bolton's death, Holloway indicates he has other work to do: " 'If it's an injection you want, Bolton, let down your trousers and I'll give you one, I have a panhysterectomy at nine' " (p. 119). After all the colloquial vagueness and imprecision of Henry's earlier language when he refers to anything sexual—"washout," "hammering away," "did it"—and his reliance on imagery and mystery in the Bolton-Holloway story, this sudden intrusion of a technical term is startling: the audience notices "panhysterectomy" and is meant to notice it. Somehow the play deals with radical sterilization, the destruction of the possibility of any existence at all, the ultimate stage of preannihilation for those "better off dead" (p. 103).

This reference, in the story, to sexual sterilization may seem unrelated to these two older men. If Holloway were a *real* Beckettian doctor, the informed listener might object, he ought to be a podiatrist. But, in fact, as an anesthetist-panhysterectomist (helping hollow out the generative insides where life originates), Holloway is an entirely appropriate kind of doctor, appropriate to Henry's fictional narrative because sterilization and abortion are abiding "ideals" in Henry's own life and are referred to a number of times in his monologue.

The first reference to abortion comes a third of the way through the play. Henry (in monologue, not in his fictional narrative) has just been speaking about his own hatred of the sea, his attempts to get away from it, his father's love of the sea and apparent suicide by drowning. He has digressed at length on his Bolton-Holloway story and then switches back suddenly to memories of his father:

> Father! (*Pause.*) You wouldn't know me now, you'd be sorry you ever had me, but you were that already, a washout, that's the last I heard from you, a washout. (*Pause. Imitating father's voice.*) "Are you coming for a dip?" "No." "Come on, come on." "No." Glare, stump to door, turn, glare. "A washout, that's all you are, a washout!" (*Violent slam of door. Pause.*) Again! (*Slam. Pause.*) Slam life shut like that! (*Pause.*) Washout. (*Pause.*) Wish to Christ she had.
>
> [Pp. 101–2]

In this flow of memory with its psychological rather than logical organization, the phrase "Wish to Christ she had" is elliptical but explicable: wish to Christ she had washed (me) out. This man who feels so keenly his father's disappointment, shares his father's sorrow that he was ever born: he should have been aborted (or perhaps prevented by douche). This wish is Henry's own ineffectual equivalent of his father's suicide. But Henry's wish for death, to have been washed from the womb and never to have lived, extends not only to his own relationship with his parents but also to his relationship with his child. Immediately after the line "Wish to Christ she had" and its pause, the monologue continues with memories about his wife and daughter: "Never met Ada, did you, or did you, I can't remember, no matter, no one'd know her now. (Pause.) What turned her against me do you think, the child I suppose, horrid little creature, wish to God we'd never had her . . ." (p. 102). He, as father, duplicates his own father's disappointment; he, too, would prefer a child never to have been born. Both important women in his life, mother and wife, should have aborted rather than delivered: "better off dead, better off dead" (p. 103).

Even the copulation which led to these unfortunate births is described with words which suggest a certain displeasure in the act: "It took us a long time to have her. (Pause.) Years we kept hammering away at it" (p. 114). In Henry's mind copulation is associated with the sea—"Where we did it at last for the first time" (p. 113)—and the sea for him is the antithesis of life.[3]

Throughout this radio drama, Henry uses sounds to drown out what he does not want to hear (or to think about). He uses the auditory fantasy of galloping horses to try to cover the sound of the waves, which remind him both of sex and of his father. He uses the story of Bolton and Holloway to try to cover the memory of his father's suicide and his own sense of worthlessness. The story allows Henry to deal indirectly with the painful struggle for release that his father must have had and with his own painful desire to escape life. Henry, however, unlike his father, is not one to commit suicide. And so he walks by the sea, where life originates and ends but does not plunge into it. Instead, he both listens to it and tries to "drown it out" with his own sounds. The extent to which Henry is tormented is revealed not by his own monologue (his "real" words) but by the story he tells himself (his "fiction").[4] And the apparently unrelated word he includes there—"panhysterectomy"—betrays his deepest feeling.

This betrayal, this dramatic revelation, is unintentional on Henry's part (and brilliant on Beckett's). Henry wants merely to distract himself with story, to cover up by narration what he does not want to hear or think about. But in the process of fabrication, he uses a word that jars Beckett's audience: where did this polysyllabic technical term suddenly come from? Why does Beckett create a character who chooses *this* term to use in this story? But, of course, medical terms, erudite references, allusions of various kinds cannot be explicated by an audience while the play is in process; they have their effect almost unconsciously. So here, "panhysterectomy" is spoken, the audience is alerted and puzzled, and the play moves swiftly on.

3. Henry describes the clashing sounds of stones and horses' hooves as preferable to the sound of the sea because "That's life! . . . Not this . . . (pause) . . . sucking!" (pp. 112–13).

4. For discussion of Henry (as "artist") in relation to his father, see Paul Lawley, " 'Embers': An Interpretation," *Journal of Beckett Studies* 6 (Autumn 1980): 35–36.

The final lines of the play, however, achieve their impact through whatever meaning "panhysterectomy" has managed to register with the audience. Henry moves toward the sea, continuing his monologue, looking at his appointment book:

> This evening . . . (*Pause.*) Nothing this evening. (*Pause.*) Tomorrow . . . tomorrow . . . plumber at nine, then nothing. (*Pause. Puzzled.*) Plumber at nine? (*Pause.*) Ah yes, the waste. (*Pause.*) Words. (*Pause.*) Saturday . . . nothing. Sunday . . . Sunday . . . nothing all day. (*Pause.*) Nothing, all day nothing. (*Pause.*) All day all night nothing. (*Pause.*) Not a sound.
>
> [P. 121]

"Plumber at nine" echoes "panhysterectomy at nine," and both plumber and doctor deal with the "waste." As is so often the case, Beckett turns a simple ordinary word into a complex pun: the waste is the drain through which the washing out occurs (whether of sink or womb), but it also refers to that which is drained off, that which is discarded because it is waste, refuse; even further, the word "waste" serves as a commentary, "the waste" meaning "such loss, what a pity!" When all is drained, when all is discarded, when all is lost, nothing remains. And this, in fact, is Henry's ideal state: "All day all night nothing. Not a sound." Parents, wives, children, all those causes and effects of reproduction, all that pervasive sucking sea is a torment for him: being a father, a lover, a child are equally intolerable (and equally fascinating). He prefers imaginary relationships, fictional events, conjured voices, absent faces rather than actual ones: narrative rather than life. He wants a panhysterectomy for his very existence, and he wants it "safely" in the form of story rather than violently in the form of suicide.

Another radio drama with an important absent face, *Words and Music,* treats the narrative element rather differently. Here there is supposedly not a "story" to be told but a series of pseudo-disquisitions recited upon various themes. But there lurks in these accounts the vestiges of a story, the recapturing of a moment in the past similar to Krapp's idyll of the lake. The dramatic situation is a simple one: two "characters"—Words and Music, one presented by human voice, the other by orchestra—are servants of

Five

a master (addressed as "My Lord" but in the script called Croak), who visits occasionally and requests them, as his "comforts," his "balms," to deliver recitations upon themes which he announces; after being much affected by their presentations of "Love," "Age," and "Face," he shuffles off, leaving them again alone together. Words's "deep sigh" marks the last sound of the play.

Like so many of Beckett's characters, Croak is an old man (about to "croak," having a croaking voice) who in declining years visits the memories of his youth and suffers painful recriminations, from himself, against himself. Here, as in so many other plays (but especially radio dramas such as *Embers* and *Cascando*) other characters can be seen as parts of the old man's mind. And here, too, the lurking story, whether fantasy or biographical anecdote, lies at the heart of the dramatic action. It is not Croak's power that is important, his ability to compel obedience from his servants, but his vulnerability to what he extracts from them. Words's and Music's own interaction (sometimes mutually helpful, sometimes hostile) gives the play interest and variety but no climax; that dramatic highpoint is reserved for Croak's reaction to them, his fleeing what they present.

And what they present is an erotic anecdote. The event begins abstractly enough, with Croak's order for an elaboration of the theme "love," and Words's formulaic response (sounding for all the world like a parody of Scholastic philosophy or a badly done exercise in combing the commonplaces):

WORDS (*orotund*): Love is of all the passions the most powerful passion and indeed no passion is more powerful than the passion of love. (*Clears throat.*) This is the mode in which the mind is most strongly affected and indeed in no mode is the mind more strongly affected than in this.
   Pause.
CROAK: *Rending sigh. Thump of club.*
WORDS (*as before*): By passion we are to understand a movement of the soul pursuing or fleeing real or imagined pleasure or pain. (*Clears throat.*) Of all—
CROAK (*anguished*): Oh!

94

WORDS (*as before*): Of all these movements then and who can number them and they are legion sloth is the LOVE is the most urgent and indeed by no manner of movement is the soul more urged than by this, to and—
    Violent thump of club.[5]

Then after some further interruption, the presentation continues:

WORDS: ... to wit this love what is this love that more than all the cursed deadly or any other of its great movers so moves the soul and soul what is this soul that more than by any of its great movers is by love so moved? (*Clears throat. Prosaic.*) Love of woman, I mean, if that is what my Lord means.
CROAK: Alas!

[P. 25]

This disquisition (interrupted by rending sighs and commanding thumps from Croak, supportive accompaniment from Music) is followed by one on "Age" (more violently interrupted and determinedly supported) culminating in a final "statement" sung by Words:

Age is when to a man
Huddled o'er the ingle
Shivering for the hag
To put the pan in the bed
And bring the toddy
She comes in the ashes
Who loved could not be won
Or won not loved
Or some other trouble
Comes in the ashes
Like in that old light
The face in the ashes
That old starlight
On the earth again.

[P. 28]

5. Samuel Beckett, *Words and Music,* in *Cascando and Other Short Dramatic Pieces* (New York: Grove Press, 1977), p. 24.

Already the "exercise" is beginning to become more personal and more like a story. Comparison with the same kind of "set piece" by an earlier playwright highlights to what very different use Beckett puts his narrative units. In *As You Like It,* Jaques presents a typical Renaissance rhetorical analysis of age and ages, the well-known passage beginning "All the world's a stage" and concluding:

> The sixth age shifts
> Into the lean and slipper'd pantaloon,
> With spectacles on nose and pouch on side,
> His youthful hose, well sav'd, a world too wide
> For his shrunk shank; and his big manly voice,
> Turning again toward childish treble, pipes
> And whistles in his sound. Last scene of all,
> That ends this strange eventful history,
> Is second childishness and mere oblivion,
> Sans teeth, sans eyes, sans taste, sans every thing.
>
> [II. vii. 157–66]

Here there is no question of Jaques's revealing anything about himself except his acerbic wit, and that is no secret. He does not "give himself away" in this passage; he merely indulges in a virtuoso performance (the kind of rhetorical caper Shakespeare so often apparently transferred from his school training to his mature art).[6] Jaques's passage is rich in imagery and metaphor, vivid illustrations of the abstract point being made, but those elements represent good poetry, good rhetoric, good pedagogy, not covert biography. Words's little poem about age, however, seems intimately connected to Croak's life: he is himself an old man (if he shuffles, he may also huddle); he, too, is haunted by a face (earlier apologizing for being late, he refers to "the tower" and "the face"); and his response to the poem continues to be very emotional. Certainly he is reminded of a real event or an important fantasy.

After a long pause, Croak's final response to the passage on age is to say again, "The face," thus announcing the last theme, one which makes the hidden story explicit. As usual, the narration

---

6. See Sister Miriam Joseph, *Shakespeare's Use of the Arts of Language* (New York: Columbia University Press, 1947).

is interrupted by Croak's groans and Music's emotional accompaniment (as well as by conflict between Words and the other two about the recitation itself). Because of the interruptions and consequent repetitions, the narrative grows incrementally. Its main elements are represented by the following segments:

Seen from above at such close quarters in that radiance so cold and faint with eyes so dimmed by ... what had passed, its quite ... piercing beauty is a little ...

... blunted. Some moments later however, such are the powers of recuperation at this age, the head is drawn back to a distance of two or three feet, the eyes widen to a stare and begin to feast again. (*Pause.*)

—flare of the black disordered hair as though spread wide on water, the brows knitted in a groove suggesting pain but simply concentration more likely all things considered on some consummate inner process, the eyes of course closed in keeping with this, the lashes ... (*pause*) ... the nose ... (*pause*) ... nothing, a little pinched perhaps, the lips ...

... tight, a gleam of tooth biting on the under, no coral, no swell, whereas normally ...

... the whole so blanched and still that were it not for the great white rise and fall of the breasts, spreading as they mount and then subsiding to their natural ... aperture—

... so wan and still and so ravished away that it seems no more of the earth than Mira in the Whale, at her tenth and greatest magnitude on this particular night and shining coldly down—as we say, looking up. (*Pause.*) Some moments later however, such are the powers—

—the brows uncloud, the lips part and the eyes ... (*pause*) ... the brows uncloud, the nostrils dilate, the lips part and the eyes ... (*pause*) ... the lips part, a little colour comes back into the cheeks and the eyes ... (*reverently*) ... open. (*Pause.*) Then down a little way ... (*Pause. Change to poetic tone. Low.*)

> Then down a little way
> Through the trash
> To where ... towards where ...

Five

Then down a little way
Through the trash
Towards where
All dark no begging
No giving no words
No sense no need
Through the scum
Down a little way
To whence one glimpse
Of that wellhead.

[Pp. 29–32]

This is no abstract discussion of "the face" (as the discussion of love had been abstract) but a very specific description of an event which seems to be erotic: a romantic scene (moonlit night, outdoors); a beautiful young woman, her face seen at close quarters from above; her hair disordered; her face lined with concentration; her eyes closed; her tooth biting her underlip; the rise of her breasts; then her eyes temporarily dimmed "by what had passed"; her recovery and resumption of amorous gazing—all this suggests an orgasmic experience, one which has led (literally, metaphorically, perhaps both) to the "wellhead": her "source" and for him who sees her a source of important experience. Interestingly enough, the language of this incident does not have the lyrical quality of Krapp's lovemaking in the boat; there is something almost clinical in the accuracy of the detail, which may itself account for why this loved one (if she is the one) "could not be won or won not loved." Whatever the nature of the trouble, Croak is personally touched by the story now and speaks her name with anguish: "Lily!" (p. 30).

Like Krapp with his memories, like Henry with his embers, Croak is left with only the ashes of a love. The emblem of his old age is a man huddled by the fire ("I wouldn't want them back. Not with the fire in me now.") seeing in its cold ash the face of a woman he loved, or wanted to love, and lost or failed. He has visited again a moment in his past, through words and music recounted to himself a critical event (whether biography or fantasy), and when the narration reaches the quick of that experience, he is devastated,

98

letting his club fall, fleeing the story he has just commanded be told. Like Krapp he has both gazed into and held at a distance "the eyes she had!" If love is indeed "the most powerful passion," affecting his mind and soul more strongly than anything else (along with its comic opposite, sloth), he has responded, like so many Beckettian men, with appropriate ambivalence, both pursuing and fleeing the object of his desire. And it is the story which allows him to perform this ritual "to and from" (p. 23) again and again, in pain and safety.

The television play *Eh Joe* is constructed similarly to *Words and Music* and contains some of the same images. The anecdote recounted presents a sequel to the one that so disturbs Croak.

The two characters in this play are Joe, a man in his late fifties (who, like Croak, wears carpet slippers) and Woman's Voice, which occupies the sound track while the camera studies Joe's face. Like the voices in *Embers,* she represents a separate character who, now dead, has become part of what he hears in his mind. The first few minutes of the play are entirely silent, made up of Joe's movements about his room as he thoroughly shuts himself in (closing window, door, cupboard, checking to be sure the room is empty, that he is alone); only then does the voice begin its long monologue, continuing till the end of the play, speaking directly to Joe, berating him.

Joe, like Henry in *Embers,* has for years had voices in his head, beginning with his father's voice, followed by a series of all the people who loved him. But rather than summon these speakers, as Henry had done, Joe practices "mental thuggee,"[7] throttling each one, till that dead person's sound fades entirely from his imagination. It would seem, in fact, that this process is his chief pleasure: "Watch yourself you don't run short, Joe . . . Ever think of that? . . . Eh Joe? . . . What it'd be if you ran out of us . . . Not another soul to still . . ." (p. 37). The current speaker is a woman he once had an erotic relationship with; she berates him for his treatment of her (suggesting it was characteristic of his relationships

7. Samuel Beckett, *Eh Joe,* in *Cascando and Other Short Dramatic Pieces* (New York: Grove Press, 1977), p. 37.

with all women). Their love began as an "idyll," with them "holding hands exchanging vows" (p. 38), and ended in narcissistic sexual exploitation and abandonment: "The best's to come, you said, that last time . . . Hurrying me into my coat . . . Last I was favoured with from you . . ." (pp. 36–37). This particular woman, however, was lucky because she found a better man: "Kinder . . . Stronger . . . More intelligent . . . Better looking . . . Cleaner . . . Truthful . . . Faithful . . . Sane" (p. 39), by her catalog implying Joe's deficiencies.

But not all his exploited women were so fortunate. Almost half of the play is taken up with the narration of an anecdote which appears to be a kind of sequel to Croak's set piece on the face, and, in a remote way, to Krapp's idyll in the boat. Common to all three anecdotes is the suggestion of an erotic moment with particular attention paid to the woman's eyes. "Let me in," pleads Krapp; "the eyes widen to a stare and begin to feast again," remembers Croak; "The pale eyes . . . The look they shed before . . . The way they opened after . . . Spirit made light . . . Wasn't that your description" (p. 41), the Woman's Voice reminds Joe. All three beloved women have been lost by these men. The fate of Krapp's and Croak's women is not specified; this girl's fate, described in vivid detail, is the story the narrating voice forces Joe to experience:

> You know the one I mean, Joe . . . The green one . . . The narrow one . . . Always pale . . . The pale eyes . . . Spirit made light . . . To borrow your expression . . . The way they opened after . . . Unique . . . Are you with me now? . . . Eh Joe? . . . There was love for you . . . The best's to come, you said . . . Bundling her into her Avoca sack . . . Her fingers fumbling with the big horn buttons . . . Ticket in your pocket for the first morning flight . . . You've had her, haven't you? . . . You've laid her? . . . Of course he has . . . She went young . . . No more old lip from her.

Camera move 8

> Ever know what happened? . . . She didn't say? . . . Just the announcement in the *Independent* . . . "On Mary's beads we plead

her needs and in the Holy Mass" . . . Will I tell you? . . . Not interested? . . . Well I will just the same . . . I think you should know . . . That's right, Joe, squeeze away . . . Don't lose heart now . . . When you're nearly home . . . I'll soon be gone . . . The last of them . . . Unless that poor slut loves you . . . Then yourself . . . That old bonfire . . . Years of that stink . . . Then the silence . . . A dollop of that . . . To crown all . . . Till His Nibs . . . One dirty winter night . . . "Mud thou art."

Camera move 9

All right . . . Warm summer night . . . All sleeping . . . Sitting on the edge of her bed in her lavender slip . . . You know the one . . . Ah she knew you, heavenly powers! . . . Faint lap of sea through open window . . . Gets up in the end and slips out as she is . . . Moon . . . Stock . . . Down the garden and under the viaduct . . . Sees from the seaweed the tide is flowing . . . Goes on down to the edge and lies down with her face in the wash . . . Cut a long story short doesn't work . . . Gets up in the end sopping wet and back up to the house . . . Gets out the Gillette . . . The make you recommended for her body hair . . . Back down the garden and under the viaduct . . . Takes the blade from the holder and lies down at the edge on her side . . . Cut another long story short doesn't work either . . . You know how she always dreaded pain . . . Tears a strip from the slip and ties it round the scratch . . . Gets up in the end and back up to the house . . . Slip clinging the way wet silk will . . . This all new to you, Joe? . . . Eh Joe? . . . Gets the tablets and back down the garden and under the viaduct . . . Takes a few on the way . . . Unconscionable hour by now . . . Moon going off the shore behind the hill . . . Stands a bit looking at the beaten silver . . . Then starts along the edge to a place further down near the Rock . . . Imagine what in her mind to make her do that . . . Imagine . . . Trailing her feet in the water like a child . . . Takes a few more on the way . . . Will I go on, Joe? . . . Eh Joe? . . . Lies down in the end with her face a few feet from the tide . . . Clawing at the shingle now . . . Has it all worked out this time . . . Finishes the tube . . . There's love for you . . . Eh Joe? . . . Scoops a little cup for her face in the stones . . . The green one . . . The narrow one . . . Always pale . . . The pale eyes . . . The look they shed before . . . The way they opened after . . . Spirit made light ... Wasn't that your description, Joe? ... (*Voice drops to whisper, almost inaudible except words in italics.*) All right ... You've had the best ... Now *imagine* ... Before she goes ... Face in the cup ... Lips on a *stone* ... Taking Joe with her ... Light gone ... "*Joe Joe*" ... No sound ... To the *stones* ... Say it now, no one'll hear you ... Say "Joe" it parts the *lips* ... *Imagine* the hands ... The *solitaire* ... Against a *stone* ... Imagine the *eyes* ... Spiritlight ... Month of June ... What year of your Lord? ... *Breasts* in the stones ... And the *hands* ... Before they go ... *Imagine* the hands ... What are they at? ... In the *stones* ... (*Image fades, voice as before.*) What are they fondling? ... Till they go ... *There's love for you* ... Isn't it, Joe? ... Wasn't it, Joe? ... *Eh Joe?* ... Wouldn't you say? ... Compared to us ... Compared to Him ... *Eh Joe?* (*Voice and image out.*)

[Pp. 39–41]

"Ever know what happened?" This is the stuff of stories, novels, not drama. Showing, not telling, the present tense, not the past is the concern of drama. But here, as in all of Beckett's plays, the narrated segment is a central part of the dramatic action, and it is a story not to be cut short. Woman's Voice is insistent that Joe listen to this story and experience *its* drama: "*Imagine* the hands ... Imagine the *eyes*...." This vivid description gives the play its dramatic climax and its thematic focus.

Not ennui, not "existential absurdity" nor free-floating *Angst* torments Joe. The malady is quite explicit: a failure of love, a failure to *accept* love resulting from despair that significant love can be given. And the primary deprivation for Joe (as for Henry and for Hamm) has been paternal love. The first beloved person to absent himself by death, and then to be throttled to death in imagination, was Joe's father. But behind him stands a more significant father, that Heavenly Father ("your Lord," the voice calls him) who is disappointingly absent and desperately wanted. ("The bastard! He doesn't exist!" Hamm says in one of his bitterest lines.) That Joe's "Lord" is the biblical God of harshness and judgment is indicated by the quotation Woman's Voice condenses to its salient words: " 'Thou fool thy soul' " (p. 39). Here again

Beckett uses a biblical story to give further point to his own storied drama.[8] In the next paragraph, Woman's Voice refers again through brief quotation to this God of death and judgment: "Till His Nibs ... One dirty winter night ... 'Mud thou art'" (p. 40).[9] The play ends with a final indictment of this God, blaming him for his failure to love Joe. The girl who gave her life "for" Joe, that suicide, is held up as a model of love beside which all others are deficient: "*There's love for you ...* Compared to us ... Compared to Him." Both human and divine fathers have failed to love Joe; he in turn cannot love anyone else. He merely "has" people ("You've had her, haven't you? ... You've laid her?"); just as his primary deficient love "has" him, a mere creature whose soul can be taken back for judgment and whose body can be decomposed by death.[10]

The biblical allusions and the conventional use of capitals for the pronoun indicate that this "Lord" is the biblical Lord; but the passage contains a typical Beckettian double meaning with sexual innuendo. The "Lord" may also refer to his penis (in the manner of D. H. Lawrence) and its judgment may be his declining sexual powers.[11] (Earlier, Woman's Voice had moved from discussion of sexual intercourse to discussion of Joe's imagined voices with the phrase, "Watch yourself you don't run short, Joe"—run short of

8. See the parable of the rich fool (Luke 12:13–21), which ends "But God said unto him, Thou fool, this night thy soul shall be required of thee: then whose shall those things be, which thou hast provided? So is he that layeth up treasure for himself, and is not rich toward God."

9. "For dust thou art, and unto dust shalt thou return" (Genesis 3:19; see also Job 7:21).

10. The importance of both the story element and the biblical associations in this play is suggested by Beckett's early notes. The word "God" and the word "story" are written large and each is circled, standing out alone, one above the other, toward the top of his notebook page. The biblical references to dust and to soul are also written out on this page. See RUL MS 1537/1, p. 5, photocopy of original document in Washington University Libraries, St. Louis, Missouri.

11. In early versions of *Eh Joe*, the phrase used was "our Lord"; by changing "our" to "your," Beckett has allowed for the religious reference "our Lord" unmistakably conveys as well as for the private and personal meaning of his double entendre. See RUL MS 1537/2, p. 2, photocopy of original document in Washington University Libraries, St. Louis, Missouri.

"hoists" and run short of voices to throttle, both suggested by this transitional remark.) "The passion of our Joe" thus refers both to sexual arousal and to physical and spiritual suffering, with Joe here parodying the role of that God who does not love him. There is no "Passion of Christ" in this play, no God who gives his life out of love; only an exploitative sexual passion and painful sense of deprivation on Joe's part, and a fragile girl who commits suicide but whose death has not in any way redeemed Joe but damns him further to torment as he listens to the recital of her story.

In one of Beckett's most recent plays to be published, *A Piece of Monologue,*[12] the absent face fades to an obscure ghost of uncertain identity. Whatever significance this absence has is revealed by the puzzling phrase "Waiting on the rip word."[13] A number of times throughout this short piece Beckett has included unusual words or unusual usages (the archaic term "haught," the medical "nevoid," the remote "spill") as well as allusions to other literature or well-known phrases. And often in these various word-plays there lurks a pun. "Rip word" condenses, in this highly condensed play, everything that "story" has meant in Beckett's other drama.

"Rip-tide" is an ordinary phrase; "rip word," a surprise that yields its meaning by comparison with the more familiar. The *Oxford English Dictionary* in its definition of the noun "rip" as "a disturbed state of the sea" makes reference to the verb form, which includes after the more immediate meanings of violent slashing or tearing the figurative meanings "to open up, lay bare, disclose, make known" and "to open *up*, rake *up*, bring *up* again into notice or discussion (esp. something unpleasant or which is to a person's discredit)."[14] Thus just as one "waits on the tide" for an appropriate flow, so here the speaker waits on the rip word, that word which will lay bare what is at the critical center of his monologue. The rip word is that disturbance in the flow of language which reveals what is hidden, the unpleasant or discreditable truth which may be disguised or submerged but never completely evaded. The rip word

12. In *Kenyon Review,* NS1, 1, no. 3 (1979): 1–4.
13. The following discussion of this play was first published as "The Rip Word in *A Piece of Monologue,*" *Modern Drama* 25 (September 1982): 349–54.
14. *The Compact Edition of the Oxford English Dictionary* (1971), 2:2554.

is sometimes just a single word, as it is in this play, but elsewhere it has been whole narratives, the stories and anecdotes that burst forth, breaks in the surface of the drama that reveal the truth of motives, feelings, themes.

The rip word in *A Piece of Monologue* is "begone," that word by which the speaker dismisses from his life what he has always really wanted. Now, at eighty-two, the speaker tells a "story" of a man, so much like himself that it is clear he is simply speaking of himself in the third person. (This old man, like the old woman in *Not I*, seems unable to face himself, to reckon with the personal nature of what he relates, always taking refuge in "he," never saying "I.") His story summarizes in its opening sentence a theme that permeates all of Beckett's previous drama: "Birth was the death of him." The two poles of his life are funeral and funeral ("they give birth astride a grave . . .").[15] This old man, speaker and subject, appears to be an invalid, confined to his room if not always to his bed. He is dressed in a white nightgown and white socks, which he wears night and day; his chief furniture is a bed and a lamp and his chief vistas are a darkened window and a blank wall. His chief preoccupation is his parents, their absent presence in his life, and their deaths.

There are five main anecdotes in the story the speaker tells, four of which involve memories of the past and one of which occurs in the present of the narrative. The first past event has to do with the old man's infancy: "At suck first fiasco. With the first totters. From mammy to nanny and back. All the way. Bandied back and forth. So ghastly grinning on" (p. 1). The anecdote depicted is that of an infant's learning to walk, but the phrase "ghastly grinning" suggests a skull, not a baby; this death imagery is appropriate, however, to his sense that "birth was the death of him" and that his progress—"on"—is from "funeral to funeral." This opening section of the play establishes a grim infancy with an even grimmer goal: as he lies in his crib he is grinning "up at the lid to come" (not at "the life to come" which that phrase echoes). The coffin in his future is already present.

15. *Waiting for Godot*, p. 57 +.

The second event from the past involves his tearing up pictures of his family which he had had pinned to the wall: "Down one after another. Gone. Torn to shreds and scattered. Strewn all over the floor. Not at one sweep. No sudden fit of . . . no word. Ripped from the wall and torn to shreds one by one. Over the years" (p. 2). A third event, referred to more than once, involves a burial: "Rain pelting. Umbrellas round a grave. Seen from above. Streaming black canopies. Black ditch beneath. Rain bubbling in the black mud. Empty for the moment. That place beneath . . ." (p. 3). And the most haunting event of all, referred to several times, involves someone lighting a lamp in his dark room:

> There in the end slowly a faint hand. Holding aloft a lighted spill. In light of spill faintly the hand and milkwhite globe. Then second hand. In light of spill. Takes off globe and disappears. Reappears empty. Takes off chimney. Two hands and chimney in light of spill. Spill to wick. Chimney back on. Hand with spill disappears. Second hand disappears. Chimney alone in gloom. Hand reappears with globe. Globe back on. Turns wick low. Pale globe alone in gloom. Glimmer of brass bedrail.
>
> [P. 3]

As the old man in the narrative thinks of these past events, he is described by the speaker as moving in and out of the darkness, staring out the dark window, standing gazing at the now-blank wall, and, most often, lighting his lamp. The first description of this act is the most detailed:

> Loose matches in right-hand pocket. Strikes one on his buttock the way his father taught him. Takes off milkwhite globe and sets it down. Match goes out. Strikes a second as before. Takes off chimney. Smoke-clouded. Holds it in left hand. Match goes out. Strikes a third as before and sets it to wick. Puts back chimney. Match goes out. Puts back globe. Turns wick low.
>
> [Pp. 1–2]

The next description of this event has all the succinctness of a stage direction: "Match one as described for globe. Two for chimney. Three for wick. Chimney and globe back on. Turns wick low. Backs away to edge of light and turns to face wall" (pp. 2–3). The narrator is part of a play, and narrating he sounds like the stage directions of a play. Beckett compresses not only the syntax of his language but the two forms, the narrative and the dramatic, which he has been employing throughout his work.

All these events, past and present, tell the audience something about this old man, his behavior, his character, the issues that preoccupy him. The description of his infancy reveals his fundamentally dour and pessimistic view of existence: the baby flat on its back in the dark (like the narrator in *Company*), has nothing to look up at but the lid of its coffin. The shredding of the photographs indicates his rejection, and probably hatred, of his parents, certainly his disappointment in them: "There was father. That grey void. There mother. That other" (p. 2). The repeated reference to the grave scene betrays the yearning that lies beneath his pessimism and hatred: the rain which falls on the grave is associated with mercy by his allusion to Portia's famous speech— "Rain . . . dropping gentle on the place beneath" (p. 2)—a mercy present in his poetic imagination but absent from his lived experience. The event with the lamp is most revealing of all, because it not only haunts his memory but he duplicates it in his life again and again as he lights and relights the lamp in his room. The lamp is, indeed, all that he has left, and even that not for long.

The play is so highly condensed that it is virtually poetry. One of the poetic techniques that gives the piece so much of its power is incremental repetition and plays on words. A pair of phrases frequently repeated is "that first night" and "this night" (which in the course of the play is shown to be his last night, the final one of those thirty thousand nights, those two and a half billion seconds he has calculated). At first it seems merely that the old man is surveying his life to date, remembering various incidents from his birth until his bleak old age. His pessimistic view of life as one long funeral is reinforced by word play such as "dying on" (rather than "living on"), repeated twice and suggesting a perpetual state of death, Tithonus with no Aurora. Another repeated set of phrases contributes to this sense of limbo: "No such thing as none" and "No such thing as whole," suggesting that neither extinction nor completion is possible. One of the most frequently repeated phrases,

repeated with important variation, is "he all but said of loved ones."
The "all but said" suggests a Freudian slip, reference to someone
loved and yet not loved. The first occurrence of this phrase comes
within the first two or three minutes of monologue, as the speaker
suggests that the old man's life consists of a succession of funerals:
"Funerals of . . . he all but said of loved ones" (p. 1). The next
comes in reference to the pictures of his parents which he shredded,
and there it is used twice. The fourth use of the phrase comes in
his anecdote of the burial in the rain, and there it is applied to the
one buried; and then twice again in his next mention of the burial,
but this time there is an interestingly ambiguous pronoun: "Till
whose grave? Which . . . he all but said which loved one's? He?
Black ditch in pelting rain" (p. 4). That "He?" raises the possibility
that the old man himself is beginning to entertain the thought that
the death which preoccupies him may be his own, not really his
parents'. The answer to the question *which* loved one may indeed
be *he*, he himself. Seconds later he introduces other possibilities:
"Coffin on its way. Loved one . . . he all but said loved one on his
way. Her way." But this diffusion of subject does not remove the
possibility that "He" may be he himself; if anything, such attempts
at disguise confirm the sense that acknowledging the true antecedent
may be too painful.

The final use of the phrase—"Ghost . . . he all but said ghost
loved ones"—comes very close to the end of the monologue and
immediately before the phrase discussed earlier, "Waiting on the
rip word," which introduces the climax of the play:

Stands there staring beyond at that black veil lips quivering to
half-heard words. Treating of other matters. Trying to treat of
other matters. Till half hears there are no other matters. Never
were other matters. Never two matters. Never but the one matter. The dead and gone. The dying and the going. From the
word go. The word begone. Such as the light going now. Beginning to go. In the room. Where else? Unnoticed by him staring
beyond. The globe alone. Not the other. The unaccountable.
From nowhere. On all sides nowhere. The globe alone. Alone
gone.

[P. 4]

Everything in the old man's life has been "ghost," that is, dead: "Ghost light. Ghost nights. Ghost rooms. Ghost graves. Ghost . . . he all but said ghost loved ones." His whole life has been dark; he tries to "stare beyond through rift in dark to other dark," but what makes the "rift" in the black veil is the rip word he must wait for. Attempts at distraction do not work ("there are no other matters"). There is only one real subject and that is death; not the death of his parents ("never two matters") but the single death, the one matter, which he has looked at, strained to pierce its veil all his life, his own death. From the moment of his birth ("from the word go") he has carried demise with him ("the word begone"). He always *knew* that, of course, at some level of himself, but from infancy focused attention elsewhere (mammy and nanny, photographs, other people's deaths, the luxury of grief over *them*); grinning that "nevoid smile" with which he has been marked from birth. But as he nears the final seconds of his final night the realization that he is looking at his *own* grave begins to intrude itself. Memories of his parents, his superiority to them (he shreds *their* pictures, attends *their* burials, but he remains) and the imaginary solace of some mysterious light, all begin to desert him. "Begone" is the real command; he has sent his parents on their way, but he himself must also be gone. Not only does the actual lamp in his room keep going out, but that other light, the unaccountable one, is also going, leaving him surrounded by "nowhere." The real globe in his actual room remains. But he is, at the end of these thirty thousand nights, himself gone, in the only way it is possible to go, alone, like Everyman, abandoned by his white socks, his white gown, his dark window, his blank wall; his brief "light gleams an instant, then it's night once more."[16]

In *A Piece of Monologue* Beckett condenses what he has stated in many of his plays and novels and brings together in one neat set of associations themes he has developed more extensively in other work: birth, the sea, and words. Twice the speaker describes the old man, combining these three elements: "Waits for first word always the same. It gathers in his mouth. Parts lips and thrusts

16. Ibid.

tongue forward. Birth. Parts the dark" (p. 3). This experience occurs in the dark and is the occasion for the emergence of a faint light which comes up gradually and then subsides. By a nice tautology, the "first word" is "birth," which like a foetus gathers itself in his mouth and then like an infant emerging from the womb parts the darkness and thrusts itself forward. Words, speech, expression are thus a kind of parturition, which here and elsewhere in Beckett's work is an unfortunate not a blessed event. These two themes, birth and expression, are associated with another thematic image Beckett has used often in his work: the sea, mixed image of life and death.[17] That word, "birth," gathers like a developing infant but also like a pool of water in a tidal basin. Birth is the beginning of the flow, but there is a companion word, a companion event, that "rip word" which disrupts the surface, showing the darkness beyond. "From the word go. The word begone," from beginning to end, from birth to death, life is surrounded by darkness and by "nowhere," "on all sides nowhere." Expression is as futile as existence. We all knew that, of course, from Beckett's earlier work, but this very recent play condenses the themes into one complex set of poetic and dramatic images, quick and painfully accurate. The usual devices of narrative are here, anecdotes embedded in a larger monologue which is in effect a whole story about a dramatic situation, a recital rather than an action. And yet the choice of form, the use of the third person pronoun is itself really the action, really the drama. The old man does not die on stage. Instead, since he and the speaker are one and the same, he tries to evade something which he is coming to understand very well: the imminence of his own death. Yet he, like the old woman in *Not I,* does not say "I," does not "own" his death, but flounders in a rip-tide of realization, trying to avoid what is beginning to engulf him, trying by recitation of a "story" about "someone else" to evade knowing "whose grave" he is looking into "from above" as the rain falls.

17. See the discussion of *Embers,* p. 92, and of *Eh Joe,* p. 101.

Reckoning Closed
and Story Ended

Come and Go, Cascando, Ohio Impromptu

E laboration of story and the subtle suppression and refinement of story—this gradual process seems to mark the development of Beckett's use of narrative in his plays. The process not only is apparent across the span of his playwriting career but also is sometimes evident in the various stages through which he brings a given play to completion. In the earlier plays there are often extended narratives—such as Hamm's and Winnie's—while in the most recent plays that story element, along with the play as a whole, has been refined to a quintessential minimum.

Usually Beckett's revisions, unlike those of someone such as O'Neill, who often wrote several entirely different drafts, are not major rethinkings or reorderings; rather he seems to write the play quite directly, almost whole, with subsequent alterations of only a word or phrase, with occasional shifting of a phrase from one spot to another. The process is largely one of refinement of expression, often involving improvement of rhythm. For example, in *Krapp's Last Tape*, the word "imagine" is changed to "fancy" ("This I fancy is what I have chiefly to record this evening"[1]), thus adding a touch of capriciousness, a sense of lightness to what the word "imagine"

1. RUL ACC 1659, p. 5.

conveys; the concept has not altered, but the nuances are clearer and the rhythm of the line is better. The phrase "little white dog" had originally been "wire-haired fox terrier" (p. 5); the brevity and emphatic stresses of the substituted phrase are clearly an improvement over the useless specificity of the rather jerky original. And the addition of "hard" into the phrase which finally reads "A small, old, black, hard, solid rubber ball" (p. 5) is again for improvement of rhythm; "solid" certainly could double for "hard" but the extra stressed syllable helps with the sense of inexorable presence in this important reference.

Changes in detail often involve a move away from specificity. In early drafts of *Play* the characters had been listed as about thirty years of age, but in later drafts they are made ageless ("Faces so lost to age and aspect as to seem almost part of urns. But no masks").[2] Thus Beckett is quite precise about what he intends, but that intended effect is itself often deliberately vague. Sometimes revision entails deletion altogether of some section, phrase, or detail which is simply too explicit, too obvious, or even (surprisingly enough) too "cute." An early play in French (c. 1956) begins by sounding like a domestic comedy except that the man is "renverse sur sa croix."[3] All the lighting of cigarettes and wrangling about sex and dinner do not help carry off this awkwardly obvious imagery, and the play was finally abandoned. Less total instances of obviousness can be found in the drafts of finished plays. The first typescript of *That Time,* for example, has the line "not a curse for the old scenes you lived in so long and the people stopping to look at you like something out of Beckett sitting there on the step in the sun."[4] In typescripts 2, 3, 4, and 5 the reference to Beckett continues, with the phrase variously recast but basically the same in effect; then in typescripts 6 and 7 the phrase "like something out of Beckett" is omitted altogether.

The condensation and deletion of explicit detail which characterizes the process of revision in most of Beckett's plays is balanced, however, by an elaboration of stage directions. Beckett usually

2. RUL MS 1528/8, p. 3.
3. RUL MS 1227/7/16/2, p. 1.
4. RUL MS 1477/2, p. 2.

seems to begin by writing dialogue first, making the story line clear; only afterwards do stage directions become detailed. For example, in *Eh Joe* the character descriptions, voice, face, and the like, and camera movements do not appear until a later typescript.[5] An exception to this process is *Ghost Trio,* which Beckett seems to have conceived visually, not aurally. There the notebook and type-script are full of details of camera shots, timing, visual details, physical manner; with virtually no spoken story nor lines—all is implication and pantomime.[6]

The overall direction of these changes, however, is toward con-cision: "Simp." as Beckett wrote in the margin of a recently revised version of *Endgame.*[7] The spoken words are usually refined in rhythm and meaning, explicit information is often suppressed, and plot line usually becomes more obscure. The result is not obfus-cation, however, but condensation. The entire play has been "boiled down" to its essence. Beckett's direction regarding Winnie's stage properties might well be used to describe his own process of writing, both in individual plays and across his playwriting career: "gen. principle: hypertrophy secondary, atrophy primary."[8]

The element of story is kept in balance with the rest of the play. As the play condenses, so too does the story, remaining, however, even in the brief plays, as important as it is in the longer ones; the hint of story becomes as effective as an entire chronicle. One play in particular, with a number of interesting drafts, demonstrates this process by which information is suppressed and story, para-mount and explicit in early versions, becomes literally a mere whisper in the final one.

In an untitled typescript of an early draft of *Come and Go,* the following rather extraordinary sections appear, read aloud by Poppy as Viola and Rose listen:

"A last maddening kiss and she tore herself from his knees and disappeared into the bedroom. Aubrey stretched out to the flames

5. See RUL MS 1537/3.
6. See RUL MS 1519/1–3.
7. RUL MS 1974-5, p. 11.
8. RUL MS 1730, p. 53.

his long hairy legs, took a sip of his brandy, relit his cigar and resumed alone the collection of obscene postcards."

"Hermione rose at last from the steaming sweet-smelling foam and stood all pink and dripping before the great cheval-glass, inspecting her luscious forms. Caressingly she passed her hands——"

"Over her splendid bosom glowing from the bath, her belly and quivering flanks, then falling to her knees plunged them between her thighs in an extasy [sic] of anticipation."

"How long she remained in this posture she never knew. Finally she sprang to her feet and, still moist, entered the bedroom."⁹

The women's interpolated conversation ("Are his trousers off already then?") and critical comments ("This is slipshod writing.") do not save the passage. A large black X annihilates each of the two pages, and Beckett as pornographer is not to be seen again. But what is interesting about the passage is the extent to which it writes large an important theme in the play, a theme and a play which get simmered down so that finally only the slightest suggestion of the original remains. In that early draft the fictional narrative, quite literally a novel, read aloud as part of the dramatic action serves to make very explicit the extent to which sexual activity interests these three women. Their aged deterioration simply heightens the sardonic effect (after reading "and, still moist, entered the bedroom," Poppy excuses herself and "goes out laboriously," her bad timing and physical heft clearly in sharp contrast with the ecstatic agility of the "luscious forms" about which she reads). All this eroticism is condensed in the final published version into two innocent phrases, "Dreaming of . . . love" and "I can feel the rings" (i.e., wedding rings).¹⁰

That the pornographic beginning was not simply a false start is indicated by another probably even earlier draft. In a typescript titled *Good Heavens* and marked "Before Come and Go," there are a series of exchanges between A and B and between B and C

9. RUL MS 1227/7/16/5 [leaf 1 r. and leaf 2 r.].
10. Samuel Beckett, *Come and Go,* in *Cascando and Other Short Dramatic Pieces* (New York: Grove Press, 1977), pp. 68 and 69.

114

suggesting that sexual activity is the secret of their apparent "good health." The suggestion is very much a matter of pun and innuendo. For example, after comments on her radiant skin and inquiry about how it is achieved, one character whispers her secret and the other exclaims, "Good heavens!" Then follow the innuendos: "I did not know he had been discharged"; "Oh very much so. (Complacent laugh.) Very much so indeed!"[11] And similar sequences follow with similar innuendos: "No cream to touch it." "I did not know he was up." "Oh very much so. (Complacent laugh.) Very much so indeed" (leaf 3 r.). The suggestion of terminal illness, which dominates the final version, is also present in this early draft, where a whispered secret elicits the ritual response "Good heavens!" followed by the somber remark "The worst kind. (*Pause*) Three months" and discussion about whether it is better to know or not (leaf 1 v.). Both eros and thanatos are much more explicit in these earlier versions than they will be in the final one.

The draft with the pornographic narrative (RUL MS 1227/7/ 16/5) also contains these sequences linking apparent good health to sexual activity. And there the details are presented quite explicitly. Each of the three women is terminally ill and does not know it; each one has a husband who is "crazed with grief," or "heartbroken," or "weeping"; each has a lover, who apparently accounts for her radiant look; and in all three cases, both lover and illness are secrets kept from others or from the one affected. That Beckett decided to jettison this excessive symmetry along with the whole pornographic sequence was probably wise. In later versions the erotic stories, either read aloud or suggestively whispered, become simply "dreaming of . . . love," a much more neutral and romantic phrase, not competing in any way with the sense of mortality which permeates the play. Yet the hint of sexual interest remains.

By tempering the sexual explicitness and reducing the play altogether, Beckett has actually intensified the sense of loss which this "dramaticule" conveys. In the early version, with its erotic novel used for imaginative escape (the three women deliberately focusing on "the little death" to avoid "the big death," eros rather

11. RUL MS 1227/7/16/4, leaf 1 r.

than thanatos), the comic grotesque elements swamp the tragic ones. In the final version, the balance is very skillful indeed; and the balance point is precisely that element of erotic interest which began as a full-fledged narrative and has been boiled down to simple references to love and marriage. The three women are no longer leering old adulteresses; they have become cartoons. Beckett has reversed the artistic process by moving his characters from flesh (with all the luscious details of story) to sketch (where the story remains only as hint), that sure deft line with which some artists begin a picture and with which others choose to end.

All of Beckett's later plays are characterized by this same concentration of length and intensity of theme, with hints and residues of story concerned almost always with the relationship between love and death. In these short plays, as in Beckett's longer ones, much of the actual drama of the piece results from the way narrative is used.

The radio play *Cascando* presents a highly concentrated example of Beckett's dramatic use of narrative. The play is *about* storytelling and also makes use of storytelling techniques. Like *Play*, it has a "character" called Opener who stops and starts the speech of others; but he, unlike the spotlight, has a voice of his own and specific words to say. Both spotlight and Opener are mysterious, almost preternatural: they are pure voice and pure light, unexplained, powerful, and compelling. What they compel is narrative.

The play begins ironically. "It is the month of May" parodies the idyllic opening of many a narrative poem and prose romance; the "dry as dust" tone of voice in which the line is delivered makes the irony unmistakable.[12] Opener has "opened" the piece; what emerges from that opening is another voice and, later, music. He will control these two "characters" by announcing "I open" and "I close," thus moving them to sound and to silence. In addition to these basic operations, Opener will also comment on his own function, in a sense "tell his own story," try to account for himself; Voice will both tell a story and grapple with the problem of sto-

12. Samuel Beckett, *Cascando and Other Short Dramatic Pieces* (New York: Grove Press, 1977), p. 9.

rytelling; and all three together will strain to bring both that story and the radio drama in which it is told to a conclusion, a conclusion at farthest extreme from the youth and love which the opening line parodies.

The problem of storytelling is very explicit in this otherwise rather elusive play. The first word Voice says (and it is almost the first word of the play, since Opener's lines are quite brief) is "story." Voice has been "turned on" midsentence, as he pants through speculations about the chief task of his life: to find the right story, to tell it, to finish it, and thus to achieve rest, sleep, and the silence of "no more stories." But this is not an easy task. He has already finished "thousands and one" stories, only to discover they were not the right ones.

This time, however, he thinks he has it, in his story about Woburn:

> this time I have it . . . I've got it . . . Woburn . . . I resume . . . a
> long life . . . already . . . say what you like . . . a few misfortunes
> . . . that's enough . . . five years later . . . ten years . . . I don't
> know . . . Woburn . . . he's changed . . . not enough . . . recogniz-
> able . . . in the shed . . . yet another . . . waiting for night . . .
> night to fall . . . to go out . . . go on . . . elsewhere . . . sleep
> elsewhere . . . it's slow . . . he lifts his head . . . now and then . . .
> his eyes . . . to the window . . . it's darkening . . . the earth is
> darkening . . . it's night . . . he gets up . . . knees first . . . then
> up . . . on his feet . . . slips out . . . Woburn . . . same old coat
> . . . right the sea . . . left the hills . . . he has the choice . . . he
> has only—
>
> [Pp. 9–10]

The salient elements of the story are these: an old man, probably derelict, infirm, makes his way to the sea at night; he wants peace, sleep; against terrific obstacles of rocks and dunes he finally gets to a boat and drifts with no tiller, no oars, heading out to the "vast deep," into complete darkness. In effect, he has chosen death. The event itself is intrinsically suicidal; and the imagery associated with it—the dark and the deep—suggests death. No May morning this, with birds singing, roses blooming, and lovers meeting. Here is

117

the extreme solitary experience, painfully sought and painfully experienced ("face in the bilge . . . he clings on").

As Woburn, within the story, struggles to end himself, Voice struggles to end the story. And in concert with Voice, Music and Opener strive to bring Woburn, the story, and this radio drama to their respective "closes":

OPENER (*with Voice and Music*): As though they had joined arms.

VOICE ⎫
MUSIC ⎭ (*together*): —sleep . . . no more stories . . . come

on . . . Woburn . . . it's him . . . see him . . . say him

. . . .

. . . to the end . . . don't let go—

. . . .

OPENER (*with Voice and Music*): Good.

VOICE ⎫
MUSIC ⎭ (*together*): —nearly . . . just a few more . . . a

few more . . . I'm there . . . nearly . . . Woburn . . .

. . . .

it's him . . . it was him . . . I've got him . . . nearly—

. . . .

OPENER (*with Voice and Music, fervently*): Good!

VOICE ⎫
MUSIC ⎭ (*together*): —this time . . . it's right . . . finish . . .

. . . .

no more stories . . . sleep . . . we're there . . . nearly . . .

. . . .

just a few more . . . don't let go . . . Woburn . . . he

. . . .

clings on . . . come on . . . come on—

. . . .

Silence.

[Pp. 18–19]

"Don't let go" is Woburn's own cry, clinging to life in the very midst of his seeking death (the difficulty of dying that Beckett writes about again and again). It is also the narrator's cry, trying not to lose his story before he has ended it (forever ended it), and it is Opener's cry, too, as he keeps Voice going, so that he does not lose the narrative by which he will end all narrative.

The very drama of this play is in the phenomenon of narration itself: the pain of being required to narrate, to tell a story, and the need to find a story which can end, and by ending annihilate all further storytelling, annihilate the storyteller, annihilate even the Opener, because then there will be nothing to open. It is the subject of all Beckett's novels,[13] here dramatized. Like the snake that swallows itself, this radio drama tries to use its own sound to bring about a final silence.

The dramatic situation in *Ohio Impromptu* demonstrates visually both the split and the connection between speaker and hearer, which has been an important motif in Beckett's work ever since the early trilogy of novels. Its text demonstrates, as well, the theme threaded through so many of his plays which makes up part of the argument of this study: that story "comforts," makes it possible indirectly to face and to deal with the pain of living. Like other very recent plays—*A Piece of Monologue* and *Rockaby*—this play involves a "doubled" character: in *Rockaby*, a woman physically on stage speaking and interacting with her own recorded voice; in *A Piece of Monologue,* a man physically on stage speaking and creating a "fictional persona" clearly identical with himself; in *Ohio Impromptu,* two visually identical characters physically on stage, one speaking, the other listening. In all cases, despite the variety of form, the effect is the same: a single character seems to "face" himself, to create himself, to deal with himself in some way and at the same time to flee. Thus a strange set of mirror images has been created. Listener and Reader, represented by actors on stage, appear to be physically almost identical; at the same time, the two men in the narrative they read seem to mirror them in situation.

In *Ohio Impromptu* the two characters are designated as L (Listener) and R (Reader), "as alike in appearance as possible."[14] They sit at adjacent sides of a rectangular table, each with "Bowed head propped on right hand. . . . Left hand on table. Long black coat. Long white hair." The only visual difference, L front and R to the

13. See especially David H. Hesla, *The Shape of Chaos* (Minneapolis: University of Minnesota Press, 1971).

14. Samuel Beckett, *Ohio Impromptu,* in *Rockaby and Other Short Pieces* (New York: Grove Press, 1981), p. 27.

side, is that L's face is hidden and R's is seen in profile; R has a book open before him and L does not. After the fade up of light and a ten second pause, L reads from the book "Little is left to tell" (p. 28), a recurrent phrase soon balanced by the last words he reads, "Nothing is left to tell" (p. 35); these are the spare limits of this very brief play. The narrative he reads refers to a man's attempts "to obtain relief" (p. 28), his separation from a "dear face" (p. 30), irrevocable isolation, terrors of night, "fearful symptoms" (p. 31), and in the midst of all this the arrival of another man sent to comfort him. At first this man read till dawn then disappeared, repeating this action on various nights. Eventually the two men "grew to be as one" (p. 33) and the Reader does not leave but sits on "without a word"; at last, however, he announces that he has been instructed not to come again: "So the sad tale a last time told they sat on as though turned to stone" (p. 34). Despite the Listener's signals to make the Reader continue reading, "Nothing is left to tell" and the now closed book remains closed.

It is important to note that the narrative read is never explicitly stated to be *about* the two men seen by the audience, and yet there is much to connect them. The two being "as one" is suggested by the physical similarity of the men on stage, and the Latin Quarter hat referred to in the narrative is actually present on the table where they sit. The very fact that the narrative describes a reader reading to a listener corresponds to the action that occurs on stage. Why this "doubling" effect? For much the same reason that it occurs, through different form, in *A Piece of Monologue:* to show characters in the process of distancing themselves from their actual lives, to let story take the place of life and action. Once again in a play by Beckett, a very interesting reciprocal confrontation and evasion has occurred, their simultaneity creating the dramatic tension of the play.

The two poles of that tension are these: that the audience "wants" to identify the characters on stage with the characters in the narrative because of the similarities just described and yet no conclusive evidence for such an identification exists. A "yes" and a "no" war with each other, probably not consciously, while the play is in progress but war nonetheless in that complex absorption which is part of an effective theatrical experience. And this tension pulling the audience between "yes" and "no" is analogous to the tension the characters in the play experience. Events are confronted (or affirmed) as narrative and evaded (or negated) as life. Story takes the place of "action" both for the audience and for the character in the play.

This phenomenon is illustrated by one of the several lines in the play which the Listener requires the Reader to repeat (throughout the play, the Listener has used a knock on the table to make the Reader repeat the previous complete sentence, with another knock as signal to resume reading). The repetition of "Then turn and his slow steps retrace" (p. 29) refers to the man physically going back (walking) over a path in his past and also demonstrates that process metaphorically (the rereading of a sentence already read). The "action" of going back over a "path" is not acted out physically—the actor does not pace up and down on stage—and yet there is a form of pacing up and down in the phenomenon of the repeated line. On stage there is very little physical motion (hands only and, at the last, heads), and yet all moves because of the narration read.

The six lines the Listener requires to be repeated express the essence of the play:

"Little is left to tell" (p. 28).

"Then turn and his slow steps retrace" (p. 29).

"Seen the dear face and heard the unspoken words, Stay where we were so long alone together, my shade will comfort you" (p. 30).

"Little is left to tell" (p. 31).

"Saw the dear face and heard the unspoken words, No need to go to him again, even were it in your power" (p. 34).

"Nothing is left to tell" (p. 35).

The fact that the Listener requires their repetition suggests the emotional charge they carry. The close proximity of the two men rules out any suggestion that the Listener simply has not heard a given line clearly. And the one line that seems syntactically awkward is reread not at the Listener's instigation but by the Reader himself trying to verify it: "After so long a lapse that as if never been. (Pause. Looks closer.) Yes, after so long a lapse that as if never been" (p. 31). (That "yes" is the Reader's only personal word in the entire play.) The six main repetitions, then, are significant to the play because they are significant to the Listener. He knows that time is passing, that little of his life is left to live or to be reread. He knows that what little life he has exists in words and memory, to be "retraced" by the story inscribed in the book to which he listens. At the heart of that life is a loved one, now dead, whose memory he had *then* (not now) tried to evade by leaving the place where they "were so long alone together." But memories pursued him, sent by—"and here he named the dear name"—to comfort him until the moment when "Nothing is left to tell," when no more memory remains, no more comfort, no more time.

At this point of utter finality the most dramatic gesture in the play occurs. "Simultaneously they lower their right hands to table, raise their heads and look at each other. Unblinking. Expressionless" (p. 35). Here the "join" between the two men is completed. In that look past and present meet, the past the Reader has narrated and the present in which the Listener lives, and by a typically Beckettian focus the "nothing left" results not simply from present and future merging (and thus, no more time) but rather from past and present merging (and thus, no more memory, that is, no more consciousness and thus, of course, no more time): at last, the blessed state when that voice in the head stops talking.

Faces until now obscured can be seen looking at each other; eyes meet. The gaze is "unblinking" not only because the look is profound but, more important, because there is nothing left to tell, to imagine. Compare, for example, the reference to blinking in *Company:* "There is of course the eye. Filling the whole field. The hood slowly down. Or up if down to begin. The globe. All pupil. Staring up. Hooded. Bared. Hooded again. Bared again."[15] This blink, described here larger than life, is repeated throughout the novel, its open position capturing the speaker's present, actual moment, and its closed position allowing for those images from

15. Samuel Beckett, *Company* (New York: Grove Press, 1980), pp. 20–21.

the past which make up his memories: "What a help that would be in the dark! To close the eyes and see that hand" (p. 20). The gaze at the end of *Ohio Impromptu* is expressionless because there is nothing left to tell, to "express." At last, the man and the voice of the one he listens to are mute, locked in a gaze, itself a kind of merger (eye beams tangling, souls meeting, to speak in the old style). "The fable of one fabling of one with you in the dark"[16] is finally ended; the comfort of story has been removed. Not only is the dear face, the dear name absent, but the comforting shade is powerless ever to return again. Two actors may be on stage at the end of the play, but their gaze has merged them into a single silent being, both two and one, like the woman in *Rockaby* who has become "her own other" (p. 19)—fixed now forever, like the narrator of *Company*, "Alone," because, just like Hamm in *Endgame*, "time is over, reckoning closed and story ended."

If expression is indeed as futile as Beckett has so often stated it is, then the extensive use of narration by characters in his plays becomes a dramatization of that fact. These narratives do not represent simply "confusion of genre," or the inability of a novelist turned dramatist to keep from falling back on his primary mode of writing. The narratives are, in fact, dramatic action, because by telling stories of various kinds, long and short, the characters are shown to be struggling with deeply personal realizations, reckoning with dangerous issues and emotions, facing them and fleeing them at one and the same time. Both the immanence and the imminence of death plagues these characters. The failure of various human relationships simply particularizes the ultimate loss which is the character's own death. Parental, and usually paternal, love is found to be deficient or entirely absent, and erotic and amorous love is often grotesque and always bungled. And yet the desire to possess these loves and the pain of their loss permanently intrudes upon the character's conscious or unconscious life. He can neither escape this nagging awareness nor face it directly (as Hamlet does, however temporarily, when reasoning about the advantages and disadvantages of suicide). Instead, he has recourse to story, in which he grieves

16. Ibid., p. 63.

over losses but claims he "wouldn't want them back." Whether long and fictional, like Hamm's chronicle and Winnie's story, or quintessentially brief and immediate, like the whispered fates in *Come and Go* which the audience does not even hear, these narratives deal with losses so great and inexpugnable that characters attend with fascination upon the very matter they seek to evade. This ambivalence is itself the dramatic action of the play.

Never Losing Track

Landscape, Silence

A
1964 issue of *Life* magazine,
in a brief article on Beckett's most recent work, *Film,* announced
that "The movie, still untitled, will run with two other short films
by avant-garde deans Harold Pinter (*The Caretaker*) and Eugène
Ionesco (*Rhinoceros*)."[1] This linking of Pinter's name with both
Ionesco and Beckett began very early in Pinter's playwriting career.[2]
Gradually the associations with Ionesco diminished, but the coupling
with Beckett has continued, not only in the popular press but also
in scholarly books and articles, where the connection is usually
taken for granted without any attempt to establish specific influence.[3] Their plays are sometimes billed together, as at the Northcott

1. *Life,* 14 August 1964, p. 85.
2. See, for example, R. D. Smith, "Back to the Text," in *Contemporary Theatre,*
Stratford-Upon-Avon Studies 4 (London: Edward Arnold, 1962), especially pp.
130–36, which discuss Beckett, Pinter, and Ionesco together; and Martin Esslin,
"Godot and His Children: The Theatre of Samuel Beckett and Harold Pinter,"
in *Experimental Drama,* ed. William A. Armstrong (London: G. Bell & Sons,
1963), pp. 128–46, which also mentions Ionesco throughout.
3. A published thesis from the University of Gothenburg devotes 162 rather
pedestrian pages to the relationship between these two authors: Per Olof Hagberg, *The Dramatic Works of Samuel Beckett and Harold Pinter: A Comparative
Analysis of Main Themes and Dramatic Technique* (1972); more recently, specific

Theatre in Exeter, where *Krapp's Last Tape* was matched, as a "drama of stoic wit," with *Landscape,* where the "struggle for survival" has "a static quality."[4] When the Samuel Beckett Theatre was proposed for St Peter's College, Oxford, sponsors included Harold Pinter along with other British artists and critics, Christopher Fry, Graham Greene, Peter Hall, Harold Hobson, Henry Moore, John Osborne, Arnold Wesker (with Buckminster Fuller donating architectural services).[5] When Jean Louis Barrault and Madeleine Renaud were, at the last minute, unable to open the 1971 exhibition on Samuel Beckett at Reading University, Pinter was asked to replace them for that important symbolic function, "because of Pinter's friendship with Beckett."[6] When Martin Esslin produced *Lessness* on BBC Radio 3, Harold Pinter was among the cast, including Nicol Williamson and Patrick Magee, whom Esslin chose knowing them "to be deeply sympathetic to Beckett's work."[7] And Pinter himself has several times referred to his great admiration for Beckett's writing: "If Beckett's influence shows in my work that's all right with me," he stated in an early interview.[8] In fact,

points of comparison between the two dramatists have been carefully developed in various scholarly articles, such as B. S. Hammond's "Beckett and Pinter: Toward a Grammar of the Absurd," *Journal of Beckett Studies* 4 (Spring 1979): 35–42; and Ruby Cohn, "Words Working Overtime: *Endgame* and *No Man's Land,*" *Yearbook of English Studies* 9 (1979): 188–203. For the most part, however, the connection between Beckett and Pinter has been mentioned by scholars *en passant* without detailed development.

4. Program notes, Northcott Theatre, Exeter, England (3 Feburary–17 March 1978).

5. Brochure for the proposed Samuel Beckett Theatre, St Peter's College, Oxford, 1971.

6. *Evening Post,* Reading, Berkshire, England, 17 May 1971. Pinter had also been awarded an honorary degree (D.Litt.) from Reading University in the previous year.

7. Martin Esslin, "Samuel Beckett and the Art of Broadcasting," *Encounter* 45 (September 1975): 45.

8. "Harold Pinter Replies," *New Theatre Magazine* 2 (1961): 8. See also Pinter's interview with Lawrence M. Bensky, first published in the *Paris Review* (1966), reprinted in *Theatre at Work,* ed. Charles Marowitz and Simon Trussler (London: Methuen, 1967), p. 99; and Pinter's statement for *Beckett at 60* (London: Calder & Boyars, 1967), p. 86.

Pinter is reported to "send his new works to Mr. Beckett, who responds with comments."[9]

Whatever the exact nature of the influence, it is quite clear that there are many ways in which these two playwrights are dissimilar, particularly in kinds of plot and subject matter and also in their use of language. And yet the following passages raise some interesting questions:

> She was with a clod, a gross pink bald whiskered clod with a gammy leg, I hope she's gone back to him. She got rid of him at the door after the usual and stood watching him hobble away. Then she ran up the steps and put her key in the door. I asked her afterwards, what possessed you to turn, why in the name of God didn't you go straight in? She said she felt eyes boring into her. Boring right into me, those were her words.

> Such male beauty I had never seen, though not strictly speaking a virgin at the time, how could I, and as the weeks sped by, and I grew to know more fully, I felt this more and more, that such male beauty I had never encountered.[10]

These passages sound much more like Pinter than Beckett; yet surprisingly enough they are from a manuscript of a more explicit version of the work that eventually became *Play*. Does this mean that the influence has been two ways? Or does it mean that Beckett naturally has "Pinteresque" tendencies which in the process of condensation he weeds out? Or does it mean that under the surface Beckett's derelict couples and Pinter's domestic ones (trailing tangles of betrayals) are more alike than they at first seem?

One point, certainly, at which similarity between Beckett and Pinter is clear is in their use of narrative sequences. Pinter, too, like the older writer he so admires, makes use of stories within his plays in order to lay bare the inner struggles of his characters, to allow them to face and to flee the painful emotions which are at the heart of the drama. Among the best examples of this similarity are Pinter's lyrical dramas, written midway in his career, dramas

9. Mel Gussow, "Beckett at 75—An Appraisal," *New York Times*, Sunday, 19 April 1981, Sec. D, p. 22, col. 6.
10. "Before *Play*," RUL MS 1227/7/16/6, p. 3.

where the narrated effort not to lose track (or heart) betrays how pained and lost the characters really are.

Plays such as *Landscape* and *Silence* are reveries made up of interlaced monologues; the "action" does not involve physical motion on stage, but rather the flow of words, the touch of memory. The splendid terse variety of lower class idiom that Pinter captures so accurately with Rose, Meg, Petey, Ben, Gus, Davies; the regional and ethnic language of Goldberg and McCann; the crisp and varied sophistications of Edward, Flora, Deeley, Anna, Mick—in short, the entire range of voices Pinter creates with such verisimilitude gives way, in these lyrical dramas, to a meditative cadence, an abundance of imagery, a dreaminess of syntax, a delicacy of diction that makes the plays almost musical, poems spoken by actors relatively motionless on stage (the same kind of effect that Beckett achieves in *Play, Not I, Eh Joe*). Characters in these plays are still differentiated from each other, but much more subtly. Sharp differences of language—such as *The Homecoming* exhibits—are not present here. Instead, all the voices are meditative, entranced in some way, and appropriately so, because what the play deals with is not event as acted out before the audience in all its temporal immediacy but the resonance of the past in the reflective present of the character's mind. These ruminating narratives make up the entire drama.

Landscape is a particularly effective piece, highly condensed, with complications of character, plot, theme reduced to their barest and most evocative terms. The fact that the play was first given as a radio drama[11] emphasizes the importance of voices, the unimportance of gesture (the play is very reminiscent of Beckett's *Embers,* broadcast on the BBC a decade earlier). That the piece also works well on stage, with the characters always sitting, "relaxed, in no sense rigid," at either side of a long kitchen table in a country house at evening,[12] indicates the extent to which Pinter's words can hold an audience, as do Beckett's, even without physical interactions. Duff, "a man in his early fifties," and Beth, "a woman in her late

11. BBC, 25 April 1968.
12. Harold Pinter, *Landscape,* published with *Silence* (New York: Grove Press, 1970) [p. 7].

forties," are presumably man and wife (though that is never explicitly stated in the text or in the stage directions). The play is made up of their interlaced monologues, but with an important difference in manner: while neither appears to hear the other's voice, Duff "refers normally to Beth" but she never looks at him. This single element of gesture bears out what would still be apparent from voice alone in radio broadcast: that Beth exists for Duff (when he says "you" he means Beth), but Duff does not appear to exist for Beth (when she says "you" the antecedent is not identifiable).[13] This distance between them is at the heart of the drama. These two people are physically present now in the same room, have for many years physically participated in the same life, yet for all that proximity they are worlds apart. Not only does the rambling narrative of each monologue indicate that fact, but the individual anecdotes within the longer meditation reveal both the nature and the cause of their alienation.

The basic situation of Beth and Duff's life is something like this. For many years they have been a pair of live-in servants, he chauffeur and general handyman, she cook and housekeeper, working for a rather lonely man, Mr. Sykes, at his estate in the country. Now they seem to inhabit the house by themselves (whether their employer is living or dead, whether they have possession of the estate or still only care for it is not clear). There is some indication Beth has been ill (and further but slight indication the illness may have been mental rather than physical); she is just now recovering, and Duff is solicitous for her welfare. His days are made up of pleasant, ordinary activities (walking the dog, fishing, going to the pub, working in the garden). Nothing is known of what Beth does, now, during the day. This summary of their situation is made up from bits and pieces of evidence scattered throughout their two monologues. They themselves, of course, are not interested in "exposition"; the focus of their thoughts is elsewhere, on the individual sets of memories and associations that make up the true drama of the play.

13. For example, compare "Would you like a baby? I said" (p. 9) and "The dog's gone. I didn't tell you" (p. 10).

Beth's thoughts center on an unidentified man with whom she made love on the beach many years earlier. So immediate and absorbing is this past event that she often uses the present tense as well as the past in musing to herself about it:

> I walked from the dune to the shore. My man slept in the dune. He turned over as I stood. His eyelids. Belly button. Snoozing how lovely.
> *Pause*
> Would you like a baby? I said. Children? Babies? Of our own? Would be nice.
> *Pause*
> Women turn, look at me.
> *Pause*
> Our own child? Would you like that?
>
> [P. 9]

Duff's reminiscences are more various and in large part concern recent events, things that happened to him that very day (seeing a couple on his walk, arguing with a fellow in a pub, the rain, the dog, the "duckshit").

Despite the fact that these two do not hear each other, there are ghostly connections between their monologues:

> BETH: I'd been in the sea.
> DUFF: Maybe it's something to do with the fishing. Getting to learn more about fish.
> BETH: Stinging in the sea by myself.
> DUFF: They're very shy creatures. You've got to woo them. You must never get excited with them. Or flurried. Never.
> BETH: I knew there must be a hotel near, where we could get some tea.
> *Silence*
> DUFF: Anyway . . . luck was on my side for a change. By the time I got out of the park the pubs were open.
>
> [Pp. 14–15]

Her "sea" and his "fish" go together (and, as the play will gradually reveal, her need to be gently wooed counterpoints with his need to learn more about that art). As her thoughts shift to another subject, hotel and tea, his take an analogous turn toward pub and pint. No, Beth and Duff do not hear each other, but their thoughts touch across the distance.

Critics have tried to guess the identity of Beth's lover: Duff himself, Mr. Sykes, or some other man? Pinter, too, has speculated about the answer, as he wrote in a letter to the director of the first German performance:

> ... the man on the beach is Duff. I think there are elements of Mr Sykes in her memory of this Duff which she might be attributing to Duff, but the man remains Duff. I think that Duff detests and is jealous of Mr Sykes, although I do not believe that Mr Sykes and Beth were ever lovers. I formed these conclusions after I had written the plays and after learning about them through rehearsals.[14]

As Pinter's own words indicate, the man's identity is a matter of speculation, not textual certainty. What is important, however, is not his past name but his present reality for Beth. Clearly, in those terms the man is not Duff as he is now or was during most of their marriage. The man on the beach represents an unnamed idyllic love, no longer present, cherished only in memory.

Duff, too, has the memory of an earlier sexual relationship, but his is quite different from Beth's. He presents that memory as part of what he says to Beth now, years later:

> Do you remember when I took him on that trip to the north? That long trip. When we got back he thanked you for looking after the place so well, everything running like clockwork.
> *Pause*
> You'd missed me. When I came into this room you stopped still. I had to walk all the way over the floor towards you.
> *Pause*
> I touched you.
> *Pause*
> But I had something to say to you, didn't I? I waited, I didn't say it then, but I'd made up my mind to say it, I'd decided I would say it, and I did say it, the next morning. Didn't I?

14. Quoted in Martin Esslin, *Pinter* (London: Methuen, 1973), p. 175.

Pause
I told you that I'd let you down. I'd been unfaithful to you.
Pause
You didn't cry. We had a few hours off. We walked up to the pond, with the dog. We stood under the trees for a bit. I didn't know why you'd brought that carrier bag with you. I asked you. I said what's in that bag? It turned out to be bread. You fed the ducks. Then we stood under the trees and looked across the pond.
Pause
When we got back into this room you put your hands on my face and you kissed me.

[P. 19]

And a few minutes later he reveals the nature of this sexual infidelity: "The girl herself I considered unimportant. I didn't think it necessary to go into details. I decided against it" (p. 22).

The event has merely been a physical act, not a personal relationship, and thus is quite different from the memory Beth cherishes, in which she speaks of "my man" and dwells lovingly and repeatedly on details ("I crept close to him and put my head on his arm, and closed my eyes. All those darting red and black flecks, under my eyelid. I moved my cheek on his skin," p. 20). But, of course, this narrative is for herself, and herself alone, not to be shared with Duff.

These two anecdotes, sexual indiscretions treated so differently, pinpoint an important difference between this husband and wife: the casual, impersonal approach to sex for him; the highly charged, deeply personal meaning for her. A second, related difference is revealed by their diction. Adjacent passages early in the play show Beth's delicacy, Duff's roughness:

BETH: They all held my arm lightly, as I stepped out of the car, or out of the door, or down the steps. Without exception. If they touched the back of my neck, or my hand, it was done so lightly. Without exception. With one exception.

DUFF: Mind you, there was a lot of shit all over the place, all along the paths, by the pond. Dogshit, duckshit . . . all kinds

of shit ... all over the paths. The rain didn't clean it up. It
made it even more treacherous.

[P. 12]

Both speak using repetitions (that carelessness of ordinary speech
Pinter captures so well), but Beth's words have a softness to them,
both in their meaning and their sound (for example, "lightly" suggests a gentleness which its long *i* and falling rhythm reinforce), and
Duff's words are harsh (his dwelling on variations of the word "shit"
with an emphatic spondee). Regularly throughout the play these
differences in language occur, illustrating a difference in perspective. Duff's anecdotes tend to be harshly worded and also to deal
with unattractive events, negative attitudes, as his story about the
man in the pub illustrates ("This beer is piss, he said," p. 15).

Beth's idyllic memories are just the opposite, as she continues
her dreamy reveling in "the lightness of your touch, the lightness
of your look, my neck, your eyes, the silence" (p. 24) while Duff
continues his vigorous disquisition on beer: "The bung is on the
vertical, in the bunghole. Spile the bung. Hammer the spile through
the centre of the bung" (p. 25). They are quite different, these
two: the woman floats, the man hammers.

The difference in mental perspective that constitutes part of the
gulf between Beth and Duff is further illustrated by various references to drawing. Beth remembers in detail a moment on the
beach:

> That's why he'd picked such a desolate place. So that I could
> draw in peace. I had my sketch book with me. I took it out. I
> took my drawing pencil out. But there was nothing to draw. Only
> the beach, the sea.
> *Pause*
> Could have drawn him. He didn't want it. He laughed.
> *Pause*
> I laughed, with him.
> *Pause*
> I waited for him to laugh, then I would smile, turn away, he
> would touch my back, turn me, to him. My nose ... creased. I
> would laugh with him, a little.
> *Pause*

He laughed. I'm sure of it. So I didn't draw him.
> *Silence*

[P. 18]

But a few minutes later she does draw something:

> I drew a face in the sand, then a body. The body of a woman.
> Then the body of a man, close to her, not touching. But they
> didn't look like anything. They didn't look like human figures.
> The sand kept on slipping, mixing the contours. I crept close to
> him and put my head on his arm, and closed my eyes. All those
> darting red and black flecks, under my eyelid. I moved my cheek
> on his skin. And all those darting red and black flecks, moving
> about under my eyelid. I buried my face in his side and shut the
> light out.
> *Silence*

[P. 20]

This real man has been her refuge, even now when he exists only
as a mental picture, an interior monologue. Her sketch of a couple
in the sand involved distance and annihilation; but once in her life
she touched someone with her eyes closed, denying the light.

Light is the problem, because it not only illuminates, it also casts
shadows, as Beth later muses:

> I remembered always, in drawing, the basic principles of shadow
> and light. Objects intercepting the light cast shadows. Shadow is
> deprivation of light. The shape of the shadow is determined by
> that of the object. But not always. Not always directly. Some-
> times it is only indirectly affected by it. Sometimes the cause of
> the shadow cannot be found.
> *Pause*
> But I always bore in mind the basic principles of drawing.
> *Pause*
> So that I never lost track. Or heart.

[Pp. 27–28]

The give-away word here is "heart." It is not parallel to "track"
in its significance. "To lose track" is quite a different idiom from
"to lose heart." The one makes sense as a motive and result of
her literally bearing in mind "the basic principles of drawing," but

the other changes the whole discussion to a kind of metaphor for her life itself. She has managed to go on living, to have the courage to continue, because she has accepted that there will be "shadows"—deprivations, losses, pain, whatever that word implies—even when she does not know their cause.

Duff, too, has had experience of shadow and light, but his experience is quite different from Beth's:

> I never saw your face. You were standing by the windows. One of those black nights. A downfall. All I could hear was the rain on the glass, smacking on the glass. You knew I'd come in but you didn't move. I stood close to you. What were you looking at? It was black outside. I could just see your shape in the window, your reflection. There must have been some kind of light somewhere. Perhaps just your face reflected, lighter than all the rest. I stood close to you. Perhaps you were just thinking, in a dream. Without touching you, I could feel your bottom.
>
> [P. 27]

Duff does not touch Beth (though Beth's man had touched her); Duff does not see her face (though Beth's man does, by turning her to him); with Duff, Beth is far away, grave ("you didn't laugh much") but she looks directly at her man, talks with him, laughs with him (p. 18). Duff does not know what Beth is looking at, but Beth describes looking at her man, willing to trust that he looks back at her even when she cannot, because of the light, see that he is looking at her (p. 29).

This discussion of drawing, the principles of shadow and light, comes just before the final, climactic lines of the play, where an incident narrated by Duff contrasts shockingly with Beth's reverie. As she recalls, dreamlike, never losing track or heart, he recalls an incident that becomes progressively harsher and more violent as he narrates it:

> You used to wear a chain round your waist. On the chain you carried your keys, your thimble, your notebook, your pencil, your scissors.
>
> *Pause*
>
> You stood in the hall and banged the gong.

Pause
What the bloody hell are you doing banging that bloody gong?
Pause
It's bullshit. Standing in an empty hall banging a bloody gong.
There's no one to listen. No one'll hear. There's not a soul in
the house. Except me. There's nothing for lunch. There's noth-
ing cooked. No stew. No pie. No greens. No joint. Fuck all.
Pause

[P. 28]

She persists with memory of her man, gently looking at her, and
Duff persists in his fantasy of a violent sexual experience with Beth:

I took the chain off and the thimble, the keys, the scissors slid
off it and clattered down. I booted the gong down the hall. The
dog came in. I thought you would come to me, I thought you
would come into my arms and kiss me, even ... offer yourself to
me. I would have had you in front of the dog, like a man, in the
hall, on the stone, banging the gong, mind you don't get the
scissors up your arse, or the thimble, don't worry, I'll throw
them for the dog to chase, the thimble will keep the dog happy,
he'll play with it with his paws, you'll plead with me like a
woman, I'll bang the gong on the floor, if the sound is too flat,
lacks resonance, I'll hang it back on its hook, bang you against it
swinging, gonging, waking the place up, calling them all for dinner, lunch is up, bring out the bacon, bang your lovely head,
mind the dog doesn't swallow the thimble, slam—

[P. 29]

All the vigor and vulgarity of his earlier language is concentrated
in these words he speaks to Beth (she may not hear him, but he
thinks she does). "Like a man," "like a woman," booting, banging,
slamming—this is his view of sexuality, all stereotypes and harsh
assault. That is what he wants, what he assumes she wants to hear
about; presumably this has been his sexual style throughout their
marriage. And she has dealt with it by simply not hearing, by
withdrawing into another fantasy of sexuality, much different in its
style. Her words, following his energetic narration, contrast with
it and give the play a quiet close:

He lay above me and looked down at me. He supported my
shoulder.
>   *Pause*
So tender his touch on my neck. So softly his kiss on my cheek.
>   *Pause*
My hand on his rib.
>   *Pause*
So sweetly the sand over me. Tiny the sand on my skin.
>   *Pause*
So silent the sky in my eyes. Gently the sound of the tide.
>   *Pause*
Oh my true love I said.

[Pp. 29–30]

The inversions and the rhythms of these lines are the stuff of
poetry; the play closes with the quiet simplicity of a lyric.

The play itself is a kind of drawing in the sand (hence "landscape" and not "portrait"), the picture of a man and a woman in
which the sand keeps slipping and images blur. There is a shadow
in this drawing, the cause of which is not apparent to either character
but is revealed to the audience by the differences in their narratives.
Quite simply, they are husband and wife who have had very different
sexual fantasies, very different attitudes toward sex. Duff is the
more insensitive of the two (the girl does not really matter to him,
and though he "refers" to Beth, he does not notice, or does not
admit, that she does not hear him), and Beth is the more remote
(she has simply withdrawn into a world of memory, or perhaps pure
fantasy; not only does she not hear Duff, she ignores his existence
altogether). And so they speak as they have lived, parallel and
interlaced narratives, words which, like their bodies, have never
really met.

Silence is a natural companion piece to *Landscape* and was first
presented with it on a double bill by the Royal Shakespeare Company, 2 July 1969. Although the script calls for three areas, each
with a chair and some limited movement among the three characters,
the play is even more dependent on the evocative nature of its
language than is *Landscape* and could also be presented as radio
drama. But despite a number of similarities, this play seems less

effective than its companion. A critical part of the difference lies in the language itself. In most other plays, including *Landscape,* Pinter's dialogue approximates "real" speech, and his fragmentary elliptical phrasing is part of that approximation. But in *Silence* the fragments and the run-on flow of words is much more literary, an almost self-conscious imitation of novelistic "stream of consciousness." The repetitions seem more mannered, more "poetic." But, in fact, the language is not poetry and thus cannot bear the burden imposed on it. Rumsey's opening speech, for example, is too dull in its rhythms to capture attention the way poetry does:

> I walk with my girl who wears a grey blouse when she walks and grey shoes and walks with me readily wearing her clothes considered for me. Her grey clothes.
>
> She holds my arm.
>
> On good evenings we walk through the hills to the top of the hill past the dogs the clouds racing just before dark or as dark is falling when the moon
>
> When it's chilly I stop her and slip her raincoat over her shoulders or rainy slip arms into the arms, she twisting her arms. And talk to her and tell her everything.
>
> She dresses for my eyes.
>
> I tell her my thoughts. Now I am ready to walk, her arm in me her hand in me.
>
> I tell her my life's thoughts, clouds racing. She looks up at me or listens looking down. She stops in midsentence, my sentence, to look up at me. Sometimes her hand has slipped from mine, her arm loosened, she walks slightly apart, dog barks.
>
> [P. 33]

The effect is a kind of stilted banality, reaching neither to the mesmerizing lyricism of Beth's last speech in *Landscape* nor to the wonderful vulgar accuracy of Pinter's other characters. Pinter can make banality dazzling, but in this speech the language fails because it is neither sufficiently banal nor sufficiently lyrical, merely awkward.

But the biggest problem with *Silence* is that there is not enough substance, in particular not enough story. Thus it is never quite clear what the evocative language is intended to evoke. There are "themes" enough in the play—reclusiveness and communion, youth and age, country and city, telling and listening—plenty of stuff to occupy the analytic mind, but none of it quite coheres. And, in any case, as soon as the working out of themes becomes the chief interest, a play has lost its drama and become a literary exercise. What would have saved this play, made the stilted language more acceptable (because less primary), made the lightly sketched characters more believable, was an event to animate them. And since this play, like *Landscape,* is composed of interlaced monologues, reminiscence rather than action occurring in the present, the characters need to remember events more fully than they do, to narrate a story (however disjointed it might be) rather than murmur free-floating details.

For example, there is the vestige of story in Bates's encounter with the noisy youths in the other room:

> I'm at my last gasp with this unendurable racket. I kicked open the door and stood before them. Someone called me Grandad and told me to button it. It's they should button it. Were I young . . .
>
> One of them told me I was lucky to be alive, that I would have to bear it in order to pay for being alive, in order to give thanks for being alive.
>
> It's a question of sleep. I need something of it, or how can I remain alive, without any true rest, having no solace, no constant solace, not even any damn inconstant solace.
>
> I am strong, but not as strong as the bastards in the other room, and their tittering bitches, and their music, and their love.
>
> If I changed my life, perhaps, and lived deliberately at night, and slept in the day. But what exactly would I do? What can be meant by living in the dark?
>
> [Pp. 35–36]

But all that these lines do is raise questions: Why are Bates and these youths in the same place? Why can't he relocate? Why do they call him "Grandad" if he is only in his mid-thirties? Since there is nothing else in the play to indicate that he is aged, decrepit,

Seven

or sexually inactive, what does this event have to do with either his character or his situation with Ellen? The revealing ironies and self-deceptions that usually accompany Pinter's anecdotes and narratives do not seem to be present here. There is not enough information for this fragment of an anecdote to make much sense or have much dramatic impact.

The same criticism can be made of the subsequent passage, a memory unit of Ellen's:

> Now and again I meet my drinking companion and have a drink with her. She is a friendly woman, quite elderly, quite friendly. But she knows little of me, she could never know much of me, not really, not now. She's funny. She starts talking sexily to me, in the corner, with our drinks. I laugh.
>
> She asks me about my early life, when I was young, never departing from her chosen subject, but I have nothing to tell her about the sexual part of my youth. I'm old, I tell her, my youth was somewhere else, anyway I don't remember. She does the talking anyway.
>
> [P. 36]

Why all the suggestions of age, as if she were quite an old woman, when she is described as being "a girl in her twenties" (p. 31)? This passage, too, merely puzzles. The details are presented but not sufficiently well connected to character and situation to be useful. It is possible, of course, to imagine a theoretical relationship between confusions about age in this play and a Proustian approach to time past,[15] to speculate that Bates and Ellen are really old (regardless of how young the actors look) and are simply recapturing the past in some of the memory units that make up their respective monologues. But the need for theory and speculation is precisely what is wrong with the play: it seems more like a strained intellectual exercise than an emotionally coherent drama. Its very failure, in contrast to the elegant coherence of *Landscape*, serves to illustrate how important narrative is in the kind of play

15. Like Beckett, Pinter has an interest in Proust's work. See *The Proust Screenplay*, written by Harold Pinter in collaboration with Joseph Losey and Barbara Bray (New York: Grove Press, 1977).

Pinter and Beckett write. The stories are not simply extraneous material but are so integral to the whole that when they are not sufficiently clear or well crafted, when the playwright loses track, the entire play fails.

"Have you heard the latest?"

The Dumb Waiter, The Birthday Party

In addition to the lyrical plays with their subtle use of narrative, either successfully achieved as in *Landscape* or awkwardly failed as in *Silence,* Pinter often makes use of crisp and witty narratives which may seem at first merely to match the patina of a crisp and witty play yet have, in fact, an underlayer of darkness and menace. The particular form of "comedy of menace" which has been seen as distinctive of Pinter's work is often achieved by these clever narratives with their threatening shadows. *The Dumb Waiter* presents a particularly sharp example of this kind of narrative because it is such a clever play. Oddly enough, it is almost a parody of *Waiting for Godot* (but a *Godot* with all the questions answered) and also something of a parody of Pinter (Pinter made easy). It makes entertaining use of both playwrights' characteristic devices such as the short line perfectly capturing the banality of ordinary speech; the play on words (puzzling for the characters, but hilariously funny for the audience); the single space, at once everywhere and nowhere; the theme of waiting and the problem of filling time; a set of characters who constitute a couple, one of whom likes to think and question; a mysterious power off stage sending recurrent messages; tragicomic situation and atmosphere; and, of course, the use of narrative to reveal something about character. Unlike *Godot*, *The Dumb Waiter* takes most of its interest from its craft, a very skillfully structured play that does not go beyond its various devices.

Both the skill and the limitation are apparent in the use of narrative segments. The play has opened with two men on stage in a basement room, Ben lying on one bed reading a paper, Gus sitting on the other tying his shoelaces "with difficulty."[1] After some initial amusing stage business involving a shoe and a matchbox (much like the business with the ladder in *Endgame* and with the boots in *Waiting for Godot*), and a newspaper and a defective toilet (off stage), the first lines of the play are finally spoken. What the audience hears is the first of three anecdotes reported from the newspaper by Ben and commented on by both men in a fashion that is quickly seen to be ritualistic. The second anecdote is reported soon after the first; together they establish the mood of the play and some important information about the two characters. The first anecdote involves a grotesque death:

> *Ben slams down the paper.*
> BEN: Kaw!
> *He picks up the paper.*
> What about this? Listen to this!
> *He refers to the paper.*
> A man of eighty-seven wanted to cross the road. But there
> was a lot of traffic, see? He couldn't see how he was going to
> squeeze through. So he crawled under a lorry.
> GUS: He what?
> BEN: He crawled under a lorry. A stationary lorry.
> GUS: No?
> BEN: The lorry started and ran over him.
> GUS: Go on!
> BEN: That's what it says here.
> GUS: Get away.
> BEN: It's enough to make you want to puke, isn't it?
> GUS: Who advised him to do a thing like that?
> BEN: A man of eighty-seven crawling under a lorry!

1. Harold Pinter, *The Caretaker and The Dumb Waiter* (New York: Grove Press, 1961), p. 85.

GUS: It's unbelievable.
BEN: It's down here in black and white.
GUS: Incredible.

[Pp. 85–86]

The situation described is at one and the same time horrible and funny; the death itself is pathetic, but its mode is pure Keystone comedy. The response of these two men is revealing. Their language (both diction and cadence) itself types them as working class (in the British sense of that term); both are fascinated and repelled by the violent event, but Ben is more matter-of-fact and accepting in his report ("It's down here in black and white") while Gus is shocked and incredulous.

The audience may belong to a somewhat different class, but it can share the response of these chaps and thus feel well disposed toward them. Their subsequent dialogue about tea and crockery continues the picture of ordinary men engaged in ordinary activity, whatever the "job" they are waiting for may be. The second anecdote parallels the first:

BEN: (*slamming his paper down*). Kaw!
GUS: What's that?
BEN: A child of eight killed a cat!
GUS: Get away.
BEN: It's a fact. What about that, eh? A child of eight killing a cat!
GUS: How did he do it?
BEN: It was a girl.
GUS: How did she do it?
BEN: She—
    He picks up the paper and studies it.
    It doesn't say.
GUS: Why not?
BEN: Wait a minute. It just says—Her brother, aged eleven, viewed the incident from the toolshed.
GUS: Go on!
BEN: That's bloody ridiculous.
    Pause.
GUS: I bet he did it.

BEN: Who?
GUS: The brother.
BEN: I think you're right.
    Pause.
    (*Slamming down the paper.*) What about that, eh? A kid of eleven killing a cat and blaming it on his little sister of eight! It's enough to—

[Pp. 87–88]

Another shocking event, horrible in its subject (the murderous impulse of a child) and comic in its method of presentation (the surprising reversal, the witty denial of expectation involved in the mistaken gender, and also the men's dogged insistence on stereotype, assuming the boy did the killing and blamed his sister). And another apparent indication of tender hearts beneath the rough exterior of these semiarticulate men. Once again they have been both fascinated and repelled by a story of violence and express outrage that such horrors should occur. "Ordinary blokes," the audience thinks, "now get on with it: what are they here for?"

Very gradually, tantalizingly, Pinter reveals what Ben and Gus are there for. The word "job" becomes progressively more ominous, various hints are dropped, as the exposition culminates in Gus's clear statement about the girl:

She wasn't much to look at, I know, but still. It was a mess though, wasn't it? What a mess. Honest, I can't remember a mess like that one. They don't seem to hold together like men, women. A looser texture, like. Didn't she spread, eh? She didn't half spread. Kaw! But I've been meaning to ask you.
    Ben sits up and clenches his eyes.
Who clears up after we've gone? I'm curious about that. Who does the clearing up? Maybe they don't clear up. Maybe they just leave them there, eh? What do you think? How many jobs have we done? Blimey, I can't count them. What if they never clear anything up after we've gone.

[Pp. 102–3]

Now the audience knows, if it had not guessed before, that Ben and Gus are hit men for an "organization." Professional murderers are not usually portrayed as comic characters, yet these two are at once both amusing and terrible.

Part of the skill of this particular play is seen in the way Pinter has exposed the essential moral quality of both Ben and Gus (as well as an important difference between them) with nondidactic accuracy. Both men deal with surfaces. Even Gus, who is troubled about the girl, focuses his interest on the physical phenomenon of her "spread" and not on the more important fact of her being a person; the relatively inconsequential matter of "clean up" engages his attention, not mourning relatives, bereft children, or wasted talents (not to mention imponderables such as right and wrong).

But the scene is not allowed to become terrifying or ponderous, because it is instantly invaded by a splendid parody of "meaninglessness": a dumbwaiter clatters down into the basement room, carrying with it a series of written orders for food (presumably there is a restaurant upstairs, and yet this lower room is an unlikely kitchen). The sudden incongruous intrusion of "Two braised steak and chips. Two sago puddings. Two teas without sugar" (p. 103) provides comic relief from the gory previous moment. This comedy grows nimbler and funnier as the orders become more exotic— "Macaroni Pastitsio. Ormitha Macarounada" (p. 108)—and as the two toughs scurry to oblige. The entire sequence is a hilarious image of unquestioning obedience to authority, the silly side of the principle which governs Ben and Gus's deadly profession.

There are two more narratives before the startling climax of the play. After the restaurant caper has run its course, Ben gives Gus his instructions:

> *Gus sighs and sits next to Ben on the bed. The instructions are stated and repeated automatically.*
> When we get the call, you go over and stand behind the door.
> GUS: Stand behind the door.
> BEN: If there's a knock on the door you don't answer it.
> GUS: If there's a knock on the door I don't answer it.
> BEN: But there won't be a knock on the door.
> GUS: So I won't answer it.
> BEN: When the bloke comes in—
> GUS: When the bloke comes in—

BEN: Shut the door behind him.
GUS: Shut the door behind him.
BEN: Without divulging your presence.
GUS: Without divulging my presence.
BEN: He'll see me and come towards me.
GUS: He'll see you and come towards you.
BEN: He won't see you.
GUS (*absently*): Eh?
BEN: He won't see you.
GUS: He won't see me.
BEN: But he'll see me.
GUS: He'll see you.
BEN: He won't know you're there.
GUS: He won't know you're there.
BEN: He won't know *you're* there.
GUS: He won't know I'm there.
BEN: I take out my gun.
GUS: You take out your gun.
BEN: He stops in his tracks.
GUS: He stops in his tracks.
BEN: If he turns round—
GUS: If he turns round—
BEN: You're there.
GUS: I'm here.
    Ben frowns and presses his forehead.
  You've missed something out.
BEN: I know. What?
GUS: I haven't taken my gun out, according to you.
BEN: You take your gun out—
GUS: After I've closed the door.
BEN: After you've closed the door.
GUS: You've never missed that out before, you know that?
BEN: When he sees you behind him—
GUS: Me behind him—
BEN: And me in front of him—
GUS: And you in front of him—
BEN: He'll feel uncertain—
GUS: Uneasy.
BEN: He won't know what to do.
GUS: So what will he do?

147

BEN: He'll look at me and he'll look at you.

GUS: We won't say a word.

BEN: We'll look at him.

GUS: He won't say a word.

BEN: He'll look at us.

GUS: And we'll look at him.

BEN: Nobody says a word.

> *Pause.*

GUS: What do we do if it's a girl?

BEN: We do the same.

GUS: Exactly the same?

BEN: Exactly.

> *Pause.*

GUS: We don't do anything different?

BEN: We do exactly the same.

GUS: Oh.

[Pp. 114–16]

These instructions constitute a different kind of anecdote from the two which opened the play. This narrative of events describes the future, something which will happen and could become a newspaper story as horrifying as the ones which so appalled Ben and Gus. But this narrative has to do with an action Ben and Gus can control, one they are directly involved in. Whatever moral sense made them "want to puke" when reading of deaths distanced as "story" seems not to operate in those murders they intend to perform. Gus's mechanical repetition of Ben's instructions emphasizes the degree to which these men are mere instruments, carrying out instructions to the letter with unthinking obedience. Their automatic ritualized approach to moral issues, issues involving passionate responses of approval or disapproval, is absolutized in the last newspaper story they read just before it is time to do their "job":

> *Ben throws his paper down.*

BEN: Kaw!

> *He picks up the paper and looks at it.*
> Listen to this!
> *Pause.*
> What about that, eh?

> *Pause.*
> Kaw!
> *Pause.*
> Have you ever heard such a thing?
> GUS (*dully*): Go on!
> BEN: It's true.
> GUS: Get away.
> BEN: It's down here in black and white.
> GUS (*very low*): Is that a fact?
> BEN: Can you imagine it.
> GUS: It's unbelievable.
> BEN: It's enough to make you want to puke, isn't it?
> GUS (*almost inaudible*): Incredible.
>
> [P. 119]

Here there is no content at all, just the empty form of ritualized response. Newspaper stories are supposed to be sensational, and so Ben and Gus respond accordingly. Their own murders are routine business, planned by others, and so they obey unthinkingly. Both the outrage and the obedience are forms of the same moral blindness, automatic responses triggered by predetermined situations.

But Gus had interrupted those instructions he was to follow exactly. He points out what he thinks is an error in Ben's narration ("You've missed something out"). True, his objection has to do with the fact that the ritual has been changed ("You've never missed that out before, you know that?"), but his place is not to reflect on the ritual, merely to perform it. From the beginning of the play Ben has had to chide Gus for his developing tendency to think ("Who took the call, me or you?" Ben says when Gus questions some of the details of an earlier explanation, p. 92). This difference between the two men is important: Ben is in charge because he does not ask questions; he just obeys (as his serious subservience to the dumbwaiter had so comically illustrated). Gus is troublesome because he tries to understand; soon ritual may not be enough for him.

In the final moment of the play, Gus, who has been off stage in the toilet, stumbles back "stripped of his jacket, waistcoat, tie, holster and revolver" (p. 121): he is the victim. There is a long silence as he and Ben stare at each other, Ben's revolver drawn, ready to do the job. The audience is shocked (there have been too few clues to make this ending easily guessed); Gus is shocked (he had no idea this would happen); and Ben? Ben does not think. At this moment in the play the two kinds of story merge: the horrifying news report about events that happen to other people and the dispassionate recital of a routine job become one and the same story for Gus. "It's unbelievable" but all too real. The emotions he mechanically acted out in response to events safely distanced from himself now intrude into a situation where he had in the past been automatically without emotion. Story becomes reality, murderer becomes victim, and this defective moral universe collapses. Comic recital of "the latest news" now suddenly becomes melodramatic fate.

This same deceptive use of "the latest news" also occurs in *The Birthday Party*. As in most of Pinter's early plays, the narrative units are still rather conventional and for the most part brief.[2] Goldberg's anecdotal memories do indeed establish elements of his character (that he is Jewish, in contrast to McCann, who is Irish), but the information is all superficial; his delight in "the nicest piece of rollmop and pickled cucumber you could wish to find on a plate"[3] does not betray inner complications and ambivalence of motive and feeling. Like anecdotes in most drama, these stories of his serve only to provide a certain "ethnic color" to the character and some comic relief for the audience.

But there is another kind of narrative that is more subtle and ultimately more revealing. And these are the stories Stanley tells in order to extract himself from a painful situation. The story, in

2. Pinter's first play, for example, does not contain the kind of arresting and revealing long narrative units that some of his later ones do. *The Room* (1960) has Mrs. Sands's lengthy account of her experience in the basement (like a story insofar as there are characters and action, scene and mood, with even something of a climax), but the function of this passage is simply expository, letting the audience and Rose know some important information to prepare for Riley's entrance later. The event is "mere experience," and the narration of it does not reveal significant elements of Mrs. Sands's character or motivation.

3. Harold Pinter, *The Birthday Party and The Room* (New York: Grove Press, 1961), p. 62.

fact, is the clue to the nature of the pain he feels. The best illustration of this kind of narrative is in one of the most splendidly comic scenes Pinter has written, the exchange between Meg and Stanley at breakfast. Meg's childlike inanity has already been well established: Petey, her husband, had read from the newspaper that "someone's just had a baby," and she replied with wide-eyed amazement, "Oh, they haven't! Who?" (p. 11). Meg's silly maternal-seductive relationship with Stanley has also been made clear: she had called him "the little monkey," "that boy," and "Stanny," and when he was late coming down to breakfast she had threatened, "I'm coming up to fetch you if you don't come down! I'm coming up! I'm going to count three! One! Two! Three! I'm coming to get you!" (p. 14); his entrance then as an unshaven man (her boarder), and not a little child, is startling and hilarious. The audience is delighted, ready for more. Meg flirts with her "boy" by ruffling his hair; he teases her when she misunderstands the word "succulent" ("You shouldn't say that word to a married woman," she tells him, coyly embarrassed and pleased, p. 18). But the lighthearted erotic-nonsensical mood changes instantly when Meg tells Stan about two gentlemen who are going to stay at her boardinghouse. Stanley's manner communicates to the audience (but not to obtuse Meg) that he is worried and frightened. He finally asserts, "They won't come" (p. 21) and tries to change the subject. But his fear remains; he deals with it by telling two stories. The first is an account of his career as a concert pianist, as he tries to impress Meg (and himself) with his own importance:

STANLEY: Played the piano? I've played the piano all over the world. All over the country. (*Pause.*) I once gave a concert.
MEG: A concert?
STANLEY (*reflectively*): Yes. It was a good one, too. They were all there that night. Every single one of them. It was a great success. Yes. A concert. At Lower Edmonton.
MEG: What did you wear?
STANLEY (*to himself*): I had a unique touch. Absolutely unique. They came up to me. They came up to me and said they were grateful. Champagne we had that night, the lot. (*Pause.*) My father nearly came down to hear me. Well, I dropped him a

151

card anyway. But I don't think he could make it. No, I—I
lost the address, that was it. (*Pause.*) Yes. Lower Edmonton.
Then after that, you know what they did? They carved me up.
Carved me up. It was all arranged, it was all worked out. My
next concert. Somewhere else it was. In winter. I went down
there to play. Then, when I got there, the hall was closed, the
place was shuttered up, not even a caretaker. They'd locked it
up. (*Takes off his glasses and wipes them on his pyjama jacket.*) A
fast one. They pulled a fast one. I'd like to know who was
responsible for that. (*Bitterly.*) All right, Jack, I can take a tip.
They want me to crawl down on my bended knees. Well I can
take a tip ... any day of the week.

[Pp. 23–24]

The story has not worked because his fear quickly changed it from
a tale of success to one of unmerited persecution. Somewhere,
somehow Stanley has failed, whether through his own fault or
because he was double-crossed (piano playing is not really the issue,
not in a cultural nowhere such as Lower Edmonton). He feels
threatened, and to deal with that feeling he tries to displace it by
attacking Meg and arousing *her* fear (if she is afraid and he is the
one with power to persecute, then he must be safe). First he insults
her ("You're just an old piece of rock cake, aren't you?"); when
that fails and she naively continues to play solicitous mother to his
poor little boy ("Aren't you feeling well this morning, Stan? Did
you pay a visit this morning?"), his attack moves from insult to
threat. He tells her a frightening story:

> *He stiffens, then lifts himself slowly, turns to face her and speaks
> low and meaningfully.*
> STANLEY: Meg. Do you know what?
> MEG: What?
> STANLEY: Have you heard the latest?
> MEG: No.
> STANLEY: I'll bet you have.
> MEG: I haven't.
> STANLEY: Shall I tell you?
> MEG: What latest?
> STANLEY: You haven't heard it?

MEG: No.

STANLEY (*advancing*): They're coming today.

MEG: Who?

STANLEY: They're coming in a van.

MEG: Who?

STANLEY: And do you know what they've got in that van?

MEG: What?

STANLEY: They've got a wheelbarrow in that van.

MEG (*breathlessly*): They haven't.

STANLEY: Oh yes they have.

MEG: You're a liar.

STANLEY (*advancing upon her*): A big wheelbarrow. And when the van stops they wheel it out, and they wheel it up the garden path, and then they knock at the front door.

MEG: They don't.

STANLEY: They're looking for someone.

MEG: They're not.

STANLEY: They're looking for someone. A certain person.

MEG (*hoarsely*): No, they're not!

STANLEY: Shall I tell you who they're looking for?

MEG: No!

STANLEY: You don't want me to tell you?

MEG: You're a liar!

[Pp. 24–25]

The scare here comes first from Stanley's manner of telling; by speaking "low and meaningfully" he slowly arouses her terror. Then he includes just enough details to suggest an ultimate fate that Meg does not want to think about: a faceless, unidentified "they" will come in a van to get someone who will need to be wheeled out. Stanley has menaced Meg with the threat of death, and like most people she denies that it will happen, at least not today. Stanley has not done anything real to protect himself, but he has defused his own fears by displacing them onto Meg. The audience believes a terrible menace lurks in Stanley's world not because there are direct signs of it, but because Stanley himself is so worried that he needs to go through the elaborate strategy of evasion which the audience has just witnessed. The audience believes the intensity of fear, even without knowing its specific form, because it has witnessed Meg's terror in response to Stanley's story.

Later, after Stanley has met the two new boarders—his inevitable fate, "If we hadn't come today we'd have come tomorrow," Goldberg says (p. 35)—he tries to talk his way out, again by telling a story, this time about himself, past and future: "I like it here, but I'll be moving soon. Back home. I'll stay there too, this time. No place like home. (*He laughs.*) I wouldn't have left, but business calls. Business called, and I had to leave for a bit. You know how it is." When McCann asks if he is in business, Stanley continues to elaborate his defensive story:

> No. I think I'll give it up. I've got a small private income, you see. I think I'll give it up. Don't like being away from home. I used to live very quietly—played records, that's about all. Everything delivered to the door. Then I started a little private business, in a small way, and it compelled me to come down here—kept me longer than I expected. You never get used to living in someone else's house. Don't you agree? I lived so quietly. You can only appreciate what you've had when things change.

After a moment, he continues nervously:

> You know what? To look at me, I bet you wouldn't think I'd led such a quiet life. The lines on my face, eh? It's the drink. Been drinking a bit down here. But what I mean is ... you know how it is ... away from your own ... all wrong, of course ... I'll be all right when I get back ... but what I mean is, the way some people look at me you'd think I was a different person. I suppose I have changed, but I'm still the same man that I always was. I mean, you wouldn't think, to look at me, really ... I mean, not really, that I was the sort of bloke to—to cause any trouble, would you? (*McCann looks at him.*) Do you know what I mean?
>
> [P. 43]

This "story" about his life is really a bargain, covertly expressed: leave me alone and I will live as if I were dead. But these hit men, angels of death, are not to be put off. Goldberg's anecdotes now begin to take on more meaning; he claims as his own that quiet town where Stanley lived ("tea in Fullers, a library book from Boots");[4] he platitudinously praises birth but actually describes death ("What are you but a corpse waiting to be washed?" p. 48), which arouses Stanley's anger and makes him try, unsuccessfully, to drive the threat away. On stage McCann and Goldberg work Stanley over with a confusing interrogation culminating in the accusation "You're dead" (p. 55) and then presumably continue the brainwashing all night (off stage), so that by morning he is in a comatose state, unable to talk or see, virtually dead and dressed for burial, ready for "Monty." This last allusion is itself an implied story, all in one word. Given the gangster language and manner that characterize Goldberg and McCann, this reference to "Monty" triggers memory of Hollywood gangster movies, Edward G. Robinson, chewed cigars, and Big Bosses. The two thugs are not taking Stanley to any doctor, as Petey well knows when he tries to interfere and gets the insidious invitation, "Why don't you come with us, Mr. Boles? ... Come with us to Monty. There's plenty of room in the car" (p. 90). The threat immobilizes Petey, as Stanley gets taken away by his ultimate captors, to that final catastrophe which he previously could face only in the disguise of story, but which now brings him to its silent but very real climax as once again "news" becomes fate.

4. Compare pp. 42 and 59.

N	I	N	E

Explanation / Manipulation / Silence

A Slight Ache, The Caretaker

Not all of Pinter's storytelling involves escapism, as do Beth's flight into idyllic sexual fantasy and Ben and Gus's fascination with news reports. Sometimes the stories are fabricated deliberately by one character in order to manipulate another; but even here there is a certain self-betrayal, an unwitting give-away, because the narrator admits by his very strategy the secret fear which prompts his manipulations in the first place. This point is made very clearly by one of the earlier plays in which the fear of death and attempts to avoid ultimate loss through self-justification are almost formulaic in their presentation.

In *A Slight Ache* Edward, responding to the threat from without (the silent matchseller, who stands before him as an embodiment of meaninglessness), desperately tries to establish meaning for his life by talking, trying to retell his life story, with an emphasis on the details which have, for him, been the bulwarks of existence: making his way in the world, getting a good woman to stick by him, and, most important, establishing his home, furnishing it, seeing that it is in good order, polished, arranged for his purpose.[1] Physical well-being makes him feel that his command is established,

1. Harold Pinter, *A Slight Ache,* in *Three Plays* (New York: Grove Press, 1962), p. 35.

his life accounted for. He thinks he is the one with power over life and death—he did, after all, kill a wasp that very morning—and thus is himself not vulnerable to dissolution (despite that slight ache in his eyes). But the power of this play comes precisely from the gap the audience perceives between Edward's assertion of control and his loss of it. His boast that he could not possibly find himself in the matchseller's place (p. 28) is not mere dramatic irony on the part of the playwright, to give the audience that interesting tickle of superiority, knowing or guessing something the character does not know or guess. The whole point of this play is to demonstrate the hidden fear, the suppressed realization which keeps an ordinary person whistling in the dark, pretending all is well, refusing to acknowledge the fact that loss, death, extinction stand just outside his gate: that no place, however well furnished, is safe.

As in other Pinter plays, the room has great significance here. After having exhibited terror at the presence of the matchseller outside his door, Edward nonetheless feels impelled to say, "Nothing outside this room has ever alarmed me" (p. 27). But no such denial can really take away his fear. He resents the presence of the matchseller on his own territory, in his own room, and in his uneasiness Edward talks repeatedly about those things dear to him, which give him a sense of security: "My den, too, was sharp, arranged for my purpose . . . quite satisfactory. . . . The house too, was polished, all the banisters were polished, and the stair rods, and the curtain rods. . . . My desk was polished, and my cabinet" (p. 35).[2] In this place he feels secure against the future: "my progress was as sure, as fluent . . . ," he says, breaking off because it appears that the silent guest is laughing (as well he might, given the irony of the situation).

That Edward's room (home) is ultimately his life and that the matchseller is ultimately the threat of death are both suggested by a variety of elements within the play. There are similarities to two scriptural images of death. The first is the incident just described,

2. For a fuller discussion of these issues and the importance of death as a theme in modern British drama, see my article in *Continuum* 5 (Autumn 1967): 538–49, on which the following paragraphs are based.

Edward reveling in the security of his possessions, like the man whose barns were full,[3] on the very night when he was to be despoiled of them (elsewhere Edward tells Flora that by nightfall he will know who the matchseller is). The second is in Edward's impassioned description of his effort to take shelter in order to compose himself (the implication of the context is that he feared the presence of the matchseller and was seeking escape from him, but concealment could not last): "the time came. I saw the wind. I saw the wind, swirling, and the dust at my back gate, lifting, and the long grass, scything together..." (p. 39). At these words, suggestive of the grass of the field which is cut down and the dust to which man returns, Edward realizes with horror that the matchseller is laughing at him. And then the transposition occurs. Despite attempts to control his situation and the matchseller by explaining his own life, Edward actually reveals and finally succumbs to his worst fear.

The characteristics of the matchseller also are suggestive of death. At first so old he appears to have lost both sight and hearing, he is himself an image of approaching death. Then, at the end, as part of the transposition, he is suddenly rejuvenated, becoming youthful and strong, as he supplants Edward, since, as death, he thrives on the taking away of life. (It is in this sense that the matchseller's conquest of Flora must be understood: the whole situation is seen from Edward's point of view, and so he loses Flora "to" his own death, along with all his other "possessions." Edward's tendency to think of Flora as an object, one of the furnishings of the security place, is indicated ironically by his words earlier to the matchseller, "Get a good woman to stick by you.... It'll pay dividends," p. 24.) The matchseller is further like death in his omnipresence in life. Flora says, "he's always there" (p. 15), and Edward calls him "My oldest acquaintance. My nearest and dearest. My kith and kin" (p. 36) and describes all sorts of occasions on which he has seen him. He is like death in the fear he inspires, a fear Edward exhibits throughout the play. He is like death in being a silent enigma that changes every time man tries to confront

3. Luke 12:16–20.

it. Edward responds in a variety of ways to him and also says, "every time I have seen you you have looked quite different to the time before" (p. 37).

An incident in the plot also suggests the basic problem is death. In the first few minutes of the play Edward traps a wasp in the marmalade pot and eventually kills it with hot water. He has been a bit cranky so far, not particularly eager to work in the garden; yet when he exhibits the dead wasp, Flora's response is "What an awful experience" but his is "What a beautiful day it is. Beautiful. I think I shall work in the garden this morning" (p. 14); only a few lines later he sees the matchseller and his fear begins. That there is a parallel between the killing of the wasp and the supplanting of Edward—both trapped in a narrow space and destroyed without there being any ultimate necessity for it—is suggested by the play as a whole and also by Edward himself illogically including mention of the event in his nervous attempt at self-affirmation before the silent guest:

> I could stand on the hill and look through my telescope at the
> sea. And follow the path of the three-masted schooner, feeling
> fit, well aware of my sinews, their suppleness, my arms lifted
> holding the telescope, steady, easily, no trembling, my aim was
> perfect, I could pour hot water down the spoon-hole, yes, easily,
> no difficulty, my grasp firm, my command established, my life
> was accounted for, I was ready for my excursions to the cliff,
> down the path to the back gate, through the long grass. . . .
>
> [P. 35]

All of these details seem to indicate that, although the immediate subject of the play is not death, the ultimate anxiety behind Edward's relationship to the matchseller is that anxiety felt in the threat of extinction. ("Blinding" the wasp is a symbol of Edward's own fate and not a cure for the ache in his own eyes.)

Part of the anxiety of death is the realization of the lack of ultimate necessity, the irrationality and impenetrable darkness of it all. A sense of meaninglessness and emptiness is conveyed throughout the play by Edward's reaction to the matchseller: the day is beautiful and Edward is ready to work, but the sight of the ever-present waiting form destroys Edward's capacity for relaxation and fruitful occupation, either physical or intellectual: he withdraws into the scullery, cut off from communication with his wife, cut off even from an honest relationship with himself by his refusal to admit the fear which eventually destroys him. In addition to his incapacity for work, either gardening or finishing the essay on "the dimensionality and continuity of space . . . and time" that he claims to have been working on for years (p. 17), he also exhibits what appears to be a somewhat hysterical perception of the world about him, a perception highly colored by his changing moods: at one moment it appears to him that the room is too hot, at another too cold; at one moment it seems the silent guest is laughing, at another, crying.

The matchseller himself is a sign of meaninglessness. His activity is pointless, standing in a back road where there is no market for his wares, day after day even though he never sells anything, offering his wet, useless matches. This futility alerts Edward and precipitates his fear: the irrationality of the peddler's activities terrifies Edward, just as the senselessness of death causes anguish. Meaninglessness is also indicated by the chain of events themselves: Edward begins his day with merely a slight ache in his eyes and ends it in shockingly unpredictable disaster, the loss of his place in the world, an end that seems to have no rational, meaningful relation to the beginning.

Even as Edward gives way before the inevitable silent threat, he struggles to save himself by talking, by explaining himself. He reveals his nervousness and anxiety by his frantic series of questions and answers:

No doubt you're wondering why I invited you into this house? You may think I was alarmed by the look of you. You would be quite mistaken. I was not alarmed by the look of you. I did not find you at all alarming. No, no. Nothing outside this room has ever alarmed me. You disgusted me, quite forcibly, if you want to know the truth.
    Pause.
Why did you disgust me to that extent? That seems to be a pertinent question. You're no more disgusting than Fanny, the

squire's daughter, after all. In appearance you differ but not in
essence. There's the same . . .
> *Pause.*

The same . . .
> *Pause.*

(*In a low voice.*) I want to ask you a question. Why do you stand
outside my back gate, from dawn till dusk, why do you pretend
to sell matches, why . . . ?

[P. 27]

Edward is ostensibly interrogating the peddler, but clearly he himself
is the one on trial, his actions, reactions, motives, his whole being.
He reveals his anxiety in his comparison between the matchseller
and "Fanny, the squire's daughter." Although he finds the one a
threatening, disgusting old man (whom he would like to escape)
and the other a beautiful young girl (the kind he would choose;
his wife, too, has flaming red hair), he tries to deny his anxiety
over the mixture of good and evil he experiences in the world by
denying there is any particular difference between these two beings.
Yet he gropes to explain how they are really the same and is unable
to. Instead of escaping his anxiety, he is reduced to the fearful
questions that reveal it: why are you here, he asks the matchseller,
who are you? Receiving no answer, he talks on, telling of his *own*
life, trying to explain. In the transposition, as the matchseller grows
younger and stronger and Edward weaker, he says, "I would like
to join you . . . explain . . . show you . . . the garden . . . explain
. . . The plants . . . where I run . . . my track . . ." (p. 39). But
explanation has not worked; the story of his life has not saved him.
Story, after all, belongs to the past; so Edward, whose day is over,
is expelled from his garden, his polished world, into the realm of
silence.

The use of story and self-explanation for purposes of manipu-
lation, and the eventual triumph of silence, is particularly effective
in *The Caretaker*. Here Pinter presents some of his most versatile
uses of language and constructs narrative units of particularly
brilliant comedy. Not only are there the usual stories and anecdotes
by which a speaker unwittingly reveals himself, there are also stories
in which the speaker himself is aware of the craft of the narrative,

deliberately employing story for his own purpose and with a sharp sense of irony. In *The Caretaker,* for the first time, Pinter has created a character who is as smart as Pinter and makes similar witty use of narrative.

Each of the three kinds of long narrative in *The Caretaker* is associated with and helps to distinguish a particular character. Davies, the complaining aggrieved derelict, relates events from the past that are supposed to illustrate how badly he has been treated, events that justify his present situation and behavior, events that the audience recognizes to be distorted or untrue. Aston, the tranquilized ineffectual, speaks very little, but occasionally his remarks are interrupted by memory of some event apparently having no connection with the present moment that he feels impelled to recount in some detail, climaxing finally in the narrative that really does account for why he is, now, the way he is. And Mick, Aston's tough and enterprising brother, narrates events that are pure fantasy and near nonsense, aimed like machine-gun blasts at Davies, whom he deliberately intends to manipulate by means of a superior use of language. Davies' narratives are unintentionally comic, Aston's pathetic, and Mick's insistently brutal; these three modes guide the play to its strong and convincing conclusion.

Davies is the least conscious of the three characters. His perceptions and responses are all predetermined by his own fixed personality traits. He is fearful of the unknown, not just foreigners and "them Blacks" next door but also the most ordinary elements of life. Turning on the electric heater terrifies him (he would rather leave it alone and be cold); however, his anxiety seems to come not from realistic assessment of that particular appliance but from his irrational fears about the gas stove:

> ASTON (*going to below the fireplace*): See this plug? Switch it on here, if you like. This little fire.
> DAVIES: Right, mister.
> ASTON: Just plug in here.
> DAVIES: Right, mister.
> *Aston goes towards the door.*
> (*Anxiously*). What do I do?
> ASTON: Just switch it on, that's all. The fire'll come on.

DAVIES: I tell you what. I won't bother about it.

ASTON: No trouble.

DAVIES: No, I don't go in for them things much.

ASTON: Should work. (*Turning.*) Right.

DAVIES: Eh, I was going to ask you, mister, what about this
stove? I mean, do you think it's going to be letting out any
. . . what do you think?

ASTON: It's not connected.

DAVIES: You see, the trouble is, it's right on top of my bed, you
see? What I got to watch is nudging . . . one of them gas taps
with my elbow when I get up, you get my meaning?

He goes round to the other side of stove and examines it.

ASTON: There's nothing to worry about.

DAVIES: Now look here, don't you worry about it. All I'll do, I'll
keep an eye on these taps every now and again, like, you see.
See they're switched off. You leave it to me.[4]

The conclusion of this sequence illustrates another of Davies's
traits: his tendency to displace his own emotions, problems, re-
sponsibilities onto another person. Here he gets rid of his own fear
by saying, and really believing, that Aston is the anxious one. These
qualities appear in the first anecdote he recounts. As soon as he
and Aston enter the latter's junk-filled room, Davies begins to
rehearse the event in the café from which Aston has just rescued
him. And although Aston had been a witness, Davies needs to
describe it all again, both to exercise his sense of outrage and also
to shore up his self-esteem. In order to prove that he ought not
to be treated "like dirt" (p. 8), he tells this little story from his
past:

All them toe-rags, mate, got the manners of pigs. I might have
been on the road a few years but you can take it from me I'm
clean. I keep myself up. That's why I left my wife. Fortnight
after I married her, no, not so much as that, no more than a
week, I took the lid off a saucepan, you know what was in it? A
pile of her underclothing, unwashed. The pan for vegetables, it

4. Harold Pinter, *The Caretaker and The Dumb Waiter* (New York: Grove
Press, 1961), pp. 25–26.

was. The vegetable pan. That's when I left her and I haven't
seen her since.

[P. 9]

Whether or not this event every really occurred is not important;
the story is a parable meant to illustrate a point. Davies really
believes his own parables, but the audience does not (having ocular
proof—and later, through both Aston and Mick, olefactory proof—
that Davies is indeed very dirty). Who cares about that supposed
wife; we can well imagine Davies himself putting dirty underwear
in a saucepan. Thus the story he tells to justify himself, solipsistically
believing that it does, actually redounds upon him.

The underlying viciousness of Davies's character is clearly expressed in another story he tells about "them bastards at the
monastery" (p. 13) who let him down "again." Complaining, aggrieved, Davies feels the world owes him a good pair of shoes, as
he explains at some length to Aston:

Can't wear shoes that don't fit. Nothing worse. I said to this
monk, here, I said, look here, mister, he opened the door, big
door, he opened it, look here, mister, I said, I come all the way
down here, look, I said, I showed him these, I said, you haven't
got a pair of shoes, have you, a pair of shoes, I said, enough to
keep me on my way. Look at these, they're nearly out, I said,
they're no good to me. I heard you got a stock of shoes here.
Piss off, he said to me. Now look here, I said, I'm an old man,
you can't talk to me like that, I don't care who you are. If you
don't piss off, he says, I'll kick you all the way to the gate. Now
look here, I said, now wait a minute, all I'm asking for is a pair
of shoes, you don't want to start taking liberties with me, it's
taken me three days to get out here, I said to him, three days
without a bite, I'm worth a bit to eat, en I? Get out round the
corner to the kitchen, he says, get out round the corner, and
when you've had your meal, piss off out of it. I went round to
this kitchen, see? Meal they give me! A bird, I tell you, a little
bird, a little tiny bird, he could have ate it in under two minutes.
Right, they said to me, you've had your meal, get off out of it.
Meal? I said, what do you think I am, a dog? Nothing better
than a dog. What do you think I am, a wild animal? What about

164

them shoes I come all the way here to get I heard you was giving away? I've a good mind to report you to your mother superior. One of them, an Irish hooligan, come at me. I cleared out. I took a short cut to Watford and picked up a pair there. Got onto the North Circular, just past Hendon, the sole come off, right where I was walking. Lucky I had my old ones wrapped up, still carrying them, otherwise I'd have been finished, man. So I've had to stay with these, you see, they're gone, they're no good, all the good's gone out of them.

[Pp. 14–15]

This harangue goes on at the same time that Aston is offering Davies a pair of shoes. Just as Davies has to claim superiority to those he fears (foreigners and them Blacks), so too he is indignant about those from whom he begs. His underlying hatred and resentment of his benefactors is betrayed by the story about the monk, but to Aston's face, Davies is obsequious (as well as choosy and vain) and regularly falls back on the cliché phrases of the street-corner bum ("Thanks anyway, mister" and "Good luck," p. 15; "Thanks very much, the best of luck," p. 24). Davies has no self-knowledge at all; his parasitism is like the hold of some blind leech clinging to whatever surface presents itself, sucking out whatever meager benefit he can get, simultaneously wanting and resenting. The intense outrage animating Davies's stories illustrates to the audience how great is the gap between his actual situation (he really does smell; he really is a bum) and his own perception of it. Ironically, grotesquely his own attempts at self-justification betray him.

Aston, too, tells stories, but unlike Davies's unintentional comedy these narratives are both bizarre and pathetic. At first, Aston seems merely laconic; his brevity does not necessarily indicate a crippled mind any more than his tinkering with the plug reveals crippled accomplishment. When, well into act 1, he tells about the brief incident in the pub, the narrative seems merely unrelated to what has previously occurred: "I went into a pub the other day. Ordered a Guinness. They gave it to me in a thick mug. I sat down but I couldn't drink it. I can't drink Guinness from a thick mug. I only like it out of a tin glass. I had a few sips but I couldn't finish it"

(p. 19). Is he merely trying to change the subject away from Davies's lament about his mistreatment in the café? Is he merely trying to deflect attention from his own generosity in slipping Davies a few bob? Is Pinter, behind it all, merely aiming for the verisimilitude of ordinary speech, characterized frequently by irrelevancy? There is no answer in the immediate moment, and the play moves on. The next irrelevant narration occurs the following morning, when out of the blue Aston recounts an event in a café:

> You know, I was sitting in a café the other day. I happened to be sitting at the same table as this woman. Well, we started to . . . we started to pick up a bit of a conversation. I don't know . . . about her holiday, it was, where she'd been. She'd been down to the south coast. I can't remember where though. Anyway, we were just sitting there, having this bit of a conversation . . . then suddenly she put her hand over to mine . . . and she said, how would you like me to have a look at your body?
>
> [P. 24]

Davies is flabbergasted. Pinter quickly turns the scene away from Aston and his bizarre story toward Davies and his grotesque response:

> DAVIES: Get out of it.
>   *Pause.*
> ASTON: Yes. To come out with it just like that, in the middle of this conversation. Struck me as a bit odd.
> DAVIES: They've said the same thing to me.
> ASTON: Have they?
> DAVIES: Women? There's many a time they've come up to me and asked me more or less the same question.
>
> [P. 25]

Once more Davies's vanity and total lack of realism make him the comic butt of the play. The point has been made, however, now unmistakably that there is something odd about Aston. His tranquility is not merely the trait of a gentle and generous spirit. Something about that calm suggests a disconnection as grotesque, in its own way, as Davies's. The very long narration that concludes

166

act 2 explains, finally, what that something is. Aston begins by talking about a café up the road:

I used to go there quite a bit. Oh, years ago now. But I stopped. I used to like that place. Spent quite a bit of time in there. That was before I went away. Just before. I think that . . . place had a lot to do with it. They were all . . . a good bit older than me. But they always used to listen. I thought . . . they understood what I said. I mean I used to talk to them. I talked too much. That was my mistake. The same in the factory. Standing there, or in the breaks, I used to . . . talk about things. And these men, they used to listen, whenever I . . . had anything to say. It was all right. The trouble was, I used to have kind of hallucinations. They weren't hallucinations, they . . . I used to get the feeling I could see things . . . very clearly . . . everything . . . was so clear . . . everything used . . . everything used to get very quiet . . . everything got very quiet . . . all this . . . quiet . . . and . . . this clear sight . . . it was . . . but maybe I was wrong. Anyway, someone must have said something. I didn't know anything about it. And . . . some kind of lie must have got around. And this lie went round. I thought people started being funny. In that café. The factory. I couldn't understand it. Then one day they took me to a hospital, right outside London. They . . . got me there. I didn't want to go. Anyway . . . I tried to get out, quite a few times. But . . . it wasn't very easy. They asked me questions, in there. Got me in and asked me all sorts of questions. Well, I told them . . . when they wanted to know . . . what my thoughts were. Hmmnn. Then one day . . . this man . . . doctor, I suppose . . . the head one . . . he was quite a man of . . . distinction . . . although I wasn't so sure about that. He called me in. He said . . . he told me I had something. He said they'd concluded their examination. That's what he said. And he showed me a pile of papers and he said that I'd got something, some complaint. He said . . . he just said that, you see. You've got . . . . this thing. That's your complaint. And we've decided, he said, that in your interests there's only one course we can take. He said . . . but I can't . . . exactly remember . . . how he put it . . . he said, we're going to do something to your brain. He said . . . if we don't, you'll be in here for the rest of your life, but if we do, you stand a chance. You can go out, he said, and live like the others. What

do you want to do to my brain, I said to him. But he just repeated what he'd said. Well, I wasn't a fool. I knew I was a
minor. I knew he couldn't do anything to me without getting
permission. I knew he had to get permission from my mother. So
I wrote to her and told her what they were trying to do. But she
signed their form, you see, giving them permission. I know that
because he showed me her signature when I brought it up. Well,
that night I tried to escape, that night. I spent five hours sawing
at one of the bars on the window in this ward. Right throughout
the dark. They used to shine a torch over the beds every half
hour. So I timed it just right. And then it was nearly done, and a
man had a . . . he had a fit, right next to me. And they caught
me, anyway. About a week later they started to come round and
do this thing to the brain. We were all supposed to have it done,
in this ward. And they came round and did it one at a time. One
a night. I was one of the last. And I could see quite clearly what
they did to the others. They used to come round with these . . .
I don't know what they were . . . they looked like big pincers,
with wires on, the wires were attached to a little machine. It was
electric. They used to hold the man down, and this chief . . . the
chief doctor, used to fit the pincers, something like earphones, he
used to fit them on either side of the man's skull. There was a
man holding the machine, you see, and he'd . . . There was a
man holding the machine, you see, and he'd turn it on, and the
chief would just press these pincers on either side of the skull
and keep them there. Then he'd take them off. They'd cover the
man up . . . and they wouldn't touch him again until later on.
Some used to put up a fight, but most of them didn't. They just
lay there. Well, they were coming round to me, and the night
they came I got up and stood against the wall. They told me to
get on the bed, and I knew they had to get me on the bed because if they did it while I was standing up they might break my
spine. So I stood up and then one or two of them came for me,
well, I was younger then, I was much stronger than I am now, I
was quite strong then, I laid one of them out and I had another
one round the throat, and then suddenly this chief had these pincers on my skull and I knew he wasn't supposed to do it while I
was standing up, that's why I . . . . . anyway, he did it. So I did
get out. I got out of the place. . . . but I couldn't walk very well.
I don't think my spine was damaged. That was perfectly all right.

The trouble was ... my thoughts ... had become very slow ... I couldn't think at all ... I couldn't ... get ... my thoughts ... together ... uuuhh ... I could ... never quite get it ... to-gether. The trouble was, I couldn't hear what people were say-ing. I couldn't look to the right or the left, I had to look straight in front of me, because if I turned my head round ... I couldn't keep ... upright. And I had these headaches. I used to sit in my room. That was when I lived with my mother. And my brother. He was younger than me. And I laid everything out, in order, in my room, all the things I knew were mine, but I didn't die. The thing is, I should have been dead. I should have died. Anyway, I feel much better now. But I don't talk to people now. I steer clear of places like that café. I never go into them now. I don't talk to anyone ... like that. I've often thought of going back and trying to find the man who did that to me. But I want to do something first. I want to build that shed out in the gar-den.

[Pp. 54–57]

Here, in a single and very long narrative, is the story of why Aston is the way he is and an explanation of his tranquility. The story serves the important function of "exposition," giving the audience information it needs about the past in order to understand the present. But unlike traditional exposition, this information comes toward the end, not toward the beginning of the play, and, most important, this passage far surpasses mere exposition. As a story, told by the victim himself, it dramatizes what that information means, in the present, to its chief exponent. The light effects complement this meaning: the room grows gradually darker, until only Aston can be seen clearly; "The fade-down of the light must be as gradual, as protracted and as unobtrusive as possible" (p. 54). Aston himself has been "faded-down" so that he is both calm and ineffectual, slow in thought, slow in speech, as unobtrusive as possible.

Aston's brother, Mick, is his opposite both in manner and in speech. Aston wears "an old tweed overcoat, and under it a thin shabby dark-blue pinstripe suit, single-breasted, with a pullover and faded shirt and tie" (p. 7). This unimaginative propriety reflects the state of quiet conformity which electric-shock treatment has imposed on Aston. By contrast, Mick's leather jacket suggests a hardy practicality well reflected in his vigorous behavior. The play opens with Mick on stage; his tough-guy leather, his slow silent movements, and carefully quiet exit when he hears the others coming generate an atmosphere of menace, which fades away during the comic interaction of Aston and Davies and violently reemerges at the end of the act with his sudden surprising attack on Davies, a *coup de théâtre* which shocks both tramp and audience. Mick's first words, "What's the game?" (p. 29) voice what everyone is wondering and then abruptly end the act. Nothing thus far has prepared the audience for the particular form of terrorizing Mick will employ as soon as act 2 begins.

Like Stanley in *The Birthday Party* terrorizing Meg with the story about the wheelbarrow, Mick is aware of the craft of narrative and can deliberately use it for his own purposes to manipulate someone else. But unlike Stanley, Mick is not himself emotionally engaged in the content of his narrative or using it to displace his own fear onto another. Instead, he maintains a detached ironic intelligence focused as pure weapon against Davies, that parasitic intruder whose opportunism threatens not Mick himself but Aston. Mick "takes care of" Aston (in the kindly sense of that phrase) by "taking care of" Davies (in the gangster sense). And he does it through narrative.

When Mick meets Davies, he attacks him both physically and verbally by forcing him down on the floor and questioning him repeatedly about his name. Davies, a nobody, offers the name Jenkins, which is not his real name, and is required to repeat that self-falsification three times and to hear it echoed back at him by Mick three times. Then, physically and psychologically cowed, he is forced to suffer a barrage of words, a nonsensical pseudostory supposedly related in some way to Davies's identity:

> You remind me of my uncle's brother. He was always on the move, that man. Never without his passport. Had an eye for the girls. Very much your build. Bit of an athlete. Long-jump specialist. He had a habit of demonstrating different run-ups in the

drawing-room round about Christmas time. Had a penchant for nuts. That's what it was. Nothing else but a penchant. Couldn't eat enough of them. Peanuts, walnuts, brazil nuts, monkey nuts, wouldn't touch a piece of fruit cake. Had a marvellous stopwatch. Picked it up in Hong Kong. The day after they chucked him out of the Salvation Army. Used to go in number four for Beckenham Reserves. That was before he got his Gold Medal. Had a funny habit of carrying his fiddle on his back. Like a papoose. I think there was a bit of the Red Indian in him. To be honest, I've never made out how he came to be my uncle's brother. I've often thought that maybe it was the other way round. I mean that my uncle was his brother and he was my uncle. But I never called him uncle. As a matter of fact I called him Sid. My mother called him Sid too. It was a funny business. Your spitting image he was. Married a Chinaman and went to Jamaica.

[P. 31]

The references to passport, to girls, to Red Indians and Chinamen suggest that Mick has been spying on Davies and Aston, listening to Davies's complaints about not having his papers, his tentative boast about women making advances, and his prejudice against foreigners. Mick terrorizes Davies by sheer quantity of words, more than the vaguely inarticulate Davies can possibly keep up with but which he senses, nonetheless, call his identity into question. Language is Mick's forte; he hits Davies with a second barrage:

You know, believe it or not, you've got a funny kind of resemblance to a bloke I once knew in Shoreditch. Actually he lived in Aldgate. I was staying with a cousin in Camden Town. This chap, he used to have a pitch in Finsbury Park, just by the bus depot. When I got to know him I found out he was brought up in Putney. That didn't make any difference to me. I know quite a few people who were born in Putney. Even if they weren't born in Putney they were born in Fulham. The only trouble was, he wasn't born in Putney, he was only brought up in Putney. It turned out he was born in the Caledonian Road, just before you get to the Nag's Head. His old mum was still living at the Angel. All the buses passed right by the door. She could get a 38, 581, 30 or 38A, take her down the Essex Road to Dalston Junc-

171

tion in next to no time. Well, of course, if she got the 30 he'd take her up Upper Street way, round by Highbury Corner and down to St. Paul's Church, but she'd get to Dalston Junction just the same in the end. I used to leave my bike in her garden on my way to work. Yes, it was a curious affair. Dead spit of you he was. Bit bigger round the nose but there was nothing in it.

[P. 32]

By following each of these attacks with a series of shorter remarks about where Davies slept and what his name is, Mick annihilates Davies by making him supply the same information again and again, as if his words had no substance, his self no substance. The final stroke of indignity in this particular sequence comes with the questions, "You a foreigner?" "Born and bred in the British Isles?" and "What did they teach you?" leaving the humiliated Davies speechless.

Using the same technique but shifting his point of attack, Mick goes on to batter Davies with a narrative about possibly renting the flat:

You're stinking the place out. You're an old robber, there's no getting away from it. You're an old skate. You don't belong in a nice place like this. You're an old barbarian. Honest. You got no business wandering about in an unfurnished flat. I could charge seven quid a week for this if I wanted to. Get a taker tomorrow. Three hundred and fifty a year exclusive. No argument. I mean, if that sort of money's in your range don't be afraid to say so. Here you are. Furniture and fittings, I'll take four hundred or the nearest offer. Rateable value ninety quid for the annum. You can reckon water, heating and lighting at close on fifty. That'll cost you eight hundred and ninety if you're all that keen. Say the word and I'll have my solicitors draft you out a contract. Otherwise I've got the van outside, I can run you to the police station in five minutes, have you in for trespassing, loitering with intent, daylight robbery, filching, thieving and stinking the place out. What do you say? Unless you're really keen on a straightforward purchase. Of course, I'll get my brother to decorate it up for you first. I've got a brother who's a number one decorator. He'll decorate it up for you. If you want more space, there's

172

four more rooms along the landing ready to go. Bathroom, living-room, bedroom and nursery. You can have this as your study. This brother I mentioned, he's just about to start on the other rooms. Yes, just about to start. So what do you say? Eight hundred odd for this room or three thousand down for the whole upper storey. On the other hand, if you prefer to approach it in the long-term way I know an insurance firm in West Ham'll be pleased to handle the deal for you. No strings attached, open and above board, untarnished record; twenty per cent interest, fifty per cent deposit; down payments, back payments, family allowances, bonus schemes, remission of term for good behaviour, six months lease, yearly examination of the relevant archives, tea laid on, disposal of shares, benefit extension, compensation on cessation, comprehensive indemnity against Riot, Civil Commotion, Labour Disturbances, Storm, Tempest, Thunderbolt, Larceny or Cattle all subject to a daily check and double check. Of course we'd need a signed declaration from your personal medical attendant as assurance that you possess the requisite fitness to carry the can, won't we? Who do you bank with?

[Pp. 35–36]

The passage begins with overt insult, then rises through ever grander improbabilities to climax in the ironic question, "Who do you bank with?" Once more Mick has outclassed Davies in his use of language, and through the narration of a pseudoevent has again impugned Davies's identity, a man with no name, no papers, no bank account, and not enough intelligence to meet irony with irony.

In act 3 Mick brings his technique to perfection by tricking Davies into a sense of security then turning the elements of that security against him. First, in response to Davies's suggestion, "You and me, we could get this place going" (p. 60), Mick describes his ideas of how to decorate the flat:

I could turn this place into a penthouse. For instance . . . this room. This room you could have as the kitchen. Right size, nice window, sun comes in. I'd have . . . I'd have teal-blue, copper and parchment linoleum squares. I'd have those colours re-echoed in the walls. I'd offset the kitchen units with charcoal-grey worktops. Plenty of room for cupboards for the crockery.

We'd have a small wall cupboard, a large wall cupboard, a corner
wall cupboard with revolving shelves. You wouldn't be short of
cupboards. You could put the dining-room across the landing,
see? Yes. Venetian blinds on the window, cork floor, cork tiles.
You could have an off-white pile linen rug, a table in ... afromosia teak veneer, sideboard with matt black drawers, curved
chairs with cushioned seats, armchairs in oatmeal tweed, a beech
frame settee with a woven sea-grass seat, white-topped heat-re-
sistant coffee table, white tile surround. Yes. Then the bedroom.
What's a bedroom? It's a retreat. It's a place to go for rest and
peace. So you want quiet decoration. The lighting functional.
Furniture ... mahogany and rosewood. Deep azure-blue carpet,
unglazed blue and white curtains, a bedspread with a pattern of
small blue roses on a white ground, dressing table with a lift-up
top containing a plastic tray, table lamp of white raffia ... (*Mick
sits up*) it wouldn't be a flat it'd be a palace.

[P. 60]

Once again he has dazzled Davies with language and mocked his
intelligence, without Davies ever realizing the insult, by his parody
of interior-decorator gush. Mick knows he has made up the word
"afromosia" but Davies does not. Davies takes "afromosia" as
seriously as he takes Mick's offer to employ him as caretaker.

The irony continues as Mick suggests, "You must come up and
have a drink some time. Listen to some Tchaikovsky" (p. 64), with
yet another kind of diction and manner outclassing Davies. And
then later, when the conflict Mick intended to precipitate between
Aston and Davies finally occurs, Davies still does not realize Mick's
intended irony in the line, "If you stank I'd be the first one to tell
you" (p. 70); Davies takes this as vindication, forgetting that only
hours before Mick *did* tell him he stank (p. 35). By very skillful
steps, Mick has lured Davies into revealing the very worst part of
his character. When Davies reaches the point of saying Aston
"should go back where he come from" (p. 71), meaning most
specifically back to the mental institution but also more generally
out of Davies's world (as indeed all foreigners should get out of
Davies's world), Mick begins to turn Davies's words against him.
"Well, you say you're an interior decorator, you'd better be a good

174

one" (p. 71). Now Davies is trapped. He *had* said, "I could decorate it out for you" but what he meant was the latter part of his sentence: "I could give you a hand in doing it ... between us" (p. 63). But Mick is calling that hand. He moves in now for the kill, using the narrative he had so fancifully constructed to torment Davies, point by point:

DAVIES: Me? What do you mean? I never touched that. I never been that.

MICK: You've never what?

DAVIES: No, no, not me, man. I'm not an interior decorator. I been too busy. Too many other things to do, you see. But I ... but I could always turn my hand to most things ... give me ... give me a bit of time to pick it up.

MICK: I don't want you to pick it up. I want a first-class experienced interior decorator. I thought you were one.

DAVIES: Me? Now wait a minute—wait a minute—you got the wrong man.

MICK: How could I have the wrong man? You're the only man I've spoken to. You're the only man I've told, about my dreams, about my deepest wishes, you're the only one I've told, and I only told you because I understood you were an experienced first-class professional interior and exterior decorator.

DAVIES: Now look here—

MICK: You mean you wouldn't know how to fit teal-blue, copper and parchment linoleum squares and have those colours re-echoed in the walls?

DAVIES: Now, look here, where'd you get—?

MICK: You wouldn't be able to decorate out a table in afromosia teak veneer, an armchair in oatmeal tweed and a beech frame settee with a woven sea-grass seat?

DAVIES: I never said that!

MICK: Christ! I must have been under a false impression!

DAVIES: I never said it!

MICK: You're a bloody impostor, mate!

DAVIES: Now you don't want to say that sort of thing to me. You took me on here as caretaker. I was going to give you a helping hand, that's all, for a small ... for a small wage, I

never said nothing about that ... you start calling me
names—
MICK: What is your name?

[P. 72]

And so the sequence wheels back toward Davies's point of particular vulnerability: his name, his identity, the fact that he is just a nobody, a sour, parasitic nobody.

Mick has achieved his goal, to get rid of Davies. And his method is a revealing one. The easiest, most obvious way would have been simply to throw him out; tough-guy Mick could easily do that, and landlord Mick has every right to. But instead he chooses a more subtle way, language rather than muscle, and for an important reason. Mick has terrorized Davies verbally not in order to make him leave voluntarily—that would never happen (at the end of the play Davies is still begging to stay). No, Mick has used his verbal strategy for Aston's sake, to force Davies to reveal himself, his viciousness, his ingratitude, so that Aston himself would make the decision for Davies to go. With the graciousness and tact that are at the heart of genuine care for another, Mick respects Aston's choices, lets him be the way he is, but since Aston is mentally impaired, Mick needs to look out for him, to help arrange circumstances (thus he provides a house for him to work on, in his own way, at his own pace, however personally irritating that may be for Mick; and thus, too, he exposes the opportunism of Davies, so that Aston can make an informed choice). Mick sarcastically pays Davies off for his caretaking work by giving him half a dollar, but Aston is the one to tell him to go.

Davies has told complaining hard-luck stories and believed himself badly treated, but the stories merely reflect further on his odious character as he unwittingly condemns himself. Aston has told bizarre, irrelevant anecdotes as well as one final harrowing tale of his mental crippling, stories which, without his realizing it, serve to make him an even more sympathetic character. And Mick, alone among them aware of the various ironies involved, is able to use verbal irony for his own purposes in the intimidating stories he invents. That accomplished, Mick with his masterful use of language

176

and narrative can safely leave the stage to Davies's inarticulate sputterings after Aston's calm condemnation, his irrevocable decision explaining why Davies must go: "You make too much noise" (p. 77). The deliberate storyteller has won and tranquil silence is restored.

The Narrative Shark Pond

The Homecoming, Old Times, No Man's Land

The anecdotes Pinter's characters recite at critical moments in the dramatic action usually serve to heighten tension both by their actual content and also by their covert relationship to whatever is currently happening on stage. Whether these anecdotes are fact or fiction is often uncertain, and that uncertainty is itself significant. Both *The Homecoming* and *Old Times,* domestic dramas of puzzling infidelities, present a placid surface under which an elusive danger seems to lurk. In *No Man's Land* an ominous fin finally breaks the surface.

Unlike *Old Times, The Homecoming* has a substantial plot made up of action that takes place on stage, all the usual business of entrances and exits, various character interactions, including physical contacts, conflicts, complication, climax. In some ways, in fact, it has all the neatness and charm of conventional boulevard comedy. But this play, too, like its later companion piece, has a number of extended narratives that stand out clearly as "story units" because of their length and apparent gratuitousness. By these story units a character conveys, or sometimes unwittingly betrays, his or her true feelings and motivations at a particular moment in the play, feelings and motivations that are of great consequence for the final scene.

The first narratives the audience encounters are conventional ones serving as traditional exposition. Max, a seventy-year-old garrulous and testy father in conflict with his snide, mocking son Lenny, needs to defend himself with stories of his past exploits: "Huhh! We were two of the worst hated men in the West End of London. I tell you, I still got the scars. We'd walk into a place, the whole room'd stand up, they'd make way to let us pass. You never heard such silence."[1] And so the conversation goes, establishing that this family had a mother (now departed) who "wasn't such a bad bitch" (p. 9), that a current interest of the men is horse racing, that Max cooks for the family (rather unsatisfactorily from Lenny's point of view). Other characters enter (Sam, Max's brother, and then the other son, Joey, a boxer) and more short narrative units are included as part of the interaction (mostly in the form of "remember this," "remember that"). Although some of the elements of the exposition may be puzzling (Max's remarks about his wife, Jessie, in particular), for the most part the audience has the sense that it is watching a fairly conventional opening scene in which some rather rough North London men reveal themselves through conversation, allowing the audience to catch up on their characters, their histories, their relationships (which they themselves know quite well and do not really need to rehearse here) so that then the drama can get underway.

The play continues with this combination of conventional dialogue forms and slightly incongruous content through the first half of act 1. The audience may wonder at the vehemence of Max's last words before the opening scene ends, but can accept them as "character revelation":

Our father? I remember him. Don't worry. You kid yourself. He used to come over to me and look down at me. My old man did. He'd bend right over me, then he'd pick me up. I was only that big. Then he'd dandle me. Give me the bottle. Wipe me clean. Give me a smile. Pat me on the bum. Pass me around, pass me

1. Harold Pinter, *The Homecoming* (New York: Grove Press, 1966), p. 8.

from hand to hand. Toss me up in the air. Catch me coming
down. I remember my father.

[P. 19]

There may be an undercurrent of "too much protest" here, but
Max's crotchety garrulousness may account for it. Nonetheless,
this father's insistence on a father's care seems strangely uneasy.

The next scene, too, is oddly both conventional and bizarre.
Lights go up on Ruth and Teddy, whose conversation continues the
play's necessary exposition: he has returned to his father's house
with his wife, who has never been there; he is unexpected, but since
his old key still works they decide to spend the night and surprise
his family in the morning. The banality of the dialogue makes the
situation not implausible. There are, however, puzzling moments
in all this banality. Accounting for the size of the living room,
Teddy explains: "Actually there was a wall, across there . . . with
a door. We knocked it down . . . years ago . . . to make an open
living area. The structure wasn't affected, you see. My Mother was
dead" (p. 21). Is the last sentence merely a non sequitur? It comes
in the place of further explanation: "the main carrying beams are
over *there*" or some such architectural fact; instead, the family
structure is mentioned. What has his mother's death to do with
the size of the living room? Is there some bizarre causal relationship,
or does the apparent illogic simply reveal Teddy's late-night post-
travel fatigue? There is no answer to this question, but the fact
that it can be raised suggests that despite its ordinary tone and
manner, this dramatic situation may not really be as ordinary as
it appears.

Teddy's meeting with Lenny, while Ruth is out for a late walk,
intensifies this sense of strangeness. There is a startling triteness
in what they say, an abnormal calm in their manner. After years
of absence, these brothers show no surprise, no enthusiasm, at their
unexpected meeting; they talk of Lenny's difficulty sleeping and
not the more important event of Teddy's visit. When Teddy finally
broaches the subject—"I've . . . just come back for a few days"
(p. 26)—Lenny shows virtually no interest; his "Oh yes? Have
you?" is the minimal remark of detached politeness. The disparity

between matter and manner grows, leaving the audience with an increasing sense that there is more on stage than meets the eye or ear. And yet there are no definite clues to the nature of that "more."

The extended narratives that occur in the last half of act 1 supply some useful hints. After Teddy has gone to bed and Ruth returns from her walk, a similarly odd encounter occurs between Lenny and the sister-in-law he has never met: rather than express surprise or interest, he talks about the weather. The inappropriateness of his detached manner is heightened by his conventional offer of a drink: "An aperitif, anything like that?" (p. 28). Not only does the word "aperitif" seem out of place in this less-than-sophisticated environment, a level of diction thus far unheard, but the kind of drink is strangely inappropriate: what appetite is it meant to awaken, what event preface? Given the lateness of the hour, "nightcap" is the drink he ought to offer her. Is Lenny merely inept, pretending sophistication, or is there design in his choice of word, despite its apparent inappropriateness? When he finally raises the critical issue, he does it offhandedly: "You must be connected with my brother in some way. The one who's been abroad" (p. 28). "Connected" is as startlingly inappropriate in its vagueness as "aperitif" was in its specificity. And the significant answer, "I'm his wife," gets no response at all; instead, Lenny launches into the first of several lengthy disquisitions:

> Eh listen, I wonder if you can advise me. I've been having a bit
> of a rough time with this clock. The tick's been keeping me up.
> The trouble is I'm not all that convinced it was the clock. I
> mean there are lots of things which tick in the night, don't you
> find that? All sorts of objects, which, in the day, you wouldn't
> call anything else but commonplace. They give you no trouble.
> But in the night any given one of a number of them is liable to
> start letting out a bit of a tick. Whereas you look at these ob-
> jects in the day and they're just commonplace. They're as quiet
> as mice during the daytime. So . . . all things being equal . . . this
> question of me saying it was the clock that woke me up, well,
> that could very easily prove something of a false hypothesis.
>
> [P. 28]

In a scene composed of very short lines, this long passage stands out. Lenny, for reasons unexplained, chooses to ignore the fact that Teddy is married. He speaks to Ruth in a way that indicates respect and intimacy (earnestly seeking her advice) and yet actually insults her by the complete inappropriateness of what he says and raises the issue of "hypothesis," the need for explanation, and the related problem of being deceived by a false explanation. Something in this scene *does* need explaining, but so far there are precious few clues to work with.

The scene continues with its blend of the banal and the bizarre, reaching a critical moment in the politely phrased but startling request: "Do you mind if I hold your hand?" (p. 30). Ruth's reply finally states aloud the question the audience has been asking with increasing frequency throughout the play, "Why?" Lenny's answer promises, at last, some kind of explanation: "I'll tell you why." Then, after a slight pause, he narrates this apparently gratuitous story:

> One night, not too long ago, one night down by the docks, I was standing alone under an arch, watching all the men jibbing the boom, out in the harbour, and playing about with the yardarm, when a certain lady came up to me and made me a certain proposal. This lady had been searching for me for days. She'd lost track of my whereabouts. However, the fact was she eventually caught up with me, and when she caught up with me she made me this certain proposal. Well, this proposal wasn't entirely out of order and normally I would have subscribed to it. I mean I would have subscribed to it in the normal course of events. The only trouble was she was falling apart with the pox. So I turned it down. Well, this lady was very insistent and started taking liberties with me down under this arch, liberties which by any criterion I couldn't be expected to tolerate, the facts being what they were, so I clumped her one. It was on my mind at the time to do away with her, you know, to kill her, and the fact is, that as killings go, it would have been a simple matter, nothing to it. Her chauffeur, who had located me for her, he'd popped round the corner to have a drink, which just left this lady and myself, you see, alone, standing underneath this arch, watching all the steamers steaming up, no one about, all quiet on the Western

Front, and there she was up against this wall—well, just sliding down the wall, following the blow I'd given her. Well, to sum up, everything was in my favour, for a killing. Don't worry about the chauffeur. The chauffeur would never have spoken. He was an old friend of the family. But . . . in the end I thought . . . Aaah, why go to all the bother . . . you know, getting rid of the corpse and all that, getting yourself into a state of tension. So I just gave her another belt in the nose and a couple of turns of the boot and sort of left it at that.

[Pp. 30–31]

The violence of the story itself is shocking, and Lenny's casual attitude toward what he narrates is equally shocking. The very fact of telling the story to Ruth constitutes an act of psychological violence against her, an attempt at intimidation and control that is clear despite its displacement into "story." Lenny is the one who has just made "a certain proposal," which Ruth rejects by questioning. His story is not an explanation of why he wants to hold her hand, but a threat indicating why she should comply. Otherwise she can expect a "belt in the nose and a couple of turns of the boot." But since Ruth remains cool and calm, withholding her hand, Lenny musters a second tale of violence:

I mean, I am very sensitive to atmosphere, but I tend to get desensitized, if you know what I mean, when people make unreasonable demands on me. For instance, last Christmas I decided to do a bit of snow-clearing for the Borough Council, because we had a heavy snow over here that year in Europe. I didn't have to do this snow-clearing—I mean I wasn't financially embarrassed in any way—it just appealed to me, it appealed to something inside me. What I anticipated with a good deal of pleasure was the brisk cold bite in the air in the early morning. And I was right. I had to get my snowboots on and I had to stand on a corner, at about five-thirty in the morning, to wait for the lorry to pick me up, to take me to the allotted area. Bloody freezing. Well, the lorry came, I jumped on the tailboard, headlights on, dipped, and off we went. Got there, shovels up, fags on, and off we went, deep into the December snow, hours before cockcrow. Well, that morning, while I was having my mid-morning cup of tea in a neighbouring cafe, the shovel standing by my

183

chair, an old lady approached me and asked me if I would give her a hand with her iron mangle. Her brother-in-law, she said, had left it for her, but he'd left it in the wrong room, he'd left it in the front room. Well, naturally, she wanted it in the back room. It was a present he'd given her, you see, a mangle, to iron out the washing. But he'd left it in the wrong room, he'd left it in the front room, well that was a silly place to leave it, it couldn't stay there. So I took time off to give her a hand. She only lived up the road. Well, the only trouble was when I got there I couldn't move this mangle. It must have weighed about half a ton. How this brother-in-law got it up there in the first place I can't even begin to envisage. So there I was, doing a bit of shoulders on with the mangle, risking a rupture, and this old lady just standing there, waving me on, not even lifting a little finger to give me a helping hand. So after a few minutes I said to her, now look here, why don't you stuff this iron mangle up your arse? Anyway, I said, they're out of date, you want to get a spin drier. I had a good mind to give her a workover there and then, but as I was feeling jubilant with the snow-clearing I just gave her a short-arm jab to the belly and jumped on a bus outside.

[Pp. 32–33]

In both cases, a woman is the object of gratuitous violence, Lenny is the perpetrator of that violence, and he comes away feeling rather pleased with himself. The stories are meant to tell Ruth something (and, as part of the play, to tell the audience something). Their very length gives them significance.

Through narrative Lenny has been able to exercise his own desire for violence and his hatred of women, neither of which he can, or does, enact physically. And through this display of disguised violence, Pinter is able to intensify the audience's realization that under the play's veneer of conventional dialogue there lurk dangerous and destructive passions.

The scene between Ruth and Lenny has now openly become a power struggle, focused on the physical placement of an ashtray and the drinking of a glass of water. When she says, "If you take the glass . . . I'll take you" (p. 34), her own counterthreat is clear. Now it is she, not he, who is on the offensive. He becomes unnerved and can only ask, "What are you doing, making me some kind of proposal?" as she successfully leaves the room on her own terms (unlike the pox-ridden slut of Lenny's first story, whose proposal left her battered). Each has threatened the other, but there is an important difference in the nature of the threat: Lenny's, however violent, was just "story," something he can express only through the distance of narrative; Ruth's threat, on the other hand, was made in the present and involves actual physical behavior. Such immediacy leaves Lenny nonplussed, while she laughs triumphantly. Ruth has called his bluff and won.

The Homecoming, like so many of Pinter's later plays, centers on power struggles between men and women involving specifically sexual issues, with a strong undercurrent of hostility directed against the women. That hostility is particularly clear in this play, not only in the stories Lenny tells but in the way Max speaks about Ruth and his own wife, Jessie. The next morning, when Teddy attempts to introduce Ruth, Max is wildly abusive: "I haven't seen the bitch [Teddy] for six years, he comes home without a word, he brings a filthy scrubber off the street, he shacks up in my house!" (p. 42). Teddy's protest, "She's my wife! We're married!" goes completely unnoticed, as Max continues his harangue: "I've never had a whore under this roof before. Ever since your mother died." In this household, all women are the same—wives, mothers, whores—just "stinking pox-ridden sluts," as Max says frequently throughout the play.

Max's long anecdote at the beginning of act 2 makes this attitude quite explicit:

> Well, it's a long time since the whole family was together, eh? If only your mother was alive. Eh, what do you say, Sam? What would Jessie say if she was alive? Sitting here with her three sons. Three fine grown-up lads. And a lovely daughter-in-law. The only shame is her grandchildren aren't here. She'd have petted them and cooed over them, wouldn't she, Sam? She'd have fussed over them and played with them, told them stories, tickled them—I tell you she'd have been hysterical. (*To Ruth.*) Mind you, she taught those boys everything they know. She taught them all the morality they know. I'm telling you. Every single bit

of the moral code they live by—was taught to them by their mother. And she had a heart to go with it. What a heart. Eh, Sam? Listen, what's the use of beating round the bush? That woman was the backbone to this family. I mean, I was busy working twenty-four hours a day in the shop, I was going all over the country to find meat, I was making my way in the world, but I left a woman at home with a will of iron, a heart of gold and a mind. Right, Sam?

Pause.

What a mind

Pause.

Mind you, I was a generous man to her. I never left her short of a few bob. I remember one year I entered into negotiations with a top-class group of butchers with continental connections. I was going into association with them. I remember the night I came home, I kept quiet. First of all I gave Lenny a bath, then Teddy a bath, then Joey a bath. What fun we used to have in the bath, eh, boys? Then I came downstairs and I made Jessie put her feet up on a pouffe—what happened to that pouffe, I haven't seen it for years—she put her feet up on the pouffe and I said to her, Jessie, I think our ship is going to come home, I'm going to treat you to a couple of items, I'm going to buy you a dress in pale corded blue silk, heavily encrusted in pearls, and for casual wear, a pair of pantaloons in lilac flowered taffeta. Then I gave her a drop of cherry brandy. I remember the boys came down, in their pyjamas, all their hair shining, their faces pink, it was before they started shaving, and they knelt down at our feet, Jessie's and mine. I tell you, it was like Christmas.

Pause.

[Pp. 45–46]

But in a matter of moments this idyllic memory turns sour:

It makes the bile come up in my mouth. The bile—you understand? (*To Ruth.*) I worked as a butcher all my life, using the chopper and the slab, the slab, you know what I mean, the chopper and the slab! To keep my family in luxury. Two families! My mother was bedridden, my brothers were all invalids. I had to earn the money for the leading psychiatrists. I had to read books! I had to study the disease, so that I could cope with an emergency at every stage. A crippled family, three bastard sons, a slutbitch of a wife. . . .

[P. 47]

Even when he wants to think well of Jessie, presenting her as a paragon of womanhood, he soon slips into a violent resentment.

This disgust, hatred, and violence give the long narrative passages their particular force. Lenny's gratuitous (and probably fictional) stories present an extreme example of "safe" expression of hostility and desire for power. Max's various references to and anecdotes about his wife are violently hostile. And even Joey, the family's not-too-bright boxer, has a story of ugly sexuality which he can tell (with a little help from the more articulate Lenny):

LENNY: Joey? Not the right touch? Don't be ridiculous. He's had more dolly than you've had cream cakes. He's irresistible. He's one of the few and far between. Tell him about the last bird you had, Joey.

Pause.

JOEY: What bird?

LENNY: The last bird! When we stopped the car . . .

JOEY: Oh, that . . . yes . . . well, we were in Lenny's car one night last week . . .

LENNY: The Alfa.

JOEY: And er . . . bowling down the road . . .

LENNY: Up near the Scrubs.

JOEY: Yes, up over by the Scrubs . . .

LENNY: We were doing a little survey of North Paddington.

JOEY: And er . . . it was pretty late, wasn't it?

LENNY: Yes, it was late. Well?

Pause.

JOEY: And then we . . . well, by the kerb, we saw this parked car . . . with a couple of girls in it.

LENNY: And their escorts.

JOEY: Yes, there were two geezers in it. Anyway . . .

Pause.

What we do then?

LENNY: We stopped the car and got out!

Ten

JOEY: Yes ... we got out ... and we told the ... two escorts
... to go away ... which they did ... and then we ... got the
girls out of the car ...
LENNY: We didn't take them over the Scrubs.
JOEY: Oh, no. Not over the Scrubs. Well, the police would have
noticed us there ... you see. We took them over a bombed
site.
LENNY: Rubble. In the rubble.
JOEY: Yes, plenty of rubble.
    Pause.
Well ... you know ... then we had them.
LENNY: You've missed out the best bit. He's missed out the best
bit!
JOEY: What bit?
LENNY (*to Teddy*): His bird says to him, I don't mind, she says,
but I've got to have some protection. I've got to have some
contraceptive protection. I haven't got any contraceptive protection, old Joey says to her. In that case I won't do it, she
says. Yes you will, says Joey, never mind about the contraceptive protection.
    Lenny laughs.
Even my bird laughed when she heard that. Yes, even she
gave out a bit of a laugh. So you can't say old Joey isn't a bit
of a knockout when he gets going, can you?

[Pp. 66–68]

The purpose of this story of rape is to establish Joey's sexual
prowess just at the time when he has been defeated by Ruth
("upstairs with [her] for two hours and he hasn't even been the
whole hog"). Joey may have stories of sexual domination, but in
this immediate physical situation Ruth has triumphed.

All the men in this family talk big but actually do very little.
Seen in this light, Teddy is not so different from his relatives as
he may at first appear. This feckless philosopher embodies a pallid
intellectual variant of the family motto: words, not deeds. His most
forceful act in the entire play is to eat Lenny's cheese-roll, an act
of "barefaced audacity" (p. 64) which precipitates not a punch in
the nose or an angry curse but yet another long pseudodisquisition
from Lenny.

The only person in the play who acts effectively is Ruth herself, as the climax outrageously and comically reveals. While Ruth is off stage—upstairs after keeping Joey from going "the whole hog"—Max, Lenny, and Joey begin to formulate another story, this one not an anecdote from the past but a plan for the future: they decide to keep Ruth, to set her up as a high-priced whore on Greek Street (Lenny's profession as pimp now emerges), and also to share her themselves; they argue about her name and her cost; they deputize Teddy to be their American representative, distributing discrete business cards to "professors, heads of departments, men like that" who might want to have "a nice quiet poke" while in London (p. 74). The fantasy builds to the point where Max exclaims, "By the time we've finished Pan-American'll give us a discount." The scene is, of course, shocking and hilarious. But when Ruth comes on stage, these would-be managers become the managed. They have "decided" Ruth's fate (without consulting her), but she is the one who really determines it. They have been playing with the idea of Ruth-as-whore, making up the story as they went along, each contributing various details until the scenario seems right to them: "we'd call her ... Dolores, or something." "Or Spanish Jacky." "No, you've got to be reserved about it, Dad. We could call her something nice ... like Cynthia ... or Gillian" (p. 74). In contrast, Ruth's lines are crisp and precise. Good businesswoman, she knows exactly what she wants and how to get it. In response to their rather tentatively worded proposal, she firmly dictates her terms: "a dressing-room, a rest-room, and a bedroom" (smartly overruling Lenny's attempt to restrict her space); a personal maid, her wardrobe, and all conveniences. And she is not going to reimburse her relatives, as Lenny suggests she should. Instead she informs them, "You would have to regard your original outlay simply as a capital investment" (p. 77). Her businesslike legal-sounding language continues: "I would naturally want to draw up an inventory of everything I would need, which would require your signatures in the presence of witnesses" (p. 77). "All aspects of the agreement and conditions of employment would have to be clarified to our mutual satisfaction before we finalized the contract"

(p. 78). "Contract": she has beaten them even at words; they fantasize while she deals with enforceable behavior.

All the hostility of the earlier narratives comes to bear on the final scene, where "woman triumphant" sits enthroned, surrounded by her subservient men. Feckless Teddy has been sent away; Sam (who reveals woman's misdeeds) lies possibly dead at her feet; Joey, still yearning for some degree of hog, kneels, head in her lap, while she touches him lightly; Lenny stands still, in attendance like the useful pimp that he is; and Max grovels at her feet, moaning and sobbing, verbally announcing his manhood ("I'm not an old man," p. 82) but acting the postures of defeat, as in his earlier anguish he had spoken their fear: "I've got a funny idea she'll do the dirty on us, you want to bet? She'll use us, she'll make use of us, I can tell you! I can smell it!" (p. 81). Ignoring his final plea for a kiss, she sits relaxed in her chair, in command of herself and of the entire situation.

No wonder these men hate women: they want something they cannot get. In actual deed, they beg and are repulsed, and so in fantasy they use words to dominate and destroy the object of their desire, making it seem worthless and thus denying its power. Mothers are dead (and thus unable to affect the structure of the house); wives are "slutbitches"; women in general are sexually revolting because "falling apart with the pox." These various fantasy narratives with all their violence are thus not really gratuitous at all, but psychologically very revealing, showing attitudes these men can express only in story. Without Lenny's "so I just gave her another belt in the nose" (p. 31), Max's "kiss me" (p. 82) loses half its dramatic power. The tableau with which the play ends combines a superficial sense of normalcy with a portentous shadow of submerged outrage and violation. Hidden just under the surface there lurks a destructive force which moves the entire play.

In *Old Times*, too, a similar sense of hidden danger is suggested by the narrative units that disrupt the banal surface "action" of the play. The piece begins with a story in process of development, proceeds through a singing match with lines from various popular songs (each a little romantic story), refers to the plot of a well-known movie, recounts at some length several personal anecdotes and fantasies, and concludes with a scene resembling a photograph, a "book illustration" or "poster" presenting the climactic moment of some of the previous narratives. Much of the critical discussion of this play deals with time relationships, sexual relationships, problems of fantasy and reality.[2] The technique that makes these various thematic elements "work"—and reveals what it is they are working at—is the innovative use of narrative within the drama.

The play opens with three characters on stage: Deeley and Kate, husband and wife, in their own living room smoking and talking; near the window in dim light, Anna, standing looking out, with her back to the audience and to the other characters. It soon becomes apparent that Anna is not physically present in the room (whether she is ever physically present is one of the interesting uncertainties of the play). It would seem that Deeley and Kate are talking about her and that Kate's first word, "Dark," must be in answer to a question asked before the play began ("What color hair does she have?"). The two proceed to establish Anna's character, to "create" her for the audience (and possibly for themselves). Physical characteristics, moral qualities, social situation are established before Anna turns to speak her first lines a third of the way into the act. What distinguishes this opening segment from standard old-fashioned "exposition" (the maid telling the butler why the master was out all night) is the fact that the exchange between Kate and Deeley seems to be more important than anything they say about Anna. Anna may or may not be a dark-haired, married, vegetarian underwear-thief; none of that information helps much when she finally begins to present herself. But in the process of describing her, Deeley and Kate have begun to reveal something about themselves: Kate's calm possession of herself and her past, Deeley's persistent and slightly testy probing, and their mutual pursuit of a verbal and imaginative game. The suggestion that Kate is inventing Anna as she goes along and that Deeley helps the process with leading questions makes the opening minutes of the play seem particularly uncertain. Deeley terminates their joint narrative with the judgment,

2. See, in particular, Alan Hughes, "Myth and Memory in Pinter's *Old Times*," *Modern Drama*, 17 (1974): 467–76, and Francis Gillen, " 'All These Bits and Pieces': Fragmentation and Choice in Pinter's Plays," ibid., pp. 477–87.

"Anyway, none of this matters."[3] But it does matter partly because the details seem provocatively irrelevant and partly because some are later shown to be of great importance. In any case, the fact that these two spend so much stage time in storytelling sets a mood for the rest of the play.

Anna's first lines suddenly erupt into the play (without any of the machinery of having her arrive) and present a memory unit from the past, the first installment of her ongoing story of her life with Kate in London twenty years earlier:

> Queuing all night, the rain, do you remember? my goodness, the Albert Hall, Covent Garden, what did we eat? to look back, half the night, to do things we loved, we were young then of course, but what stamina, and to work in the morning, and to a concert, or the opera, or the ballet, that night, you haven't forgotten? and then riding on top of the bus down Kensington High Street, and the bus conductors, and then dashing for the matches for the gasfire and then I suppose scrambled eggs, or did we? who cooked? both giggling and chattering, both huddling to the heat, then bed and sleeping, and all the hustle and bustle in the morn-ing, rushing for the bus again for work, lunchtimes in Green Park, exchanging all our news, with our very own sandwiches, innocent girls, innocent secretaries, and then the night to come, and goodness knows what excitement in store, I mean the sheer expectation of it all, the looking-forwardness of it all, and so poor, but to be poor and young, and a girl, in London then ... and the cafés we found, almost private ones, weren't they? where artists and writers and sometimes actors collected, and others with dancers, we sat hardly breathing with our coffee, heads bent, so as not to be seen, so as not to disturb, so as not to distract, and listened and listened to all those words, all those cafés and all those people, creative undoubtedly, and does it still exist I wonder? do you know? can you tell me?
>
> [Pp. 17–18]

This breathless rush of memory sets a scene, establishes characters and suggests various events, all of which will develop into a more specific narrative as the play proceeds. The passage ends with an

3. Harold Pinter, *Old Times* (New York: Grove Press, 1971), p. 17.

important question: "does it still exist?" It does, indeed, and the play will show how narrative (both memory units and fantasies) make the existence of the past possible in the present.

The audience, however, may not yet realize to what extent the play is made up of stories or appreciate how important selectivity is even in factual narratives; and certainly the subtle distinctions between fact and fantasy are not yet apparent. But Pinter helps alert attention to the narrative elements by repeated use of the word "listen"[4] and by sharpening the focus momentarily on specific words, words that have a literary ring to them. "The word lest. Haven't heard it for a long time" (p. 19). "The word gaze. Don't hear it very often" (p. 26). After these clues, Anna and Deeley participate in a song duel, singing lines from popular tunes of the thirties (Jerome Kern, Rogers and Hart), all of which make use of a diction and syntax which is partly colloquial ("I've got a woman crazy for me") and partly literary ("And someday I'll know that moment divine"), the total effect resembling the unobtrusive stilt-edness of "lest" and "gaze." This medley of songs presents a composite "story" of romance: yearning for love, lost and yet ever present, complete with scenic detail ("smoke gets in your eyes") and characters and events ("They asked me how I knew / My true love was true, / I of course replied, / Something here inside / Cannot be denied," p. 28). The audience begins to sense that these slightly antique formulas of romantic love suggest a situation which is, like the diction of the songs, familiar and yet a bit odd. What is going on here? Why these games of speculation and memory? First, the story-making sequence that opened the play, now a song contest, both brought to formal conclusion with a judgment by Deeley (in the latter case, "They don't make them like that any more," p. 29). The audience begins to suspect that all these safely distanced exchanges carry a burden of half-hidden motive and feeling—not mere nostalgia, but power and dominance (who can outwit whom, who can remember the most, who can achieve the most). And what makes such covert admissions possible for these characters is the

4. "Listened and listened to all those words" (p. 18); "Listen. What silence," "listen very carefully" (p. 19).

fact that they are dealing with "stories," not direct experience, telling, not doing.

After the silence that ends this particular dramatic sequence, the audience feels relief when Deeley announces, "What happened to me was this" (p. 29). At last, something straightforward and clear (never mind that it seems gratuitous). Then what follows is the first of several extended narratives, quite clear as self-contained story but puzzling in relation to the play. Deeley tells Anna about his meeting with Kate:

> What happened to me was this. I popped into a fleapit to see
> Odd Man Out. Some bloody awful summer afternoon, walking in
> no direction. I remember thinking there was something familiar
> about the neighbourhood and suddenly recalled that it was in this
> very neighbourhood that my father bought me my first tricycle,
> the only tricycle in fact I ever possessed. Anyway, there was the
> bicycle shop and there was this fleapit showing Odd Man Out
> and there were two usherettes standing in the foyer and one of
> them was stroking her breasts and the other one was saying
> "dirty bitch" and the one stroking her breasts was saying
> "mmnnn" with a very sensual relish and smiling at her fellow
> usherette, so I marched in on this excruciatingly hot summer
> afternoon in the middle of nowhere and watched Odd Man Out
> and thought Robert Newton was fantastic. And I still think he
> was fantastic. And I would commit murder for him, even now.
> And there was only one other person in the cinema, one other
> person in the whole of the whole cinema, and there she is. And
> there she was, very dim, very still, placed more or less I would
> say at the dead centre of the auditorium. I was off centre and
> have remained so. And I left when the film was over, noticing,
> even though James Mason was dead, that the first usherette ap-
> peared to be utterly exhausted, and I stood for a moment in the
> sun, thinking I suppose about something and then this girl came
> out and I think looked about her and I said wasn't Robert New-
> ton fantastic, and she said something or other, Christ knows
> what, but looked at me, and I thought Jesus this is it, I've made
> a catch, this is a trueblue pickup, and when we had sat down in
> the café with tea she looked into her cup and then up at me and
> told me she thought Robert Newton was remarkable. So it was

Robert Newton who brought us together and it is only Robert Newton who can tear us apart.

[Pp. 29–30]

This extended narrative by Deeley is later countered by one of Anna's, addressed alternately to Kate and Deeley:

Don't tell me you've forgotten our days at the Tate? and how we explored London and all the old churches and all the old buildings, I mean those that were left from the bombing, in the City and south of the river in Lambeth and Greenwich? Oh my goodness. Oh yes. And the Sunday papers! I could never get her away from the review pages. She ravished them, and then insisted we visit that gallery, or this theatre, or that chamber concert, but of course there was so much, so much to see and to hear, in lovely London then, that sometimes we missed things, or had no more money, and so missed some things. For example, I remember one Sunday she said to me, looking up from the paper, come quick, quick, come with me quickly, and we seized our handbags and went, on a bus, to some totally obscure, some totally unfamiliar district and, almost alone, saw a wonderful film called Odd Man Out.

[P. 38]

Each has negated the other and gained Kate according to his or her version of the event. It does not matter which account is "true" (nothing in the play would provide a conclusive answer), but Anna's response to Deeley's story contains a significant observation: "There are some things one remembers even though they may never have happened. There are things I remember which may never have happened but as I recall them so they take place" (pp. 31–32). Deeley may object to this cool observation with an incredulous "What?" but in fact he is playing the same game. Both he and Anna tell stories about "past events" in order to gain power and control in the present.

Their response to each other's stories indicates to some extent how this power-play operates. Deeley's challenge "It is only Robert Newton who can tear us apart" (that is, "No friend from the past can threaten my marriage") is met with Anna's "F. J. McCormick was good too." Thus by ignoring the challenge, she negates its significance. Deeley does a similar thing to her account of salad days with Kate. By ignoring her story altogether—saying irrelevantly "Yes, I do quite a bit of travelling in my job" (p. 38)—he denies its very existence and pulls attention back to himself.

But the stories are more than mere strategies for attention, more than struggles for center stage. The content is revealing, allowing the speaker, particularly Deeley, to voice anxiety while at the same time establishing himself with bravado. The inclusion of details about the usherettes is significant. Why remember this and retell it in such detail, why this rather than the contents of the candy counter or the pattern in the rug? By describing two women who work together—as Kate and Anna lived together, a piece of information which earlier seemed to disturb Deeley (p. 16)—and by emphasizing their sensuality (the stroked breast, the sensual relish, the smile, the exhaustion), he can give vent to his unspoken fear that there may have been a lesbian relationship between his wife and her old friend while at the same time subordinating that element of the narrative to what he hopes is the more important fact, his "trueblue [and permanent] pickup."

Anna asserts that her past with Kate ("Don't tell me you've forgotten") is more important than the present with Deeley. His old neighborhood is, after all, "some totally obscure, some totally unfamiliar district" to them. And regularly throughout the play she establishes her past world as if it were present, excluding Deeley altogether. "Don't let's go out tonight" (p. 43), she says toward the end of act 1, beginning a sequence of play-acting from the past which Deeley's interruption ("Hungry? After that casserole?" p. 44) cannot destroy. Later on, in act 2 the same sequence is continued when Kate suddenly says, "Well, I've decided I will stay in tonight anyway" (p. 60). After an extended re-creation of the past, Deeley must break in again to bring the discussion back to the present (p. 64).

Ignoring Deeley and taking Kate back into the past with memories both recounted and re-enacted are two of the ways Anna establishes her dominance. One of her most important memory-stories is the extended narrative which she tells right after Deeley's story about seeing Odd Man Out:

This man crying in our room. One night late I returned and found him sobbing, his hand over his face, sitting in the arm-chair, all crumpled in the armchair and Katey sitting on the bed with a mug of coffee and no one spoke to me, no one spoke, no one looked up. There was nothing I could do. I undressed and switched out the light and got into my bed, the curtains were thin, the light from the street came in, Katey still, on her bed, the man sobbed, the light came in, it flicked the wall, there was a slight breeze, the curtains occasionally shook, there was nothing but sobbing, suddenly it stopped. The man came over to me, quickly, looked down at me, but I would have absolutely nothing to do with him, nothing.

Pause.

No, no, I'm quite wrong . . . he didn't move quickly . . . that's quite wrong . . . he moved . . . very slowly, the light was bad, and stopped. He stood in the centre of the room. He looked at us both, at our beds. Then he turned towards me. He approached my bed. He bent down over me. But I would have nothing to do with him, absolutely nothing.

[P. 32]

This extended narrative continues through a series of exchanges between Deeley and Anna, Deeley curious about what kind of man he was, Anna describing his leaving and his return, his lying across Kate's lap, his final departure ("as if he had never been"), and then Deeley's raunchy nervous joke, "Of course he'd been. He went twice and came once." By commenting, "Well, what an exciting story that was" (p. 34), Deeley attempts to reduce the narrative to mere fiction, a diversion, denying it could have any relation to "real life." But, in fact, the struggle being dramatized in this play is the struggle for dominance, to see who will "possess" Kate and who will be odd man out. Anna's story, bizarre as it seems, threatens Deeley by describing a scene in which the two women remain and the man leaves. Deeley may dismiss the story as mere fiction, but he persists in trying to find out what the man looked like because he feels in peril. Is Anna's "exciting story" really a parable, meant to warn him about something?

Act 1 has ended with Anna appearing the stronger of the two contestants. She has kept pace with Deeley in the singing match, trivialized his story by ignoring its threat and countering its accuracy very casually somewhat later (as if it did not deserve a direct answer); she has succeeded several times in luring Kate into reliving past memories, and she unnerves Deeley with her own original narrative that suggests there may be more than one story about an odd man out. The act ends with Kate off stage taking her bath, Anna and Deeley on stage, looking at one another, with a look that must embody all the threats and evasions they have thus far presented only in narrative form.

In act 2 Deeley introduces another extended narrative, one designed to reestablish his own dominance. As Kate is still off stage at her leisurely bath, Deeley and Anna sit in the bedroom talking. Deeley explains that their beds are "susceptible to any amount of permutation" (p. 48) and pursues the question of whether a husband or another woman would dry Kate best, knowing "how and where and in what density moisture collects on women's bodies" (p. 56). In the midst of this sexually charged "small talk," Deeley tries to include himself in Kate and Anna's earlier life by inventing a story in which he knew them. Anna keeps denying his invention ("I don't think so," p. 48; "I don't honestly think so," p. 49; "Never," p. 50), but he persists. The main portion of the story is delivered in a single long narration, interrupted once briefly:

DEELEY: We've talked before. In that pub, for example. In the corner. Luke didn't like it much but we ignored him. Later we all went to a party. Someone's flat, somewhere in Westbourne Grove. You sat on a very low sofa, I sat opposite and looked up your skirt. Your black stockings were very black because your thighs were so white. That's something that's all over now, of course, isn't it, nothing like the same palpable profit in it now, it's all over. But it was worthwhile then. It was worthwhile that night. I simply sat sipping my light ale and gazed . . . gazed up your skirt. You didn't object, you found my gaze perfectly acceptable.

ANNA: I was aware of your gaze, was I?

DEELEY: There was a great argument going on, about China or something, or death, or China *and* death, I can't remember which, but nobody but I had a thigh-kissing view, nobody but you had the thighs which kissed. And here you are. Same woman. Same thighs.

Pause.

Yes. Then a friend of yours came in, a girl, a girl friend. She sat on the sofa with you, you both chatted and chuckled, sitting together, and I settled lower to gaze at you both, at both your thighs, squealing and hissing, you aware, she unaware, but then a great multitude of men surrounded me, and demanded my opinion about death, or about China, or whatever it was, and they would not let me be but bent down over me, so that what with their stinking breath and their broken teeth and the hair in their noses and China and death and their arses on the arms of my chair I was forced to get up and plunge my way through them, followed by them with ferocity, as if I were the cause of their argument, looking back through smoke, rushing to the table with the linoleum cover to look for one more full bottle of light ale, looking back through smoke, glimpsing two girls on the sofa, one of them you, heads close, whispering, no longer able to see anything, no longer able to see stocking or thigh, and then you were gone. I wandered over to the sofa. There was no one on it. I gazed at the indentations of four buttocks. Two of which were yours.

[Pp. 51–52]

Anna's comment on this narration matches Deeley's earlier comment on her account of the crying man. After a pause she says, "I've rarely heard a sadder story" (p. 52), thus once again denying any truth in what he says, just as her interruption—highlighting the word "gaze"—indicates that she recognizes Deeley's anecdote as literary invention, a mere fiction. His next line, "I agree," and their next set of lines (Anna: "I'm terribly sorry." Deeley: "That's all right.") have a double meaning. At the literal level they apply to the content of the story (her sympathy for his sad experience). But they also serve to comment on the fact that both Anna and Deeley know and covertly acknowledge that this story is indeed just an invention (yes, it's a pretty unconvincing piece; I'm sorry I wasn't able to let myself be taken in by it; that's all right, we both are doing our best).

Ten

It is clear that Deeley cannot keep up the play-acting as well as Anna. As they discuss which one of them should dry and powder Kate, his voice changes from the sophisticated banter of "It's quite common to powder yourself after a bath but it's quite uncommon to be powdered" to the grim realism of "My mother would have a fit" (p. 56) and moments later to the exasperated judgment muttered to himself, "Christ" (p. 57). Anna seems to be winning as she and Kate go once again into a long sequence of reliving the past. And when Deeley forces them back to the present their conversation is still about the past, with Anna speaking at length and Deeley only briefly. The talk is suggestive, Anna telling a story about telling Kate stories of sexual experience:

> I had borrowed some of her underwear, to go to a party. Later that night I confessed. It was naughty of me. She stared at me, nonplussed, perhaps, is the word. But I told her that in fact I had been punished for my sin, for a man at the party had spent the whole evening looking up my skirt.
> [Brief interruption by Deeley.]
> But from that night she insisted, from time to time, that I borrow her underwear—she had more of it than I, and a far greater range—and each time she proposed this she would blush, but propose it she did, nevertheless. And when there was anything to tell her, when I got back, anything of interest to tell her, I told her.
> [Brief interruption by Deeley asking if she would blush then.]
> I could never see then. I would come in late and find her reading under the lamp, and begin to tell her, but she would say no, turn off the light, and I would tell her in the dark. She preferred to be told in the dark. But of course it was never completely dark, what with the light from the gasfire or the light through the curtains, and what she didn't know was that, knowing her preference, I would choose a position in the room from which I could see her face, although she could not see mine. She could hear my voice only. And so she listened and I watched her listening.
> [Pp. 65–66]

Deeley not only begins "to find all this distasteful" (p. 66), he is quite unnerved. Trying to change the subject and establish himself as a person of consequence, he ends his tirade with a garbled boast:

"I have my eye on a number of pulses, pulses all round the globe, deprivations and insults, why should I waste valuable space listening to two—" (p. 67). Deeley does not get to finish his remark. Up until now the dialogue has been largely between Deeley and Anna. Kate has been laconic and fairly noncommittal. Now suddenly she begins to dominate the play. She cuts Deeley short (before he can say the critical word) by telling him, "If you don't like it go" (p. 67). Few lines in this play have been supplied with directions for delivery, but Pinter prefaces Kate's words with "Swiftly." Like a cobra floating sleepily in space, then striking suddenly, Kate attacks. And Deeley's response acknowledges her superiority in this fight: "Go? Where can I go?" (and not, "Why should I?"). She remains firm, calm (and it becomes clear that her laconic manner has not been the result of passivity but of strength): "To China. Or Sicily." Deeley continues to be unnerved and trivial: "I haven't got a speed boat. I haven't got a white dinner jacket" (p. 68). Deeley tries to revive his bond with Kate by telling her his Wayfarers Tavern story, but this time his speech is fragmentary, not confidently coherent:

Yes, we met in the Wayfarers Tavern. In the corner. She took a fancy to me. Of course I was slimhipped in those days. Pretty nifty. A bit squinky, quite honestly. Curly hair. The lot. We had a scene together. She freaked out. She didn't have any bread, so I bought her a drink. She looked at me with big eyes, shy, all that bit. She was pretending to be you at the time. Did it pretty well. Wearing your underwear she was too, at the time. Amiably allowed me a gander. Trueblue generosity. Admirable in a woman. We went to a party. Given by philosophers. Not a bad bunch. Edgware road gang. Nice lot. Haven't seen any of them for years. Old friends. Always thinking. Spoke their thoughts. Those are the people I miss. They're all dead, anyway I've never seen them again. The Maida Vale group. Big Eric and little Tony. They lived somewhere near Paddington library. On the way to the party I took her into a café, bought her a cup of coffee, beards with faces. She thought she was you, said little, so little. Maybe she was you. Maybe it was you, having coffee with me, saying little, so little.

[P. 69]

Rather than face the current situation, rather than deal directly with the fact that his wife has just rejected him, Deeley has recourse to a story, preferring to talk about relationships rather than to live them. And the story does not work any better with Kate than it did with Anna.

As Kate and Deeley discuss the story, the past rather than the present, Anna, wanting to regain position, interrupts, and Kate strikes her down even more effectively than she did Deeley: "(To Anna.) But I remember you. I remember you dead" (p. 71). Though Anna still moves, she never speaks again. Kate has silenced both contestants for her attention. The rest of the play is hers.

Now, for the first time, Kate speaks at length. What she tells is the most extended and puzzling story in the entire play:

> I remember you lying dead. You didn't know I was watching you. I leaned over you. Your face was dirty. You lay dead, your face scrawled with dirt, all kinds of earnest inscriptions, but unblotted, so that they had run, all over your face, down to your throat. Your sheets were immaculate. I was glad. I would have been unhappy if your corpse had lain in an unwholesome sheet. It would have been graceless. I mean as far as I was concerned. As far as my room was concerned. After all, you were dead in my room. When you woke my eyes were above you, staring down at you. You tried to do my little trick, one of my tricks you had borrowed, my little slow smile, my little slow shy smile, my bend of the head, my half closing of the eyes, that we knew so well, but it didn't work, the grin only split the dirt at the sides of your mouth and stuck. You stuck in your grin. I looked for tears but could see none. Your pupils weren't in your eyes. Your bones were breaking through your face. But all was serene. There was no suffering. It had all happened elsewhere. Last rites I did not feel necessary. Or any celebration. I felt the time and season appropriate and that by dying alone and dirty you had acted with proper decorum. It was time for my bath. I had quite a lengthy bath, got out, walked about the room, glistening, drew up a chair, sat naked beside you and watched you.
> *Pause.*
> When I brought him into the room your body of course had gone. What a relief it was to have a different body in my room,

a male body behaving quite differently, doing all those things they do and which they think are good, like sitting with one leg over the arm of an armchair. We had a choice of two beds. Your bed or my bed. To lie in, or on. To grind noses together, in or on. He liked your bed, and thought he was different in it because he was a man. But one night I said let me do something, a little thing, a little trick. He lay there in your bed. He looked up at me with great expectation. He was gratified. He thought I had profited from his teaching. He thought I was going to be sexually forthcoming, that I was about to take a long promised initiative. I dug about in the windowbox, where you had planted our pretty pansies, scooped, filled the bowl, and plastered his face with dirt. He resisted . . . with force. He would not let me dirty his face, or smudge it, he wouldn't let me. He suggested a wedding instead, and a change of environment.

    Slight pause.

Neither mattered.

    Pause.

He asked me once, at about that time, who had slept in that bed before him. I told him no one. No one at all.

[Pp. 71–73]

This surrealistic narrative contains many elements from earlier parts of the play (much as a dream is made up of recognizable pieces, however bizarre the whole may be). In the first segment, Kate speaks to Anna about death, dirt, and cleanliness. Unlike Anna, she does not seem to consider their friendship to be "very old and treasured," something "to celebrate" (p. 68). Instead, it is a corpse for which neither last rites nor any celebration is necessary. Kate may have felt earlier that Anna and Deeley were talking about her as if she were dead (p. 34), but Anna is the one who is dead. And Anna's experience of Kate "so shyly poised over [her], looking down at [her]" (p. 35)—which had disturbed Deeley—is not a gesture of tender intimacy but an act of unfeeling scrutiny and rejection. Anna may have borrowed Kate's underwear and tried her "little tricks," but she does not really succeed. Anna is, in fact, the very opposite of Kate: Anna, of the volcanic island, Kate, of a silent coast (p. 22); Anna, dirty, Kate, clean; Anna dead, Kate sitting upright, alive.

In the second segment, the woman's corpse has disappeared. Kate finds it a relief to bring a different kind of body—living and male—into *her* room. But regardless which bed they sleep in, no matter how much the unidentified man thinks he is different from Kate's previous woman, there is an element both partners share: a face plastered with dirt (either actually or potentially). Kate's story indicates that she has not been sexually "forthcoming" (another one of those mannered, slightly literary words, like Anna's "gaze") and that her "little trick" associates sexuality with dirt. The heterosexual solution to whatever may be Kate's problem is a wedding and a change of environment; she apparently did give it a try, because she makes a definite judgment, using the past tense: "Neither mattered."

Deeley is not named in Kate's anecdote about the mud-smeared man (nor in Anna's about the crying man). This "story" does not purport to describe their marriage, but the connection is unavoidable. The audience has witnessed Deeley's anxiety about the crying man, his distress about the implied intimacy between Kate and Anna, his complex combination of distance from his wife ("My work takes me away quite often, of course. But Kate stays here," p. 19) and his uneasy possessiveness ("Oh no they can't take that away from me," pp. 27, 58). Kate is saying something in dreamlike story form which the audience can well believe relates to her life with Deeley. And he believes it, too. After Kate's critical last line, Deeley starts to sob. When she says, "no one. No one at all" had slept in Anna's bed before the unidentified man, she is not simply denying her lesbian relationship, she is denying sexuality altogether. Both male and female partners share the same dirty face in Kate's personal associations; she implies she found no difference between them in bed. Throughout it all, she has remained clean, glistening, watching. "No one at all" has ever really touched her, certainly not possessed her.

With these words, Anna is both silenced and felled (eventually she lies down on one of the divans). Deeley clinches his connection (whether real or imaginary is not important) with the weeping man by himself beginning to sob and then lying down across Kate's lap (p. 74; see p. 33).

The play ends as a still photo illustrating the outcome of the power struggle that has occurred. The lights go "up full sharply. Very bright," catching the characters in their fixed positions (and contrasting with the dim light of the play's opening). Anna, who had been standing at the beginning of act 1 is, after various moves on stage, now prostrate. Deeley and Kate are in their original positions, but now Deeley's slump seems the posture of defeat, not the casual comfort of a man at home. Kate, who had earlier been described as "curled" on the sofa, is now sitting, and all the preceding action certainly suggests she is upright. Her silence of act 1, her physical immobility of act 2 (she has been sitting on the divan since almost the beginning of the act) indicate not the weakness both Anna and Deeley would like her to have but rather a powerful self-possession. The others have jockeyed for position, recounted anecdotes designed to establish their personal dominance without having to reveal directly, to themselves or to others, what is at stake. She has merely waited them out, taken elements of their stories, and formulated a narrative that annihilates them both. Now Kate controls the stage, the stage which the audience sees and the one on which these characters play out their lives.

Except for a bath off stage, some coffee-drinking, and a minimum of moving around on stage, this play has been virtually all reminiscence. Much of that reminiscence has been in the form of stories, anecdotes that may or may not be true. The play is thus almost all narrative; its drama lies in the fact that these characters have chosen to relate to each other this way, that talk is their form of action, story their mode of self-protective self-revelation. And here, too, as in *The Homecoming,* the movement of passions under the surface has constituted the real action of the play.

In *No Man's Land* Pinter uses a metaphor vividly appropriate to describe the way narrative functions in his later plays. Spooner, the seedy pickup, speculating on his vulnerable position in the wealthy household into which he has been brought, uses the cryptic phrase "the shark in the harbour."[5] Here, better perhaps than in

5. Harold Pinter, *No Man's Land* (New York: Grove Press, 1975), p. 60. For a fuller discussion of this metaphor see my article "Pinter, Albee, and 'The Maiden in the Shark Pond,'" *American Imago* 35 (1978): 259–74.

any other phrase, is an image to describe the narratives that fill
Pinter's work: the word "harbour" suggests placidity and safety,
just as the superficial action and atmosphere in many of the plays
seems banal and unthreatening, but the shark indicates danger and
violence, a predatory force lurking beneath the surface, occasionally
showing itself for a moment as an ominous fin breaking the deceptive
tranquility. Just as these flashes on the surface betray a world
underneath which cannot be escaped and which may indeed be
more fateful than anything reflected from the world above, so these
narrative units, apparent interruptions in what would traditionally
be taken as the "action" of the drama—the plot—actually indicate
that the real moving force, the real conflict, the real action lies in
the events that are narrated and not in those that "occur" on stage.
There is no physical violence in No Man's Land, and yet the play
is intensely violent; there are no women characters on stage, and
yet they are central to what actually "happens." Spooner and Hirst's
real battleground is not the comfortable room of the stage set but
the dangerous territory of their memories. The past, erupting into
the present through narrative, is what the play is about.

The specific danger in this past are the women whom Spooner
and Hirst remember: to these men, women have seemed like rav-
aging predators; in response, the men feel a profound hostility and
fear, hostility and fear so disturbing that they cannot deal with it
directly but, like Deeley, must transform painful feelings into
"story."

As is usual in Pinter's dramatic structure, No Man's Land is
composed of a series of conversation-units which have an overt
subject and a hidden emotional tension progressing toward some
kind of climax. In many of these units in this particular play, women
are the ostensible subject, violence the emotional tension, and
references to death or drowning the climax. For example, in the
first scene two aging strangers are drinking and talking. Hirst, to
whose home they have come, is laconic; Spooner, his seedy pickup,
is ingratiating and loquacious. Spooner's monologue progresses
through discussion of a series of personal characteristics which he
genially attributes to himself: strength, poetic "life," freedom, and
(by association) serenity. But the backbone of all these is strength,

which he owes, he says, to the fact that he has never been loved. And it is here that a woman is mentioned for the first time in this no man's land: "I looked up once into my mother's face. What I saw there was nothing less than pure malevolence. I was fortunate to escape with my life" (p. 26). Whatever fear (or hostility) is embodied in this primal experience, Spooner quickly covers with another memory of his mother's attractiveness and a longer idyll of his wife's moving through a world where nothing can ail. The references to women become a bizarre combination of the idyllic and the morbid as Hirst refers to his memory concerning his village church hung with garlands "in honour of young women of the parish, reputed to have died virgin" (p. 29). Spooner then wrenches the subject away from Hirst and attacks him savagely by making insulting comments about his wife and their marriage, an attack which reaches its climax in Spooner's accusing Hirst of impotence. The conversation thus reaches a point farthest removed from its initial subject—Spooner's strength—and it has done so through a process of casual discussion which seems comfortably formless and appropriate to the late hour and the drunken state of these two recent acquaintances.

Spooner's derelict erudition and courtly manner have occasionally produced startling and mixed metaphors earlier in the scene, but here, at its moment of climax, he introduces an odd allusion of great significance: "Let me perhaps be your boatman. For if and when we talk of a river we talk of a deep and dank architecture. In other words, never disdain a helping hand..." (p. 33). These and other unexplained images of aid come at a time when Hirst stands rigidly upright, gripping a cabinet, frozen with emotion, immediately after the accusation of impotence. Spooner's now-jaunty manner concerning the wife who will not come back contrasts strongly with Hirst's stunned reply: "No man's land ... does not move ... or change ... or grow old ... remains ... forever ... icy ... silent" (p. 34). The scene ends with Hirst felled and crawling from the room, Spooner remaining alone and still. Thus the conversation that comprises the opening scene has moved through several topics, but linking the parts together is the ambivalent reference to women as malevolent and attractive, as virginal and dead or married and mistreated. In each case, the woman is physically absent, present only in the memories and imaginations of these two men who polarize as strength and impotence. The final words of the scene involve water, a river which will be mentioned again later in the play, and a description of the titular phrase which seems to apply to Hirst himself: "icy . . . silent," a stasis suggestive of death just as "deep and dank architecture" suggests a grave.

The connections between women and this water-ice-death allusion become even more pronounced in Hirst's own fantasy sequence later in the play. In act 1, returning to the room refreshed, having slept, Hirst recounts a dream he has just had: "Waterfalls. No, no, a lake. Water. Drowning. Not me. Someone else" (p. 44). But he immediately brushes the depression away by memories of friends in the past, friends now captured forever unchanging in his photograph album. Once more, the memory is idyllic: "What was it informed the scene? A tenderness towards our fellows, perhaps. The sun shone. The girls had lovely hair, dark, sometimes red. Under their dresses their bodies were white. It's all in my album" (p. 44). The pattern of this sequence reverses the earlier one, which had progressed from memories of women to fears of drowning. In both the climax is stasis: frozen unchanging no man's land; the photograph album "of my youth, which can never leave me" (p. 45).

This sequence of the dream and the album is introduced by Hirst's genial account of the pleasures of going to sleep early (he implies, as he returns to the room refreshed, that he has in fact gone to bed right after tea, like a good old man, but the audience knows how self-deceived he is, having just seen him drinking heavily with Spooner till the early hours of the morning). His account of this sleep is warmed with contentment: "After tea and toast. You hear the faint beginnings of the evening sounds, and then nothing. Everywhere else people are changing for dinner. You're tucked up, the shutters closed, gaining a march on the world" (p. 44). The memories are as much that of a child's afternoon nap as that of an old man's early sleep, with one exception: the notion of "gaining a march on the world" is adult in its imagery and perhaps also in its competitiveness. But what march is this? Where is this heavy-drinking sixty-year-old man moving except toward death? As he speaks of this "march" his pleasant mood suddenly turns to depression and he remembers the frightening part of his dream.

Despite Hirst's efforts to drive the depression away by memories of the past, references to his album, the grim reality of the dream keeps intruding: "Brightness, through leaves. Gambolling. In the bushes. Young lovers. A fall of water. It was my dream. The lake. Who was drowning in my dream?" (p. 46). And finally the association is made between drowning, freezing, and women's sexuality:

> It was blinding. I remember it. I've forgotten. By all that's sacred and holy. The sounds stopped. It was freezing. There's a gap in me. I can't fill it. There's a flood running through me. I can't plug it. They're blotting me out. Who is doing it? I'm suffocating. It's a muff. A muff, perfumed. Someone is doing me to death.
>
> [P. 46]

Here, all in one frantic paragraph, Hirst brings together his fears, and in his next lines he expresses his consequent hostilities: "She looked up. I was staggered. I had never seen anything so beautiful. That's all poison. We can't be expected to live like that" (p. 46). Hirst at one and the same time identifies with women ("There's a gap in me. . . . I can't plug it") and feels intimidated by them ("I was staggered"). Specifically, he feels destroyed, done to death, by female sexuality (the muff, a centuries-old slang term for female genitals, though characteristically he is not conscious of that meaning in his dream); yet his response is ambivalent for he feels both attraction ("beautiful") and repulsion ("poison"). Since the requirements of this sexuality are more than he feels he can meet, since he cannot live like that, his alternative is a form of death, freezing.

Hirst progresses yet another time through his sequence of denial, resurgence of memory (this time, however, he recalls not an actual woman, but a man, Boris, wine waiter at the Ritz), and climactic allusion to water, when Spooner interrupts him in an effort to save him: "It was I drowning in your dream." As Hirst collapses,

Ten

Spooner attempts to reassure him: "You saw me drowning in your dream. But have no fear. I am not drowned" (p. 48). But this messianic announcement of triumph over death does not allay Hirst's basic fears and haunting memories, which recur as dramatic climax in the last moments of the play.

But before examining this climax, it will be useful to note two important related elements in the play. One is the strong suggestion of homosexuality among all four men; the other is the expression of hostility among the men when they speak of their various sexual relationships with women. The homosexual relationships in the play are only suggested, not explicit, yet they seem obvious enough. The play opens with what is clearly the continuation of a drinking session begun with a pickup ("Do you often hang about Hampstead Heath?" Spooner asks Hirst in their first few minutes on stage). Spooner's attempts at elegant wit and his seedy appearance suggest an aging no-longer-successful sexual entrepreneur. The apparently wealthy household into which Spooner has been introduced is one composed entirely of men: the sixty-year-old Hirst and his two younger companion-caretakers, Briggs, tough and violent, Foster, clever and feminine (he is called "cunt" by Briggs). This *ménage à trois* is quite self-sufficient; Spooner is clearly a rival-intruder toward whom the two younger men direct their hostility in defense of their territorial rights. They are nurse, bodyguard, cook, house-keeper, drinking companion, secretary, and perhaps even lover and procurer for Hirst (Briggs met the young Foster on a street corner and recommended him to Hirst). These various suggestions of homosexuality are also strengthened by the use of a typical ste-reotype: Spooner, Foster, Hirst are poets or present themselves as poets. Pinter has given Spooner, in particular, that mincing effem-inate manner associated in the popular mind with "aesthetic types."

Underlying the relationships among these four men is a strong current of violence. Some of it is explicable in ordinary social terms. When Briggs and Foster returning home find Spooner, they treat him with great contempt because, it would appear, this is not the first time Hirst has picked up a derelict. Even their talk of kicking his head off is understandable in light of their function as protectors (much as Mick terrorizes Davies with mock threats in Pinter's *The*

210

Caretaker). Understandable, too, is the hostility Foster and Briggs occasionally turn against each other, the natural clash between pretty boy and tough guy. Less explicable is the rudeness Briggs and Foster sometimes show toward Hirst, when their servile role is replaced by a suggestion of equality or even dominance; yet even the rudeness can be seen as benign strategy to prevent Hirst from drinking too much. The violent clashes that are most puzzling and also most violent are those between Hirst and Spooner. And these always concern women.

It is not at all clear in the play—and the obscurity is integral— if Spooner and Hirst have known each other in the past. Perhaps they are fabricating their memories, each feeling out the other, building on clues, half-wondering if the other *really* remembers, and trying hard to keep up. Whether or not the memories are factually accurate is not important. What does matter is the use of these memories in the present, weapons of hostility. The two men meet in no man's land, circle, and fight over women. Spooner's opening attack on Hirst's wife and Hirst's virility, already discussed in detail, constitutes round one, in which Spooner occupies the territory triumphantly. (Act 1 ends with Spooner again alone in possession of the stage, but this time alone because he has been abandoned and left in the dark by Hirst's henchmen, not because he has driven Hirst from the room. In the first part of act 1 Spooner had waged a war of subtle psychological violence; in the last part he has, at best, held off threats of physical violence.)

Act 2 opens with Spooner once again sparring with the tough and openly hostile Briggs. With Hirst's reentry, the subtle violence between the two principals begins again. Hirst's jovial old-boy greeting, covering two and a half pages of uninterrupted text and considerable stage time, moves immediately from typical generalities ("My goodness, it's years," p. 68) to two specific questions: "Did you have a good war?" and "How's Emily?" The allusions to war are brief and on the surface at least seem simply to typify Hirst's age and attitude. The reference to Emily triggers a long ramble in which Hirst recounts his seduction of this woman, assumed to be Spooner's wife ("Don't suppose you ever knew about it, what? Oh, we're too old now for it to matter, don't you agree?"). Then

211

after copious details Hirst moves from her "unparalleled ardour" to a few less charged memories, concluding finally with his earlier question: "You did say you had a good war, didn't you?" This is one of the few times in the entire play when Hirst speaks at length. The passage initiates what becomes a violent verbal exchange between the two men, with Spooner again on the skillful offensive, leading Hirst through a series of brief questions and answers that indict him as a ruthless seducer of women, subjecting them to an "insane and corrosive sexual absolutism" (p. 76). Hirst thus appears as a powerful and victorious tyrant in the "war" between the sexes. After having been accused of every perversion, homosexual as well as heterosexual, and after having had his poetic abilities attacked, Hirst struggles between violent outrage and the need for civilized self-control; his only refuge is in his album. The play thus circles back to an earlier set of references, that tranquilizing album with its pictures, and finally moves on to the climactic image of drowning and stasis.

But in the meantime a considerable portion of the action of the play has been taken up with these memories of women and the sexual relationships Hirst and Spooner had with particular women in their past. In terms of sheer bulk, sheer amount of stage time, the discussion of women is clearly one of the most important elements in the play: women are "in" the play not as agents but as significant absences. They are the occasion for and subject of violent verbal exchange between the men. Of all those "good ghosts" at his altar of the dead, that photograph album where Hirst attempts to mummify the past, the women are the ones who will not stay dead: they reemerge in dreams, and memories of them arouse destructive emotions in the present. The only escape for Hirst is into a world where there are no men and thus also no women, a world where the fluid life of youth and sex is frozen into personal immobility, no man's land "forever icy and silent."

Thus the puzzling final scene of the play actually makes sense: Hirst's "changing the subject for the last time" leaves him frozen forever in the present with no options for change ("nothing else will happen forever. You'll simply be sitting here forever," Foster tells him, p. 94). His lake of memory, with its drowned body, yields

212

to no man's land, icy and silent. The live and ravening shark-woman is disguised as a drowning body which is then dismissed as "nothing." Hirst has come near to seeing both himself (as sexual subject) and woman (as sexual object) in terms of drowning: victim and victimizer have shared the same imagery in the protagonist's memory, and the term of this fantasy become reality is death.

Both Hirst and Spooner are driven by an unrecognized fear and hostility toward women which they unwittingly reveal in the associations they make and in the stories and anecdotes they tell: war and wives, malevolence and mothers, orgasm and death. Gradually Pinter winds his play down to a point of absolute zero; the final rhythms grow slower and slower, emotional pitch declines, quiet and winter prevail. Hirst had earlier associated himself with the dead, the "good ghosts" of his album: "They possess all that emotion . . . trapped. Bow to it. It will assuredly never release them, but who knows . . . what relief . . . it may give to them . . ." (p. 79). He imagines them sealed in glass jars and would tender them as he himself wants to be tendered now. And so he goes voluntarily into a kind of death, a stasis both physical and emotional, in order to avoid the thing in the water, the body of woman which had so horrified and intimidated him in the past. And Spooner, who shares Hirst's fear and hostility, becomes an accomplice and chief attendant in this ritual of perpetual death, freezing the shark pond in order to remain unravaged. There will be no threats in the present nor in the future because there will no longer be any stories from the past. Like Beckett's May in *Footfalls* or Listener in *Ohio Impromptu*, Hirst has achieved Hamm's goal, and there will be no change of subject: story itself is ended and with it, life.

"I'll probably
call it a day
after this canter"

Family Voices

Ｔhe few plays of Pinter's that
have appeared since *No Man's Land* have not appreciably utilized
or contributed to this new dramatic technique of employing narrative for subtle psychological revelation. Aside from the rather
artificial gimmick of presenting the play in reversed chronology,
Betrayal (1978) is a conventional piece in almost every respect;
what stories there are serve the function of exposition both for the
audience and for the characters within the play. *The Hothouse*
(written in 1958 but not produced until 1980) is an undistinguished
piece from Pinter's past, interesting chiefly as an over-long example
of themes and techniques he would develop more skillfully in later
work. But now with *Family Voices,* Pinter's work again resembles
Beckett's in its evocate brevity and in its telling use of narrative.

   Family Voices is a radio drama made up of a series of monologues.
The speakers, designated in the script as a young man, a woman,
and a man, are indicated by context to be a son, his mother, and
his father. Unlike other radio dramas, such as *A Slight Ache,* in
which the characters speak to one another in a dramatic situation
that could be staged as well as broadcast, the three voices here do
not represent speech at all but letters which are somehow read out

by the writer. Pinter had previously made use of the dramatic situation in which characters in the same room speak but apparently do not hear each other (in *Landscape*), but in this play he distances the characters even further by separating them both spatially and temporally: the son at an urban boardinghouse writes to his mother, presumably at an address he knows since she is at home; the mother writes to the son, having received no letters from him, with no idea where he is and therefore with no way to address her letter once it is finished; the father writes to the son from the grave, a ghostly letter which the son will not receive and which he would have no way of answering. Thus these three intimately related people express themselves in isolation, connected still by powerful emotional ties but unable either to speak directly to each other or even to communicate effectively in writing. The structure of this creation is complex: Pinter has written a script to be perceived visually by the actors who will then read the words aloud in a broadcast to be perceived aurally by an audience, the play itself concerning words which presumably are written, or intended to be written in letter form, to be perceived by the eye of the recipient, yet which actually have their dramatic existence as sound, as if the very interiors of the writers "spoke." This interplay of visual and aural makes *Family Voices* a particularly interesting example of various forms of narration. At one extreme lies "narrative" meaning story, something from the past fixed in an account which is printed (the kind of usage that makes the word "narrative" synonymous with "fiction" or "novel" as generic or library classifications). And at the other extreme lies "narrative" meaning recital, the existence in the present of events which have happened in the past, with the emphasis here on the lively and necessarily evanescent oral nature of that recital (the kind of usage that associates the word "narrative" with the storytelling tradition of scops and bards). The first of these usages is essentially visual, the second, aural. What Pinter has done quite interestingly in *Family Voices* is translate the spatial fixity of writing (the composed letter) into the temporal fluidity of speech; in the conjunction of these two modes lies the drama of the play.

All three characters write with the stilted vacuousness of genteel conventionality (the standard "I am having a very nice time"[1] of post cards and uninspired letters). There is an occasional "vivid" word or slang term ("I hope you're feeling well, and not as peaky as you did, the last time I saw you") but these, too, have long since become trite. Even the passages that aspire to more elegance ("an utterly charming person, of impeccable credentials," p. 10) seem false and mannered. And throughout all these various shades of banality run meaningless phrases which dull further what has just been said ("more often than not," p. 9).

Among the various stories told in this stilted language is the boy's account of his afternoon with Lady Withers and the buns (pp. 15–17), basically a tea-time metaphor for sexual temptation, excitement, and frustration: "Jane withdrew her feet, my bun clasped between her two big toes" (p. 17). This is followed immediately by another story about a searching mother and sister. To be more precise, this latter is a story within a story; the boy writes to his mother about an event a fellow boarder, Riley, tells him:

> While I way lying in my bath this afternoon, thinking on these things, there was apparently a knock on the front door. The man with black hair apparently opened the door. Two women stood on the doorstep. They said they were my mother and my sister, and asked for me. He denied knowledge of me. No, he had not heard of me. No, there was no-one of that name resident. This was a family house, no strangers admitted. No, they got on very well, thank you very much, without intruders. I suggest, he said, that you both go back to where you come from, and stop both-ering innocent hardworking people with your slanders and your libels, these all too predictable excrescences of the depraved mind at the end of its tether. I can smell your sort a mile off and I am quite prepared to put you both on a charge of mali-cious mischief, insulting behaviour and vagabondage, in other words wandering around on doorsteps knowingly, without any visible means of support. So piss off out of it before I call a copper.
>
> [Pp. 17–18]

1. Harold Pinter, *Family Voices* (London: Next Editions, 1981), p. 9.

216

"He then sat on the edge of the bath and recounted to me what I've just recounted to you" (p. 18) the boy disingenuously writes, as if there were no connection between his mother and the searchers. Yet he ends the letter with the remark, "It interests me that my father wasn't bothered to make the trip" (p. 18), thus implicitly acknowledging that it was indeed his mother and sister at the door. He seems, however, not at all concerned about them but only about his absent father.

The mother's letter grows increasingly shrill and virulent. She moves from "Darling. Where are you" and "I miss you" (p. 12) through hopeful fantasies such as "perhaps you will arrive here in a handsome new car, one day, in the not too distant future, in a nice new suit, quite out of the blue, and hold me in your arms" (p. 17) to threats such as "The police are looking for you. . . . I have stated my belief that you are in the hands of underworld figures who are using you as a male prostitute. . . . You will be found, my boy, and no mercy will be shown to you" (p. 25), culminating finally in the decision "I've given you up as a very bad job" (p. 26). Her B-movie parting question, "Do you think the word love means anything?" (p. 26) supplies by its accusing and self-righteous tone adequate reason for the son to have fled home.

The father is "heard" only twice, within the last few minutes of the play. His letter, written "from the grave," is full of clichés ("A quick word for old time's sake. Just to keep in touch," p. 24) despite the unusual and grim situation from which he so cheerily sends his message. His jovial tone is darkened only for a moment at the end when he describes a recurrent event ("I still hear, occasionally, a dog barking") and his emotional response ("Oh, it frightens me," p. 24). Yet even this association with death[2] is introduced by a sentence suggesting the trite banality of everyday life: "There's only one thing bothers me, to be quite frank." Can that really be the *one* thing wrong with death? And is "bother" a strong enough response? This very banality betrays how self-

2. "Oh keep the Dog far hence, that's friend to men, / Or with his nails he'll dig it up again!" T. S. Eliot, *The Wasteland*, I, The Burial of the Dead, ll. 74–75.

deceived he is, intending to be frank but actually muting feelings and dulling expression.

What is clear from these various letters is the fact that in this triangular relationship the son flees the mother and yearns for the father, the mother pursues the son and despises the father, and the father, so inept as to be "dead," cannot begin to make contact with anyone. The message he sends his son is so hackneyed, so indicative of emotional poverty, that it epitomizes everything wrong with relationships in this family. All he can muster, in this chthonic cry from the grave, is "Lots of love, son. Keep up the good work" (p. 24). Here is the meaningless pseudo-abundance of adolescents, the pseudo-heartiness of politicians and schoolmasters. Fewer phrases could be emptier or less personal.

The play ends with the son longing to clasp his father's shoulder, "to have a word with him." But this father acknowledges that he is "quite dead": "What I have to say to you will never be said" (p. 26).

No, none of it will be *said*, spoken, because these alienated three—father, mother, and son—will never meet. They can only *write* accounts, distanced narratives about their complicated feelings of love and hatred. The mother can only send histrionic threats and accusations to a son who longs for a home where women treat him well ("Mrs. Withers and Jane smiled at me. . . . Oh mother, I have found my home, my family. Little did I ever dream I could know such happiness," pp. 19–20). The father can only send meaningless advice and empty expressions of love to a son yearning for recognition and contact. All three—weak father, termagant mother, fugitive son—deal in clichés because such formulaic language takes the place of genuine feelings and direct expression. Fixed narrative is all they can offer each other, not live contact; story, not touch; the temporal and spatial distance of written word, not the perilous immediacy of speech. And so these "family voices" go unheard, not voices at all, silent words, dead letters sent from afar.

After sending his "old hullo out of the dark. A last kiss from Dad," the father had begun to extricate himself from his letter by further clichés: a folksy Estragon, he writes, "I'll probably call it a day after this canter. Not much more to say" (p. 24). He, too, like Beckett's and Pinter's other characters, has taken an excursion into narrative. Like Hamm, like Winnie, like Krapp and Henry and May, like Beth, Deeley, Davies, Lenny, Hirst and Spooner, like so many characters in twentieth-century drama, he has used story to avoid direct confrontation with subjects that nonetheless fascinate him, little canters into the dangerous territory of love and death, emerging, finally, silent, "safe."

Selected Bibliography

Admussen, Richard L. *The Samuel Beckett Manuscripts.* Boston: G. K. Hall & Co., 1979.

Anderson, Michael. *Anger and Detachment: A Study of Arden, Osborne, and Pinter.* London: Pitman, 1976.

Baker, William, and Stephen E. Tabachnick. *Harold Pinter.* New York: Barnes & Noble, 1973.

Barnard, G. C. *Samuel Beckett: A New Approach.* London: J. M. Dent & Sons, 1970.

Bensky, Lawrence M. "Harold Pinter: An Interview." *Paris Review* 10 (Fall 1966): 12–37. Reprinted in *Theatre at Work,* ed. Charles Marowitz and Simon Trussler. London: Methuen, 1967.

Brater, Enoch. "Still/Beckett: The Essential and the Incidental." *Journal of Modern Literature* 6 (1977): 3–16.

————. "Time and Memory in Pinter's Proust Screenplay." *Comparative Drama* 13 (1979): 121–26.

Brown, John Russell. *Theatre Language.* London: Allen Lane, 1972.

Cohn, Ruby. *Just Play: Beckett's Theater.* Princeton, N.J.: Princeton University Press, 1980.

————. "Outward Bound Soliloquies." *Journal of Modern Literature* 6 (February 1977): 17–38.

————. *Samuel Beckett: The Comic Gamut.* New Brunswick, N.J.: Rutgers University Press, 1962.

————. "Words Working Overtime: *Endgame* and *No Man's Land.*" *Yearbook of English Studies* 9 (1979): 188–203.

Diamond, Elin. "The Fictionalizers in Beckett's Plays." In *Samuel Beckett,* edited by Ruby Cohn, pp. 111–19. New York: McGraw-Hill Book Co., 1975.

Dick, Kay. "Mr. Pinter and the Fearful Matter." *Texas Quarterly* 4 (Autumn 1961): 257–65.

Duckworth, Colin. *Angels of Darkness: Dramatic Effect in Samuel Beckett with Special Reference to Eugène Ionesco.* London: George Allen & Unwin, 1972.

Esslin, Martin. "Godot and His Children: The Theatre of Samuel Beckett and Harold Pinter." In *Experimental Drama,* edited by William A. Armstrong, pp. 128–46. London: G. Bell & Sons, 1963.

————. *Pinter: A Study of His Plays.* 3d ed. London: Methuen, 1977.

————. *Samuel Beckett: A Collection of Critical Essays.* Englewood Cliffs, N.J.: Prentice-Hall, 1965.

————. "Samuel Beckett and the Art of Broadcasting." *Encounter* 45 (September 1975): 38–46.

————. *Theatre of the Absurd.* New York: Doubleday & Co., 1961.

Federman, Raymond, and John Fletcher. *Samuel Beckett: His Works and His Critics.* Berkeley: University of California Press, 1970.

Friedman, Melvin J. *Samuel Beckett Now.* Chicago: University of Chicago Press, 1970.

Gale, Steven H. *Butter's Going Up: A Critical Analysis of Harold Pinter's Work.* Durham, N.C.: Duke University Press, 1977.

————. *Harold Pinter: An Annotated Bibliography.* Boston: G. K. Hall & Co., 1979.

Ganz, Arthur, ed. *Pinter: A Collection of Critical Essays.* Englewood Cliffs, N.J.: Prentice-Hall, 1972.

Gontarski, S. E. *Beckett's Happy Days: A Manuscript Study.* Columbus, Ohio: Ohio State University Libraries, 1977.

————. " 'Making Yourself All Up Again': The Composition of Samuel Beckett's *That Time.*" *Modern Drama* 23 (1980): 112–20.

Graver, Lawrence, and Raymond Federman. *Samuel Beckett: The Critical Heritage.* London: Routledge & Kegan Paul, 1979.

Hagberg, Per Olof. *The Dramatic Works of Samuel Beckett and Harold Pinter: A Comparative Analysis of Main Themes and Dramatic Technique.* University of Gothenburg, Department of English, 1972.

Hammond, B. S. "Beckett and Pinter: Toward a Grammar of the Absurd." *Journal of Beckett Studies* 4 (Spring 1979): 35–42.

Selected Bibliography

"Harold Pinter Replies." *New Theatre Magazine* 2 (1961): 8–10.

Harvey, Lawrence E. *Samuel Beckett: Poet and Critic*. Princeton, N.J.: Princeton University Press, 1970.

Hayman, Ronald. *Samuel Beckett*. New York: Frederick Ungar, 1973.

Hesla, David H. *The Shape of Chaos: An Interpretation of the Art of Samuel Beckett*. Minneapolis: University of Minnesota Press, 1971.

Hoffman, Frederick J. *Samuel Beckett: The Language of Self*. London: Southern Illinois University Press, 1962.

Kennedy, Andrew. *Six Dramatists in Search of a Language*. London: Cambridge University Press, 1975.

Kenner, Hugh. *Samuel Beckett: A Critical Study*. New ed. Berkeley: University of California Press, 1968.

Knowlson, James. " 'Krapp's Last Tape': The Evolution of a Play, 1958–75." *Journal of Beckett Studies* 1 (Winter 1976): 50–65.

————. *Light and Darkness in the Theatre of Samuel Beckett*. London: Turret Books, 1972.

Knowlson, James, ed. *Samuel Beckett: Krapp's Last Tape (Theatre Workbook 1)*. London: Brutus Books, 1980.

Knowlson, James, and John Pilling. *Frescoes of the Skull: The Later Prose and Drama of Samuel Beckett*. New York: Grove Press, 1980.

Lahr, John, ed. *A Casebook on Harold Pinter's "The Homecoming."* New York: Grove Press, 1971.

Mercier, Vivian. *Beckett/Beckett*. New York: Oxford University Press, 1977.

Morrison, Kristin. "Neglected Biblical Allusions in Beckett's Plays: 'Mother Pegg' Once More." In *Samuel Beckett: Humanistic Perspectives*, edited by Morris Beja, S. E. Gontarski, and Pierre Astier. Columbus, Ohio: Ohio State University Press, 1982.

————. "The Rip Word in *A Piece of Monologue*." *Modern Drama* 25 (September 1982): 349–54.

————. "Defeated Sexuality in the Plays and Novels of Samuel Beckett." *Comparative Drama* 14 (Spring 1980): 18–34.

————. "James's and Lubbock's Differing Points of View." *Nineteenth-Century Fiction* 16 (1961): 245–55.

————. "Modern Drama: Death as Theme." *Continuum* 5 (Autumn 1967): 538–49.

————. "Pinter, Albee, and 'The Maiden in the Shark Pond.' " *American Imago* 35 (1978): 259–74.

————. "Pinter and the New Irony." *Quarterly Journal of Speech* 55 (1969): 388–93.

Selected Bibliography

Pilling, John. *Samuel Beckett*. London: Routledge & Kegan Paul, 1976.

Quigley, Austin E. *The Pinter Problem*. Princeton, N.J.: Princeton University Press, 1975.

Robinson, Michael. *The Long Sonata of the Dead: A Study of Samuel Beckett*. New York: Grove Press, 1969.

Rosen, Steven J. *Samuel Beckett and the Pessimistic Tradition*. New Brunswick, N.J.: Rutgers University Press, 1976.

Samuel Beckett Collection. Library. University of Reading. Reading, England.

Smith, R. D. "Back to the Text." In *Contemporary Theatre*. Stratford-Upon-Avon Studies 4. London: Edward Arnold, 1962.

Taylor, John Russell. *Anger and After*. London: Methuen, 1962; rev. 1969.

Zeifman, Hersh. "Being and Non-Being: Samuel Beckett's *Not I*." *Modern Drama* 19 (1976): 35–46.

Zilliacus, Clas. *Beckett and Broadcasting: A Study of the Works of Samuel Beckett for and in Radio and Television*. Abo: Abo Akademi, 1976.

Index

Index

Index

Index

Index

Index

Index

Joe (*Eh Joe*), 10, 12, 99–104
Joey (*The Homecoming*), 179, 186–90

Kate (*Old Times*), 191–92, 194–98, 200–205
Krapp (*Krapp's Last Tape*), 10, 12–14, 54–65, 87, 93, 98–100, 219

Lenny (*The Homecoming*), 7, 179–90, 219
Lucky (*Waiting for Godot*), 19, 21, 23–26

McCann (*The Birthday Party*), 128, 150, 154–55
Magee, Patrick, 126
Marcel (*A la recherche du temps perdu*), 9–11, 13, 59
Max (*The Homecoming*), 179–80, 185–87, 189–90
May (*Footfalls*), 69–72, 213, 219
Meg (*The Birthday Party*), 128, 151–54, 170
Mick (*The Caretaker*), 128, 162, 164, 169–76, 210
Mildred, or Milly (*Happy Days*), 12, 48–50, 53–54
Minnie (*All That Fall*), 75, 77, 81
Moll (*Malone Dies*), 25
Monologue, 2 n, 23–25, 54, 62 n, 67–70, 74, 84, 90, 92–93, 99, 104–10, 128–29, 134, 139–40, 206, 214
Moore, Henry, 126
Mother (*Footfalls*), 69–72
Mother Courage (Brecht), 6
Mother Pegg (*Endgame*), 34
Mouth (*Not I*), 65–68, 74

Nagg (*Endgame*), 31–33, 36–37, 39, 42
Narrative and dramatic genres, 7

Narrative elements in drama, 3–4, 13, 52, 65, 74–75, 82, 123–24, 215
Nell (*Endgame*), 42

O'Neill, Eugene, 2–3, 52, 111
Osborne, John, 126

Paradise Lost (Milton), 44
Petey (*The Birthday Party*), 128, 155
Pinter, Harold: *Betrayal*, 214; *The Birthday Party*, 142, 150–55, 170; *The Caretaker*, 125, 156, 161–77, 211; *The Dumb Waiter*, 142–50; *Family Voices*, 214–19; *The Homecoming*, 7, 128, 178–90, 205; *The Hothouse*, 214; *Landscape*, 125–26, 128–40, 142, 215; *No Man's Land*, 126 n, 178, 205–14; *Old Times*, 4, 178, 190–205; *The Room*, 150 n; *Silence*, 125, 128, 137–42; *A Slight Ache*, 156–61, 214
Plot, 6, 14, 75, 113, 128, 178, 206
Point of view, 82, 158
Pozzo (*Waiting for Godot*), 19, 21, 26–27
Proust, Marcel, 9–13, 140

Radio plays, 7, 53, 74–75, 88, 116–19, 128–29, 137, 214
Renaud, Madeleine, 126
Resnais, Alain, 42
Riley (*The Room*), 150 n
Robinson, Edward G., 155
Rooney, Mr. (*All That Fall*), 76–81
Rooney, Mrs. Maddy (*All That Fall*), 75–81
Rose (*The Room*), 128, 150 n
Rubáiyát of Omar Khayyám, The (FitzGerald), 44
Rumsey (*Silence*), 138
Ruth (*The Homecoming*), 7, 180–86, 188–90

227